OPERATION: JUSAN

A Story of Rescue and Repatriation from Islamic State

T0323077

The Momentum Publishing Company

OPERATION: JUSAN

JUSAN

A Story of Rescue and Repatriation from Islamic State

Erlan Karin

Operation: Jusan by Erlan Karin

This edition has been published in 2021 in the United Kingdom
by The Momentum Publishing Company.

www.momentumbooks.co.uk

1 2 3 4 5 6 7 8 9 10

ISBN 9781911475538

A CIP catalogue record for this book is available from the British Library.

Original jacket design modified by James Nunn
www.jamesnunn.co.uk | @Gnunkse

Printed and bound in Great Britain

This edition has been published with the support
of the National Bureau of Translation, Kazakhstan.

CONTENTS

FOREWORD

In 2014, after several months of research in Afghanistan, Turkey, France and the US, and having taken dozens of interviews with witnesses, I completed my work on the book *Soldiers of the Caliphate: Myths and Reality*. It tells the story of a terrorist group that included several Kazakhstanis. Having finished putting the book together, I was sitting in a Starbucks in Washington with my friend Jacob Zenn, senior analyst at the Jamestown Foundation and a well-known expert on terrorism. We were discussing my book, and the problems of violent extremism in the world. It was then that Jacob told me: 'You've done a great job in reconstructing the sequence of events, researching the make-up of one terrorist group, but that is already history. It is important to understand what is happening right now.' He was referring to Syria; conflict was already flaring up and radicals had just begun arriving there from all over the world, including Kazakhstan.

At the time, I had no intention of taking on the 'Syrian case' – I wanted to draw a line under this topic and move on to something lighter. But Jacob's words stuck in my mind. When I returned from Washington, I gathered a small team and we began looking for data and facts about Kazakhstanis travelling to Syria. Initially, we monitored social networks, gleaning any information that pointed towards citizens of Kazakhstan in various radical groups in Syria and Iraq. We were helped by our colleagues from Turkey, the US and Europe. They shared with us any data they came across regarding our nationals in Syria. In addition, we analysed videos shot by Kazakhstanis themselves. Back then, we were trying to understand the scale of the problem and determine the approximate number of our citizens who had left for Syria. Next, we began classifying them according to the groups they joined. By that time, our network of experts had widened, with new colleagues joining the research. We established good working relations with our intelligence agencies, thus gaining access to certain information on ongoing operations.

In early 2015, we began interviewing Kazakhstanis who had been convicted for participating in terrorist activities in Syria and Iraq. We managed to record a few dozen such interviews. The focus of our research slowly shifted. We realised we should turn our attention to the radicalisation of women and children, and how they are used by terrorist groups. After the release of the infamous ISIS propaganda video showing a boy from Kazakhstan carrying out the execution of two people in Syria, our research team began concentrating on the phenomenon of Kazakhstani jihadis departing for Syria with their wives and children.

Our search for information on the fate of women and children in Syria brought us into contact with a Turkish foundation caring for the families of ex-ISIS fighters. At a meeting with representatives of the foundation, they refused to provide us with a full list of Kazakhstani nationals under their care, although they did confirm that they were working with Kazakh families. On the basis of this data, in 2016 we prepared the first report, titled 'Our People in Somebody Else's War'. The paper discussed the problem of radicals leaving for Syria and Iraq with their families, and mentioned that, sooner or later, the question of what became of women and children in these radical groups would need tackling. Our research was presented in the Royal United Services Institute for Defence and Security Studies in London (2016), the French Institute of International Relations in Paris (2017), and at the Central Asia Program at George Washington University (2020).

At the end of summer 2018, Kazakhstan's National Security Committee (NSC) contacted me about a special operation to repatriate Kazakhstani nationals from Syria. The operation was in the early preparation stages, and they invited me to join the team. I would like to take this opportunity to express my thanks to the head of the NSC, Karim Massimov, for giving me the chance to take part in this operation and conduct this research.

The first attempt to repatriate Kazakhstanis from Syria was made at the beginning of October. However, the military transport planes had to turn back mid-flight because the situation at the point of evacuation suddenly deteriorated dramatically. For months on end, the operation was repeatedly postponed for several weeks, and it was not until the beginning of January 2019 that the first phase of the operation could be completed, thanks to which several dozen women and children were returned to their homeland.

In some way, this episode is also connected to a personal story for me. In September 2018, as Operation: Jusan[1] was unfolding, I was approached by a woman from the Karaganda region. Her name was Ganibet. She told me that her brother and sister-in-law had gone to Afghanistan some time ago, and both had died there soon after. Their children remained in the care of a Kazakhstani woman, who later took them with her to Syria. Ganibet had been searching for traces of her niece and nephew for several years but was only able to get in touch with them in August 2018. She asked me to help her bring the orphans home.

When Operation: Jusan was in the planning stages, Ganibet's niece and nephew were still in an ISIS camp, and getting them out seemed impossible. Moreover, the evacuation was top secret, so I could not divulge any information regarding measures our intelligence agencies were planning in order to repatriate Kazakhstani citizens. And so Ganibet's story was unfolding in tandem, and at the time I myself did not think it would be possible to repatriate children being held in ISIS-controlled territory. There was only a very slim chance that the children could be brought across scores of kilometres to a relatively safe zone – and, even if they were, it was not clear how they could

---

1. *Jusan* is the Kazakh word for wormwood (Artemisia), a genus of plant found in abundance on the Eurasian steppe.

be picked up from there. But they got lucky. During the third stage of Operation: Jusan, in May 2019, Ganibet's niece and nephew were brought back home. This is an unlikely rescue story. It was a miracle that young, parentless children stranded in the midst of a war in a foreign land could be plucked from this hell and reunited with their relatives.

Now Ganibet is raising her niece and nephew alongside her own children. They are going to school and she is doing her best to give them the childhood they were deprived of. Yes, she is facing certain problems of a legal nature: she is fighting for the right of custody. Nevertheless, these are the difficulties of a peacetime life, not war. A couple of years ago, nobody could have imagined that we would be able to bring home children who had been stranded abroad, caught in the crossfire unleashed by ISIS. This story gave me yet another, almost personal, motivation to continue my work. That is why, every time discussions arise about whether or not it was right to repatriate our nationals from Syria, I think of these two children, Ganibet's little niece and nephew – and for me, there can be no question. Children must not pay for the mistakes of their parents.

Operation: Jusan has become a unique example of a state's care for its citizens. Unprecedented in its scale and complexity, it will no doubt go down in history as one of the most successful special operations. Having witnessed all stages of it, I was impressed over and over again by the professionalism, dedication and patriotism of the officers and staff of Kazakhstan's intelligence agencies, by our military and diplomats. Hot on the heels of the completion of the operation, before the details and circumstances were forgotten, I decided to record the main steps taken to prepare and implement it. I believe that it is important for people to know about the intense and often invisible work of the state agencies. This book is dedicated first and foremost to all those who worked behind the scenes in this dangerous but noble mission.

I was tasked with gathering the relevant information for the research. We interviewed more than 100 women repatriated as a result of this humanitarian mission. All that data has been compiled, analysed and presented in this book. From time to time, the rationale behind the evacuation of our nationals from Syria and Iraq is questioned. I hope that this book will answer at least some of those questions, and, most importantly, will ensure that the mistakes, tragedies and disillusionment of the individuals described are not repeated, and that nobody else's children will have to die or suffer in somebody else's war.

Erlan Karin
Almaty, 2020

I

FAMILY JIHAD

The Syrian crisis began as an episode of the Arab Spring. It quickly transformed into a full-scale civil war that impacted directly not only the regional balance of power but also on the structure of international relations. At first glance, this is nothing special. Conflicts that affect the global distribution of power are nothing new in the history of humanity. But the events in Syria became not only the most prolonged conflict but also one of the largest as, according to various estimates, it drew in dozens of states, directly or indirectly. Essentially, what happened and is still happening in Syria is nothing short of an asymmetric war. Radical groups are serving as conduits for the interests of competing world and regional powers that are settling scores between themselves on foreign territory. That is why modern terrorism is primarily the result of shadow politics and geopolitical wrangling.

The US State Department's annual report on international terrorism notes that 'the civil war in Syria became one of the factors contributing to the activation of terrorism on a global scale'. Ongoing fighting in this conflict zone impacted on the radicalisation of nationals of other countries, and this drew increasingly large numbers of people into terrorist activities. One of the peculiarities of this process is the phenomenon known as 'foreign terrorist fighters'. According to data presented in 2016 by the global intelligence and security consultancy The Soufan Group, the number of people leaving for Syria and Iraq to join ISIS or other radical groups may have topped 30,000.[1] This exceeds the total number of foreign fighters who went to Afghanistan after the beginning of the war in 2001. Unfortunately, Kazakhstan is included in the unenviable list of eighty-six countries whose nationals went to the Syrian conflict zone to take part in armed jihad; jihad that serves somebody else's interests.

Meanwhile, the 'jihadi' movement in Central Asia has its own history directly linked to the genesis of new independent states subsequent to the collapse of the Soviet Union. My previous book, *Between ISIS and al-Qaeda: Central Asian Fighters in a Syrian War* (written in co-authorship with Jacob Zenn), presents a detailed chronology and classification of the extremist underground emerging in the region. It covers three stages: the North Caucasian, Afghani and Syrian periods.

However, unlike the first two, the Syrian phase shows a distinct difference – whole families went to the war zone. The specifics of 'family jihad', therefore, are of particular interest in studying the processes of social transformation taking place in the Central Asian region.

One of the first confirmations of 'family jihad' was a propaganda video released by the ISIS terrorist group. It concerned '150 Kazakhstanis', allegedly members of the same family, who went to Syria for jihad. The video was published by Western mass media in October 2013, but the screaming headlines turned out to be not entirely accurate; the Kazakhstani nationals were in fact identified as belonging to several families. Like other countries in the region, Kazakhstan had previously faced the problem of male fighters travelling to Afghanistan to join terrorist groups; but now, for the first time, families, including those with minors, began leaving for Syria.

The exodus of our nationals for the conflict zone peaked in 2013–15; and, from 2017, the flow of departures to Syria was successfully

---

1. The terrorist group Islamic State of Iraq and al-Sham [the Levant] (ISIS) is banned in Kazakhstan.

curbed. Currently, authorities in Central Asian republics are working with independent institutions to find ways to resolve a new problem triggered by the departure of citizens to the Middle East. After the fall of ISIS's so-called Islamic Caliphate, ex-fighters and members of their families began returning home, so now it is imperative to develop methods to successfully reintegrate them into society. At the same time, questions surrounding the causes and factors that motivated people to leave remain unanswered.

Several studies as well as expert evaluations link the problem of radicalisation, and subsequent departure of Central Asian nationals to the active combat zone, primarily with the issue of national self-identification. After the collapse of the Soviet Union, the ensuing ideological vacuum created a crisis of identity in the new republics, and the majority experienced a religious renaissance during the post-Soviet period. At the dawn of independence, several nations in the region even considered establishing a Sharia-based state. This thorny issue was resolved relatively peacefully in Uzbekistan; however, one serious consequence of those events was the emergence of the first jihadi organisation in the region, the Islamic Movement of Uzbekistan (IMU). Subsequently, the IMU went on to fight on the side of the Taliban in Afghanistan and impacted significantly on the rise of radical cells in neighbouring republics. In Tajikistan, the civil war reached a head in 1992–93, and ended with the signing of a peace treaty in the summer of 1997. Tajikistan was the only republic in the region to have an Islamic party. The Islamic Renaissance Party of Tajikistan (IRPT) existed until 2015. Today, all Central Asian states have chosen the secular development model. Nevertheless, the question of national self-identification, in which religion plays the key role, still remains topical in the social discourse.

On the other hand, independent studies confirm that there is yet another factor that leaves a person vulnerable to those recruiting for radical groups: unfavourable socio-economic conditions. We know that a number of those who departed for Syria were work migrants from Kyrgyzstan, Tajikistan and Uzbekistan. Many of them initially went to Russia in search of work. Finding themselves in an alien social milieu, they easily fell prey to the influence of destructive discourses; taking their families, they left for the Middle East. Radicals from Kazakhstan were predominantly from the country's western and central regions. Although rich in oil and gas reserves, Kazakhstan lags behind other countries in many socio-economic criteria. Furthermore, the relatively high prices for goods consume a considerable portion of the local population's already meagre income. For many years, the cities of Satpayev and Zhezkazgan in central Kazakhstan have been considered depressed areas where, against the backdrop of decreased mining of natural mineral resources, jobs are being cut and unemployment is on the rise.

But for most of those who left, the economic factor was not the crucial point. For example, according to one study of 350 Kazakh nationals who went to Syria, 295 were from middle-income or business families.[2] In other words, at least 84 per cent had an income and were not in dire straits. In neighbouring Tajikistan, a high-up offical, commander of the Tajik riot police (OMON) Colonel Gulmurod Khalimov, joined ISIS and became one of the group's leading military commanders. This caused quite a stir when the news broke in 2015. In a specially recorded video, he explained his decision, which was reported as follows: [he was] 'opposing the methods of the Tajikistan Ministry of Internal Affairs, such as a ban on the fivefold *namaz* prayers and the donning of traditional Muslim dress. He criticised the policies of the Tajikistan authorities, and [the Tajik capital, i.e. government] Dushanbe's ties to Russia and the USA.'[3] In 2016, his second wife and four children went to Syria. It is known that Khalimov's wife, Khumairo Mirova, captain of the Ministry of Internal Affairs, was head of the customs agency press centre.[4]

---

2. 'Central Asian Security: modern dynamics of radicalisation among young people in Kazakhstan, Kyrgyzstan and Tajikistan': https://ia-centr. ru/publications/bezopasnost-tsentralnoy-azii-sovremennaya-dinamika-radikalizatsii-sredi-molodezhi-v-kazakhstane-kyrg/.
3. 'How a Tajik riot policeman became an IS leader': https://ru.sputniknews-uz.com/world/20170908/6257930/Tajikskii-omonovec-stal-glavarem-ig. html.
4. Ibid.

Another example that appeared in an ISIS propaganda video: before leaving for Syria with his family, one Kazakhstani radical was a Russian schoolteacher in the Turkestan Oblast (administrative region) of Kazakhstan (former South Kazakhstan Oblast). According to his relatives, his family enjoyed an average income and suffered no hardship. Like the main bulk of Kazakhstani radicals, he left in 2013, whereas the worsening socio-economic situation in Kazakhstan – the devaluation of the national currency, price hikes and falling wages – began in 2014. Cases like this demonstrate that a lack of favourable socio-economic conditions is not the main driving force behind leaving for Syria.

We should not overlook personal and psychological factors. Some of the radicals 'discovered religion' when they found themselves in a difficult situation not necessarily linked with financial hardship. Some lost loved ones, some were experiencing emotional stress due to problems associated with personal growth, and all of them were in need of moral support, which 'brothers in faith' were on hand to provide. It is safe to say that a significant proportion of those who left for Syria were lonely, lost souls who got caught in the nets of recruiters from radical cells. Many of them lacked profound religious knowledge, and so they readily accepted simplified religious concepts.

As a response to the problem of Central Asian nationals becoming involved in terrorist activities abroad and the potential risk of experienced militants returning home, governments of the region tried to tighten state control over religious affairs somewhat. In 2014, the Ministry of Education of Tajikistan issued a mandate forbidding men under the age of fifty from wearing a beard in educational institutions. In Uzbekistan, the authorities forbade minors under eighteen from participating in Friday prayers and other services held in mosques throughout the country, including during the summer holidays. In 2018, the parliament of Kazakhstan debated a draft law on religious activities and religious congregations. New amendments establishing a ban on demonstrating 'external signs of destructiveness' in public places, and a ban on reading the marriage sacraments in places other than religious premises, were proposed. Admittedly, this draft legislation was later taken off the agenda.

These harsh measures did, to some extent, help the states to maintain domestic stability. There have been no terrorist incidents in Uzbekistan since 2005, for instance, despite the common border with unstable Afghanistan and the uneasy situation in the Middle East. To a certain extent, this was achieved thanks to large-scale state control. As a result, the radicals were pushed beyond the country's borders – many Uzbek nationals fought in the ranks of the IMU in Afghanistan, and in new groups such as the Imam Bukhari Division and Katibat al Tawhid wal-Jihad in Syria. So, it comes as no surprise that radically disposed individuals, both inside and outside the countries of the region, use any cases or facts connected with limiting the right to freedom of religion as a tool in the ideological struggle. Such people argue that the Central Asian states allegedly waged war against Muslims. That is why attempts made by governments of Central Asia in the sphere of religion to some extent also facilitated the 'mass exodus' to Syria and Iraq of those adhering to radical Islamic creeds.

The interpretation of the Syrian war in jihadi sermons played a role in the fight for hearts and minds. In extremist propaganda, the Syrian conflict was portrayed as a forerunner to the Apocalypse or Judgement Day. According to Islamic concepts, before the end of the world, Mahdi, the last successor to the Prophet Muhammad, will appear, and there will allegedly be a decisive battle between Mahdi and Dajjal (the False Messiah, akin to the Antichrist). It is said that this battle will take place in the lands of ancient ash-Sham, i.e., Syria and Iraq. So, many jihadis sincerely believed that by going to Syria and joining ISIS, they were becoming warriors in Mahdi's future army. This is yet another reason why the Syrian war became a magnet for radicals from all over the world. Experts, of course, do not see the desire to draw nigh to the Messiah as a valid explanation for the actual and deep causes underlying radicalisation. However, when the perception of the world is simplified in the minds of marginalised youth, a parabolic interpretation of narratives, religion and life in general easily resonates with them.

Be that as it may, it is difficult to give a clear answer as to what became the main factor in motivating people who were not hard-up and often even prosperous to abandon their homes and work and go to an unstable, dangerous region. According to Simon Haselock, an expert on countries that have gone through violent conflicts, these criteria can change in the future:

> [T]he causes for tomorrow's radicalisation may differ from those of today. For example, now we are talking about religious extremism connected mainly with Islam. But the world changes, and the causes for radicalisation could change, too. So, even now, there is a developing tendency in several countries that racial identity is on the increase while in others it is decreasing. So, society reacts to this radicalisation, they want to have an identity they can be proud of. It is possible that in the future, religious extremism will decrease, and national or ethnic extremism will increase.[5]

Moreover, by analysing interviews with citizens who left for Syria and Iraq we can see that, for them, the key issue was in fact the ideological factor rather than the religious one. We should assume, then, that at some point the spiritual quest can lead to an understanding of the need to change something in one's life. In our case, many who left did so in search of new conditions, in accordance with their (religious) views. This was a kind of social protest against the reality around them, and the policies of the state. Furthermore, according to those who decided to join the Islamic Caliphate in Syria, they went in search of a just life for Muslims.

Here is a quotation from an interview with a Kazakhstani woman who returned home.

> My husband and I only decided to go to Syria *to live in a society with the same values as ours*; to bring up our children without state interference. After all, Syria is an Islamic state... It is very difficult for Muslims to live in Kazakhstan. The authorities do not understand that prohibitions only lead to more people violating

---

5. 'Terrorists are just waiting to be written about in the mass media': http://theopenasia.net/articles/detail/terroristy-tolko-i-zhdut-chto-o-nikh-budut-pisat-smi-ekspert/.

them. It is always like this, in civic society, too. When something is forbidden, people always strive to get it.[6]

A general pattern emerges from the dozens of interviews conducted with ex-fighters and their wives: for them, the only path to a just Muslim society is the creation of an Islamic Caliphate. At some point, it seemed possible to do this on the territories of Syria and Iraq. According to the 'returnees', the current civic regimes in Central Asian republics do not meet the needs of the growing and strengthening Muslim section of society. Consequently, their views on the ideal Muslim society boil down to the corresponding state model: the Islamic Caliphate. But such a regime runs counter to civic society. As a result, a section of society chose a 'life befitting a Muslim' in Syria. That is precisely why Central Asian radicals often burnt their passports in ecstasy, posing in front of video cameras, thereby cutting ties with their past, with the institute of the civic state, and with their homeland.

It would seem that the majority sincerely believed that they came to Syria not so much for military jihad but to build a new state – an Islamic Caliphate. And that is why they took their wives and children with them. This is a very important point if we want to understand not only the phenomenon of foreign terrorist fighters, but also what motivated them. For most of them, by going to Syria or Iraq, they were making a choice in favour of their identity, seeing themselves as part of the new state. In their view, they did not leave for jihad but undertook *hijra* – a relocation, as the Muslim *umma* (community) once did under the leadership of the Prophet Muhammad. And in this value system, they were not potential fighters but 'Muhajirs', Muslims who performed *hijra*. They were convinced that this is their right, and they consider jihad as a holy duty prescribed for Muslims to protect the fledgling state.

Here, we must point out that many Kazakhstani women evacuated as part of Operation: Jusan remained in the ranks of ISIS to the

---

6. 'I'll take off my niqab tomorrow, but you will put it on': http://www.uralskweek.kz/2016/12/14/zavtra-ya-snimu-nikab-a-vy-nadenete-2/.

very end, right until the Kurds took the town of al-Baghuz, the last stronghold of the Islamic State in Syria.

Relatively convenient logistics also facilitated the departure of radicals together with their families. To get to Afghanistan, for instance, radicals had to go via Ukraine and Turkey to Iran, and then from there over the mountains to Pakistan. Altogether, the journey took between fifteen and forty-five days, because the recruits had to wait for days or sometimes weeks at each transit hub – in Istanbul, for instance, or the Iranian town of Zahedan – for fake documents or visas. The journey from Iran to Pakistan was not easy, either; they had to cross mountain trails on foot or in pickup trucks. Life in Waziristan was hard, too, as the radical groups were based in already overpopulated small towns. There was not enough accommodation for everyone, so the militants were cooped up together in barracks or rented houses. Attempts to ferry their wives over to Afghanistan often ended in failure since direct routes – via Bishkek, for example – were under the surveillance of intelligence agencies, who blocked anyone crossing into the active combat zone.

Compared with the Afghan route, the journey to Syria was much easier. It was enough to take a direct flight to Istanbul, board a coach and, after several hours, you found yourself at the Turkish-Syrian border. Many Central Asian countries enjoyed a visa-free travel regime with Turkey, making it even easier for the new recruits.

The Syrian route was convenient not just in terms of logistics; it was much more attractive financially, too. Jihadis only had to pay for a flight to Istanbul, and a taxi or coach to Hati, the Turkish province bordering Syria. To get to Afghanistan, on the other hand, Central Asian radicals had to spend on average $5,000 (including cost of tickets, paying for fake documents, lodging in transit points, and guides). That is why male radicals left for Afghanistan alone, and would save up for the journey for several months. Comparing the routes that radicals took to Afghanistan and Syria, some experts dubbed the Turkish route to Syria the 'Jihadi Highway'.

As a result, hundreds of families from Central Asia immigrated to the Middle East. They were motivated by the desire to find a better, righteous life for Muslims on Syrian territory, to help 'oppressed brothers and sisters', and to fulfil themselves. Some of them were indeed ready to take up a gun in 'the war against infidels'. There is no precise data on the numbers of radical families that left, but even the available data that occasionally made its way into the mass media show that this was a large-scale affair.

According to the Committee on Women and the Family under the Government of the Republic of Tajikistan, at the beginning of August 2016 there were 200 Tajik families in Syria and Iraq.[7] These included seventy-three families from the Republic's Sughd Region and forty-three from the Khatlon Region. The Norwegian Refugee Council reported that, in autumn 2017, there were women and children from Central Asian republics in a temporary refugee camp in Iraq: thirty-one families from Tajikistan and sixteen families from Uzbekistan.[8]

In 2015, sixty-three instances of entire families leaving were discovered.[9] In December 2018, Kyrgyz media reported that hundreds of women and children from Kyrgyzstan were in a UN-controlled refugee camp in the Syrian province of al-Hasakah.[10] These represent just a few announcements taken from official sources.

In total, over 5,000 people from Central Asian republics left for the Middle East. Many of the men died, and their families found themselves in temporary camps for displaced people. Hundreds more children were born there in the space of a few years, and many know neither their native tongue nor anything about their own country.

---

7. 'Tajik family devastated after presumed departure of brother and sister to Syria': http://central.asia-news.com/ru/articles/cnmi_ca/features/2017/10/20/feature-01.

8. 'Dozens of families of IS fighters from Tajikistan and Uzbekistan in the Refugee Camp near Mosul': http://www.fergananews.com/news/26869.

9. 'Kyrgyz nationals took 83 children to the active combat zone in Syria': https://ru.sputnik.kg/society/20150908/1018051039.html.

10. 'A Kyrgyz woman wants to leave Syria (Кыргызстандык келин Сириядан кеткиси келет): https://www.azattyk.org/a/syria_kyrgyz_women/29635490.html.

Those who left Central Asia for the Middle East

Country	Total number	Died	Returned
Kazakhstan	around 870[11] (not including children)	over 300 (not including children)	613 (Operation: Jusan)
Kyrgyzstan	850[12]	150	60[13]
Tajikistan	1,900[14]	Over 500[15]	147[16]
Turkmenistan	500	-	-
Uzbekistan	3,000[17]	-	220 women and children (Mehr Operation)

Thus, the issue of religion is not the main reason for the radicalisation of citizens. If we examine the social characteristics of those who left for the Middle East, we can find some similarities in their discontent

11. 'Will the wives and children of Kazakhstani ISIS fighters return home?': https://www.zakon.kz/4938659-budut-li-zheny-i-deti-kazahstanskih.html.
12. 'National Security Committee (NSC): "150 Kazakhstani nationals perished in the war in Syria"': https://rus.azattyk.org/a/29324938.html.
13. 'The religious situation in Kyrgyzstan: challenges and risks for Central Asia': https://newtimes.kz/obshchestvo/61320-religioznaya-situatsiya-v-kyrgyzstane-vyzovy-i-riski-dlya-tsentralnoj-azii.
14. 'Truck carrying al-Nusra Front fighters and munitions, NSC archive photo: almost 2000 Tajik nationals fought for ISIS in Syria and Iraq': https://tj.sputniknews.ru/country/20181119/1027461743/tajikistan-syria-iraq-gknb-uchastie-isis-terroristy.html.
15. 'Rakhom told how many Tajik nationals died in Syria and Iraq': https://ru.sputnik-tj.com/main/20180512/1025541889/rahmon-rasskazal-skolko-grazhdan-tajikistan-pogiblo-sirii-irak.html.
16. 'Former USSR countries became largest "providers" of fighters for Syria and Iraq': https://ca-news.org/news:1412533.
17. 'Mufti of Uzbekistan: around 3,000 Uzbeks are fighting in the Middle East': https://eadaily.com/ru/news/2019/06/10/muftiy-uzbekistana-na-blizhnem-vostoke-voyuyut-okolo-3-tys-uzbekov.

with their own social status. These people may well have felt rejected and outcast in their society and country, and their search for the underlying causes of this isolation led them to Syria and Afghanistan. As such, if we want to glean an average portrait of the typical person who left for Syria, we cannot ignore the individual stories of people and whole families who joined jihad.

Terrorism in Kazakhstan

Kazakhstan first encountered an upsurge in terrorist activity in 2011–12. This was primarily linked to the activities of Kazakh radicals in Kazakhstan and, in particular, to the Jund al-Khalifa group (Soldiers of the Caliphate), whose members planned several terrorist acts in Kazakhstan. In addition, 'sleeping' radical cells also plotted a series of terrorist acts inside the country. According to data from the National Security Committee of the Republic of Kazakhstan (NSC RK), from 2013–17, thirty-eight violent extremist acts of a terrorist nature were prevented or thwarted in the early planning stages.[18]

Prevented Acts of Terrorism

Period	2013	2014	2015	2016	2017	2018	2019
Number	8	3	4	12	11[19]	3[20]	3[21]

---

18. 'National Security Committee, NSC, unveils a plan to fight extremism and terrorism': https://tengrinews.kz/kazakhstan_news/knb-predstavil-plan-deystviy-borbe-ekstremizmom-terrorizmom-311730/.
19. Eleven terrorist acts thwarted in Kazakhstan in 2017.
20. 'Three terrorist acts prevented in Kazakhstan since the start of the year': https://kursiv.kz/news/obschestvo/2018-08/v-kazakhstane-predotvrascheno-tri-terakta-s-nachala-goda.
21. 'Three acts of terrorism frustrated in Kazakhstan': https://tengrinews.kz/kazakhstan_news/tri-terakta-sorvali-v-kazahstane-386360/.

Research into the problems of religious extremism and terrorism in Kazakhstan (2014)[22] revealed that, in most cases, law enforcement agencies succeeded in preventing acts of terrorism and did not allow terrorist groups active on the territory of Kazakhstan to join forces. Some extremist groups were neutralised by law enforcement agencies while attempting to commit common crimes – theft, robbery, armed robbery – or during routine police work. For example, one group was uncovered when traffic police stopped a car to check documents.

Unfortunately, the country continues to be plagued by low law-abidance, indifference, and lack of responsibility on the part of citizens. In each of the criminal cases studied, we find at least three to five individuals who either knew of the planned terrorist acts or saw weapons in the possession of criminals. There were also cases of citizens storing these weapons for them. None of these individuals alerted the law enforcement agencies. The terrorist attack perpetrated in Aktobe, in the west of the country, in June 2016 is a clear example of this. Eighteen individuals appeared before the judge, having known about the impending criminal acts but having failed to inform the corresponding authorities.[23] Two more were sentenced for harbouring criminals.

We can draw several conclusions by analysing the movements of Kazakhstani citizens in the territory of Kazakhstan:

First: Terrorist groups in Kazakhstan acted autonomously, without a unified centre for decision-making and coordination. There was no stable financial route, either. At the same time, the analysis revealed the existence of certain horizontal connections between groups active in various regions of the country and destroyed in

---

22. The socio-biographical data of 227 people (including 150 convicted) were studied within the framework of this research. The study also analysed information about 77 individuals who were mentioned in criminal documents and who were involved in terrorist activities to varying degrees. All criminal cases relate to the period 2007–13, with the exception of one case from 2004.
23. 'Twenty-nine people tried for the terrorist act in Atkobe': https://www.ktk.kz/ru/news/video/2016/10/07/72786/.

the period 2011–12. From 2002 onwards, these connections had been fostered for several years under the influence of external forces, i.e., international terrorist organisations.

Second: Most cases and incidents that took place during the period studied cannot easily be classified as acts of terrorism. With the exception of some cases (an armed attack in Taraz in 2011 and explosions in Atyrau in the same year), they were spontaneous criminal offences. By and large, all the incidents were responses to law-enforcement intelligence-gathering activities, covert operations, etc., and some included exchanges of gunfire. Intelligence agencies and law enforcement agencies managed to prevent terrorist groups active on the territory of Kazakhstan from joining forces and gaining strength. Most were destroyed in the initial stage of formation, and any planned actions were effectively thwarted.

Third: Radical groups active in the territory of Kazakhstan were formed mainly from professional criminal gangs who made a living from armed robbery, theft and burglary, and who later transformed into extremist groups under the influence of their leaders or some other factors.

Fourth: The radicalisation of some groups played out against the backdrop of an absence of consistent state involvement in religious affairs. Religious communities, or even just random sponsors, were constructing places of worship (mosques) unchecked, and, in some regions, completely unlawfully. Such associations acted without the required permits or used fake documents, and sometimes preached radical ideas openly. Furthermore, in some regions, preachers of non-traditional Islamic movements were conducting ideological work freely and unhindered. In the early 2000s, several lectures by the well-known Salafist[24] Said Buryatsky, who later became one of the main ideologists of the armed underground of the North Caucasus,

---

24. From *Salafism*, a Sunni fundamentalist movement advocating a return to the traditions and practices of the *salaf*, the first three generations of Muslims.

were organised in Aktobe and various regions of the Aktobe Oblast. While relevant steps are being taken today, local executive bodies have still not fully grasped the import of this situation.

Fifth: Public opinion holds that the main targets for terrorist attacks are law enforcement agency staff, and this has given rise to the false belief that ordinary citizens are not at risk from terrorism. However, analytical data shows that, although terrorist acts are indeed often directed at defence and law enforcement agencies, the victims were in fact most often ordinary citizens – taxi drivers, businessmen, shop workers – whereas special forces staff died while in the course of covert operations.

The study also analysed the activities of nineteen extremist groups active in the territory of Kazakhstan from 2002–13. These groups were tentatively divided into three categories:

Sabotage units. These typically act according to a clear plan and are hierarchical in structure. For example, the Jamaat Mujahideen of Central Asia were responsible for a series of terrorist attacks in Uzbekistan in summer 2003. The group was created by two members of the Islamic Jihad Union who arrived in Kazakhstan from Afghanistan on the orders of al-Qaeda.

Jamaats. Groups of this type formed on the basis of shared religious outlooks, and usually consisted of young people who attended the same mosque. Such groups always had an elected emir as their head. But these groups lacked a clear plan of action, were often poorly equipped, and acted spontaneously.

Gangs. Most extremist groups active in Kazakhstan engaged mainly in common criminal activities – racketeering, armed robbery, attacks on trade centres, and assaults on businessmen. These groups had self-proclaimed leaders who were generally the most experienced; under their influence, ordinary criminal gangs transformed into extremist groups. A clear example is the organised crime syndicate headed by Ruzembay Ishimbetov, responsible for a series of armed robberies in Almaty. Later, Ishimbetov developed an interest in the ideas of jihadism. However, we cannot rule out the possibility that this was merely a cover for his true criminal goals.

As we have already noted, Kazakhstani intelligence agencies successfully prevented the jihadi underground in Kazakhstan from becoming institutionalised, and this in turn helped prevent the formation of stably functioning extremist groups. However Jund al-Khalifa (Soldiers of the Caliphate) – established in the Afghan-Pakistan region in summer 2011 with the participation of Kazakhstani nationals – could be considered an exception. This group was not purely a Kazakhstani one, though; its leader was the Belgian national Moez Garsallaoui and his deputy was the French national David Drugeon. The Soldiers of the Caliphate did not last long; having announced themselves with fanfare in 2011, they disbanded completely in 2012, following the death of Garsallaoui. Nevertheless, the history of this group shows the Kazakh radicals' drive for institutionalisation and their marked desire to play a more prominent role in promoting jihadi ideas.

In general, at the height of terrorist activity in Kazakhstan (2011–12), the idea of jihad against the authorities lacked a clear institutional and ideological basis. I should also point out that this surge of violent extremism was largely prompted by a fatwah issued by the radical ideologist Abu Munzir ash-Shanqiti. Published in November 2010, it called for jihad against Kazakhstani police. The fatwah spread through jihadi Internet channels at the beginning of 2011. Moreover, the same ideologue issued a 'fatwah on joining Mujahid in Syria', published on the Internet in 2012. Together with similar calls from other 'sheikhs', this served as the basis on which Salafists from various countries, including Kazakhstan, immigrated to Syria. Kazakh radicals who left for Afghanistan most often melted into other groups, rarely forming their own jamaats. They usually joined other ethnic groupings within other larger groups.

However, the Syrian conflict changed this trend, marking a new stage in the institutionalisation of 'Kazakh jihadis'. The first reports of the exodus of Kazakhstani nationals to Syria appeared in 2013. The video that caused the greatest furore, 'Muslim family of 150 people moved to Sham', was published on YouTube on 15 October 2013. And, from that moment, more reports on the so-called Kazakh Jamaat in ISIS followed. People began announcing that they recognised relatives and acquaintances, especially among those shown in the notorious video about '150 Kazakhstanis'. It became clear that Kazakhstanis went to Syria in groups or whole families. For example, it was revealed that several young men from the village of Kengir in the Karaganda Oblast headed to the Syrian conflict zone 'for jihad'. Three brothers from the city of Zhezkazgan – Erkebulan, Erkemurat and Jasulan Sarsenbeks – also left for Syria. The eldest died in Syria in October 2013, and the two other brothers were positively identified later on video.

From that moment, Kazakh fighters regularly appeared in ISIS propaganda videos. Moreover, unlike those of the Afghan period, the Syrian videos featuring Kazakhstani fighters more frequently called for jihad against the government in Kazakhstan. Of nine militants who returned on their own accord, one was detained while planning an act of violence in Kazakhstan. Later, Kazakhstani jihadis would begin using their own children in propaganda for Caliphate ideology. We cannot rule out the possibility that people were paid to participate in such videos. As a result, a stream of propaganda content appeared that highlighted Kazakhstani fighters and their young children. One of the returnee women reported that a video about Kazakh children studying in a children's military camp was propaganda and that there was no such camp. Here is a quote from her interview:

One time they got everyone into the car, as if that kind of thing happened every day, but it never did. If you look carefully, you can see the kids can't even write. They wanted to set up a children's camp, more than once, but there were lots of arguments about it.

And here is an excerpt from an interview with another woman: 'The only thing that worried me were those terrifying videos they were making. They said they were to frighten the enemies. But in fact, there weren't really any of those establishments they filmed, those *muaskar* [training camps]. There weren't any.'

Nevertheless, recent information and data from interviews with women returnees testify to the fact that some military camps engaging children from Kazakhstan and other countries did exist on ISIS territory – though they were soon disbanded. One reason for their closure was instances of violence, including sexual violence, from older boys towards younger ones, and other transgressions against the norms of Sharia. It should be noted that children of the 'Kazakh Jamaat' leaders were also caught in acts of abuse. We also know that almost all the Kazakhstani children who were filmed in the videos or underwent training in such camps have died.

The Syrian conflict did indeed become a departure point for terrorist organisations in changing their ideological approach towards mass and family recruitment. Following the release of the video about Kazakh families, the Grand Mufti of Syria, Ahmad Hassoun, declared that 250 Kazakhstani nationals were fighting against government forces in Syria.[25] Concurrently, according to the Anti-Terrorist Centre of the National Security Committee of Kazakhstan, in October 2013 there were around 100 Kazakhstanis in active combat zones aboard.[26] In 2014 it was announced that 300 Kazakhstanis had joined terrorist groups in the Middle East, and that half were women.[27]

In March 2016, new data were presented confirming that around 200 Kazakhstanis were fighting in Syria and Iraq; they had wives, militants' widows and children with them.[28] In general, there was a

25. Meeting of Grand Mufti of Syria, Ahmad Badreddin Hassoun, with the representative of the Imperial Orthodox Palestine Society in Moscow, October 2013: http://www.interfax.ru/world/337260.
26. 'NSC announces checks on "jihadis"': http://rus.azattyq.org/content/knb-proverki-video-kazakhskiye-jikhadisty/25146593.html.
27. '300 Kazakhstani nationals fighting in Syria and Iraq': http://rus.azattyq.org/content/knb-proverki-video-kazakhskiye-jikhadisty/25146593.html.
28. '"200 Kazakhstanis together with their families fight in Syria and Iraq" – Secretary of Security Council': https://l.facebook.com/l.php?u=https%3A%2F%2Fvlast.kz%2Fnovosti%2F16060-200-kazahstancev-vmeste-s-semami-vout-v-sirii-i-irake-sekretar-sovbeza.html%3Ffbclid%3DIwAR0oaodl2l6LHZWKoqB8sIVdv-KEHS12kK15dYDMyfJjioLF4qNK-Lg1fXY&h=AT2EzA8GZi3OSxyKFKu_kUniCjnEtKQ3ARXlYxrhU6dzGZk

steady increase in the number of citizens leaving for the Middle East until 2017, and then the flow abated.

Number of Kazakhstani Nationals in the Middle East

Sources	2013	2014	2015	2016	2017	2018
Official bodies	100	300	400	200 (+200 women, children)	500 (137 men, the rest, women and children)	800
Independent structures	250	400	500	550	500	-

Over the whole period of the Syrian conflict, starting from 2011, more than 300 Kazakhstani nationals died in the fighting.[29] At the same time, attempts made by 546 Kazakhstani recruits to travel to the zone of terrorist activity were thwarted[30] (168 in 2013, 136 in 2014, 151 in 2015, 91 in 2016, 62 in 2017). Around 125 people returned from flashpoints of their own accord, fifty-eight of whom were subsequently tried and convicted.[31]

According to official data from the NSC RK, by the end of 2019 'around 40 militants from Kazakhstan and around 65 of their

---

pLILqrvTBFlKc83khEILeSnVbRzh8kpANXgg_RRuqFC7JasduKTvWUcas RAogXohX3vAw2P5rdpOXnT24R_ll1yA98vadjwL6neLqrQ

29. 'Over 220 Kazakhstani nationals died in fighting in the Middle East': https://www.zakon.kz/4893699-svyshe-220-grazhdan-kazahstana-pogiblo.html.
30. 'NSC reveals plan of action in fight against extremism and terrorism': https://tengrinews.kz/kazakhstan_news/knb-predstavil-plan-deystviy-borbe-ekstremizmom-terrorizmom-311730/.
31. 'NSC Vice President explains why terrorists are not being stripped of their citizenship for now': https://informburo.kz/novosti/zamglavy-knb-rasskazal-pochemu-terroristov-poka-ne-lishayut-grazhdanstva.html.

family members and wives remain abroad in the ranks of terrorist organisations.'[32]

ISIS marketing

The stream of ISIS propaganda materials featuring Kazakhstani nationals fighting in Syria and Iraq became a serious challenge for Kazakhstan's security. Terrorist groups published a series of videos in which Kazakhstani fighters took part.

Before the release of the scandalous video about '150 Kazakhstanis in Syria', in July 2013, the SITE Intelligence Group website published a video showing a Kazakh-speaking fighter calling for recruits to take part in the war in Syria. It has not been confirmed that this individual was a Kazakhstani national.

A Kazakhstani fighter rallies people to participate in the war in Syria

A second video was released in October 2013. The French television network France 24 ran a report on a video posted by the ISIS terrorist group. The 20-minute videos talks of 150 Kazakhstani nationals – men, women, teenagers and children – who arrived in Syria in an orderly manner to perform jihad. Fighters in the video declare that they arrived with their families in order to die a martyr's death in the name of jihad. On the one hand, the video underlined that Kazakhstanis were

---

32. '40 Kazakhstanis still in the ranks of fighters abroad – NSC': https://tengrinews.kz/kazakhstan_news/40-kazahstantsev-ostayutsya-v-ryadah-boevikov-za-rubejom-knb-386363/.

Timeline for the Publishing of Propaganda Videos about Kazakhstani Militants in Syria and Iraq

Date	Content	Group	Media Resource	Language	Duration
17 July 2013	Fighter calls people to join jihad in Syria in the Kazakh language	ISIS	-	Kazakh	-
15 October 2013	Video claims '150 Kazakhstanis' arrived in Syria to take part in combat.	ISIS	H-Center.info	Kazakh, Russian	20 min. 23
March 2014	About the death of a 19-year-old fighter from Abu Hurairah Kazakhi group	Jaish al-Muhajireen wal-Ansar	Akhbar Sham	Arabic	03 min. 19
16 July 2014	16 people, some masked, stand with arms in hands. Abu Sina speaks in Kazakh, saying that many Kazakhs are fighting in Sham and calls for jihad in Syria.	ISIS	al-Hayat Media Center	Kazakh, Russian, subtitles	08 min. 05
22 November 2014	About 'Kazakh Jamaat' in Syria. Footage of minors training with weapons. Some give interviews in Kazakh.	ISIS	al-Hayat Media Center	English and Russian subtitle Kazakh	14 min. 55

Date	Content	Group	Media Resource	Language	Duration
January 2015	Execution of two allegedly Kazakh-born Russian FSB agents, in which a child from Kazakhstan takes part.	ISIS	al-Hayat Media Center	Russian, English subtitles	07 min. 38
28 February 2016	Children of Kazakh jihadists level threats at the country's leadership	ISIS	Furat Media	Russian, Kazakh	06 min. 37
May 2016	About 'Turkestani Jamaat'. Depicts the activities of fighters and recent events on controlled territories	Kazakh Islamic Jihad	-	Russian, Kazakh	04 min. 04
January 2018	Video of Kazakh fighters in a training camp. A blind fighter from Kazakhstan works as a masseur helping others in physical rehab.	ISIS	-	Kazakh, Arabic subtitles	-

leaving for Syria en masse; on the other hand, it foregrounded the role of children. However, the wife of one of those '150 Kazakhstanis', Aziza Azmametova, who later returned to Kazakhstan, stated that all members of the Old Turkestan group were forced to take part in making this video in August 2013. According to her, members of the CIS Brigade and the Daud Brigade, also known as 'Kazakh Jamaat', participated, too.

> My husband was called to the set, but he did not even know why he had to travel there. Initially, everyone was told that an address to all emirs would be recorded, nobody guessed that the video would be used for jihad propaganda. Refusing to participate was out of the question.[33]

This is one of the first candid interviews about the lives of Kazakhstanis fighting in Syria. It was precisely this interview that confirmed to some extent one version of events, maintaining that some of the Kazakhstanis who left for Syria were misinformed or tricked. Relatives and friends of those who emigrated said the same.

Still from the video about '150 Kazakhstanis' who arrived in Syria

In April 2016, Azamat Shalkarbai's user page on the social network VK posted photos of fighters in Syria; some of them (Amanzhol Zhansegirov and Teimur Balashakiyev) had been spotted earlier in footage about '150 Kazakhstanis'. Close examination of the photos

---

33. 'Wife of Kazakhstani sentenced for calling for jihad gives candid interview': https://www.lada.kz/another_news/18992-zhena-osuzhdennogo-za- prizyvy-k-dzhihadu-kazahstanca-dala-otkrovennoe-intervyu.html.

showed that they were taken at the same time as the video was being shot, in summer 2013.

Kazakh fighters in Syria

In July 2014, a third video about Kazakhs fighting in Syria and Iraq appeared on social media linked to ISIS. The footage shows sixteen armed people, some of whom are masked. One man, Abu Sina, speaks in Kazakh, saying that there are many Kazakhs fighting in Sham, and calls for jihad in Syria. He declares that they 'will start in Sham and come to Kazakhstan'. It was subsequently reported that four Kazakhs caught in this video, allegedly, committed acts of terror and died, including the militant who called for jihad. This video had probably been put together earlier, in 2013 or early 2014. This is suggested by the fact the fighters shown in the video, members of ISIS, do not mention the group's recent military operations in Iraq in their recorded messages.

Fighter calls for jihad in Kazakh language[34]

---

34. Video: https://vk.com/club69751505?z=video-71849371_168972742%2 F662a415905ee03a8a7.

Fighters who died in Syria and Iraq

At the end of the video, a threat was levelled at Central Asian intelligence agencies – the National Security Committee of Kazakhstan and the National Security Committee of Kyrgyzstan.

Still from the video: 'Address from Kazakhstani brothers in Sham'
Caption on the still: Assassination of Sefevid secret service agent,
Baghdad (Message for NSC of Kazakhstan: 'we remember you, scum!')

If in previous videos with Kazakhstanis they spoke of holy duty, the suppression of Muslims, and called people to join their brothers fighting in Syria, in the video from July 2014, for the first time, Kazakh fighters called people to jihad on the territory of their own country. This video became the touchstone triggering the agitation of Kazakhstani nationals.

In November 2014, another video about Kazakhs fighting in Syria appeared: 'Race towards Good'. The American SITE Intelligence Group was the first to report on it. The Kazakhstani media later quoted this source in articles discussing the video of an alleged Kazakhstani national calling for jihad in July 2013. The SITE Intelligence Group was also the initial source for information on the terrorist group Soldiers of the Caliphate in 2011. The video from November 2014 showed fighters undergoing general training in camps, after which they switched to special training, learning how to use various types of weapons, especially sniper rifles. In the video, one of the instructors said in Russian that he was in a 'Jamaat of Kazakh Brothers' and they were 'studying all known types of rifle – American, Russian and Austrian'. He also stated that the first group of fighters had already completed their training and would soon join the ISIS terrorist group.

Screenshots from the November 2014 video

Once again, the focus of the video is on children, presenting about thirty of them. Children are shown during lessons in ISIS madrasas learning the Qur'an, tajwid (rules on the orthoepic reading of the Qur'an), and the Arabic language. The video also states that the children undergo physical and military training and learn how to handle weapons. In the interviews, the children speak in Kazakh, saying they will become 'mujahids who kill kaffirs [infidels]'.

Screenshots from the November 2014 video

It must be noted that the fifteen-minute video was filmed and put together in a professional manner with the use of modern technologies and is in high resolution. It was published on the ISIS media outlet al-Hayat Media Center. Most probably, the video was shot in summer or autumn 2014, because it uses the group's then-currrent name – the Islamic State; as we know, the group changed its name from 'Islamic State of Iraq and Syria' (ISIS) to 'Islamic State' (IS) in June 2014.

In 2015, ISIS released another video featuring children from Kazakhstan. This video will be discussed in detail in the following chapter on minors. Later, at the end of February 2016, the ISIS media outlet Furat Media, aimed at viewers from the post-Soviet areas, released a series of so-called messages to the countries of the Central Asian region, including Kazakhstan. In the seven-minute video titled 'Heartfelt message to the lads of Kazakhstan', the Kazakh fighter Marat

Maulenov from the Turkestan Oblast, spoke in Russian about life in the Caliphate. He calls his home country 'Kaffirstan', from the word 'kaffir' ('infidel'), a dreadful sin in Islam. At the end of that video, teenagers (it later became known that these were in fact Maulenov's two underage sons) voice threats to the leadership of the Republic. It subsequently came to light that Maulenov's elder son died 'as a *shahid* [martyr]', as his father said. In the documentary *In Search of Faith* (directed by Asiya Baigozhina) produced with state support, Maulenov's brother talks about Marat and his family, mentioning that fighters rejoice and congratulate each other when their children become *shahids*. He goes on to say that his brother hopes his younger son will follow in the footsteps of his older, twenty-two-year-old son. Unfortunately, in this particular case, the propaganda video foregrounded fanatics ready to sacrifice their own innocent children. Maulenov died in 2017 and his surviving family members were evacuated during the covert Operation: Jusan.

Marat Maulenov

At the beginning of 2018, yet another propaganda video from Daesh (an abbreviation for ISIS from Arabic) showed radicals from Kazakhstan. They called to overthrow the country's government: 'It [the government] had no right to destroy Muslim identity and govern with laws imported from Russia.'[35] Alongside the 'functioning' Kazakh

---

35. https://ent.siteintelgroup.com/Multimedia/kazakh-is-fighters-call-on-fellow-countrymen-to-rise-up-in-video.html.

fighters, the video shows a blind man called Abu Bakr al-Kazakhi. According to the video, he is the masseur who helps wounded fighters recover; he has two wives. The ISIS message is clear: thanks to faith, even the blind, sick, or outcast can find fulfilment in the Caliphate.

Abu Bakr al-Kazakhi

'My brothers and sisters, o, my brothers in faith! What happened to you? Where are you? Haven't you dreamed of the Caliphate for many years? And here it is, the Caliphate Allah has granted us!' says Abu Bakr al-Kazakhi in the video.[36]

However, the story of Erbol from Zhezkazgan, as told by those who recognised 'al-Kazakhi', differs from that narrated in the video. A man named Askar, interviewed by researchers Noah Tucker and Serik Beisembayev, stated that the local mosque collected money to pay for massage courses to help Erbol gain regular income. But Erbol did not easily find work and his friend advised him to go to Syria.

Besides 'official' ISIS propaganda videos, fighters from Kazakhstan also released their own amateur footage about military activity in Syria and Iraq on the Internet.

---

36. 'ISIS use a BLIND jihadist to make new attack threats weeks after a one-legged fanatic said having a disability was "no excuse" for not fighting': https://www.dailymail.co.uk/news/article-5301205/ISIS-use-BLIND-jihadist-make-new-attack-threats.html.
[36] Ibid.

Screenshots from a video of Kazakh fighters in Syria and Iraq

On 19 May 2016, a video titled 'Battle for Sham' was posted on YouTube. It claimed to be about the Turkestani jamaat in Syria. In Russian and Kazakh with subtitles in both languages, it spoke of the activities of the fighters and recent events in the controlled territories. According to an analysis of chronological data, the video was filmed in 2015 by a member of the al-Nusra Front. In May 2015, this group had captured the Syrian town of Ariha mentioned in the video, which as they said was the last to fall in Idlib Province.[37] The video also reports on travelling to another town, Muhambil, captured by al-Nusra Front in June 2015.[38] It should be noted that most of the militants are wearing masks or are filmed from behind, and only some, including fighters from Palestine, are showing their faces. The name of a group founded and active in Afghanistan – Kazakh Islamic Jihad – can be seen written on a wall in one scene in the video. According to the credits and video effects, the video was made in a video-editing programme 'iMovie' on a smart phone.

Screenshots from the video, 19.05.2016

37. 'Rebels capture last Syrian town in Idlib province': http://www.reuters.com/article/us-mideast-crisis-syria-ariha-idUSKBN0OD2LK20150529.
38. 'Syrian regime air strikes kill 49 in Idlib': http://www.trtworld.com/mea/syrian-regime-air-strikes-kill-49-idlib-2703.

A general analysis of the 'official' propaganda and 'unofficial' amateur videos about Kazakh fighters in Syria and Iraq reveals the following general traits:

Video quality: Targeted distribution of high-quality videos. Compared with analogous videos posted by fighters in Afghanistan and the Caucasus, these materials are of higher resolution and are not amateur but of professional quality. 'Official' videos are put together professionally with the use of special effects, slow motion, the sounds of explosions, and music. The majority of videos show footage of military action, training and calls for jihad.

Equipping and kitting out the fighters: Compared with similar content from Afghanistan and the Caucasus, where militants are shown wearing traditional local garments, in Syria they are dressed in military uniform.

Выходцы из Центральной Азии, присоединившиеся к радикальным группировкам в Афганистане

Центральноазиатские отряды в Сирии хорошо экипированы и оснащены современным оружием

Natives of Central Asia who joined radical groups in Afghanistan

Central Asian detachments in Syria, well-kitted and equipped with modern weapons

Fighters are well-armed and taught to use a variety of modern weapons, which testifies to the fact the radicals in Syria had good supply lines, at least at the beginning of the military conflict there. Moreover, fighters are using refitted cars equipped with artillery and mortar launchers.

The main language of propaganda is Russian: Even when fighters in the video address the viewer in Kazakh, their words are accompanied by subtitles in Russian. In most cases, the main credits are given in Russian and Kazakh. Such propaganda materials, like analogous videos from Afghanistan and the Caucasus, are aimed at the much larger Russian-speaking audience. Nevertheless, later videos begin using the Kazakh language more often, and this bears witness to the changing social portrait of radicals leaving for Syria.

Minors as a powerful ISIS propaganda weapon: Unlike other foreign fighters, including other Central Asian nationals, Kazakh fighters increasingly show their children in propaganda videos. The two last 'official' ISIS videos show minors holding weapons.

Frequency of video releases: During the course of one year, ISIS released at least two videos at intervals of three or four months. The last video was published in January 2018.

Unfortunately, as a result of the widespread presence of ISIS and other terrorist groups on the Internet, young people aged between twenty-two and thirty became the main victims of radical propaganda. Some followed the ideology of violence and led propaganda and recruitment activities in Kazakhstan itself. In November 2015 alone, several citizens were simultaneously convicted for propagating terrorism in general and the radical ideas of ISIS in particular. Four residents of the Burlinsk district of the West Kazakhstan Oblast were sentenced to five and a half years in a general correction facility. The investigation revealed that they 'gathered in a rented flat in Aksay, watched videos about terrorist activities in Iraq and Syria.

Furthermore, one of the accused was in touch with a native of Aksay who is now fighting with ISIS, and he himself was planning to leave for Syria.'[39]

Here are some examples of sentences given in 2015 for violent extremist propaganda and terrorism:

- In the Kostanay Oblast, a resident of the town of Rudniy was sentenced to six years for spreading propaganda about ISIS on social media.[40] The investigation revealed that, from January 2014, he posted videos promoting terrorism and extremism on his pages in social networks.
- Two twenty-seven-year-old residents of Nur-Sultan [here and afterwards used as the standard name for the capital of Kazakhstan] were sentenced to five years. According to the case files, A. from Zhezkazgan and G. from the Chechen Republic of the Russian Federation, preached 'the radical religious ideology of joining the ranks of the international terrorist organisation Daesh' to three men from July–August in 2015 in a hotel in Nur-Sultan.[41]
- A twenty-three-year-old woman from the town of Zyryanovsk in East Kazakhstan Oblast was sentenced for attempting to send her younger brother to Syria.[42]

---

39. 'Four residents of Southern Kazakhstan sentenced for terrorist propaganda': https://www.kt.kz/rus/crime/chetvero_zhitelej_zapadnogo_kazahstana_osuzhdeni_za_propagandu_terrorizma_1153612554.html.
40. 'A lawyer from Rudniy sentenced to six years for propaganda of Daesh ideas': http://tengrinews.kz/crime/yurista-rudnogo-prigovorili-shesti-godam-propagandu-idey-284303/.
41. 'Two residents of Astana sentenced to five years for terrorist propaganda': http://www.dailynews.kz/acidents/crimes/za_propagandu_terrorizma_osuzhdeny_na_pjat_let_dvoe_zhitelej_astany.
42. 'Young woman from Zyryanovsk in East Kazakhstan Oblast found guilty of promoting extremist propaganda and attempting to send her younger brother to war in Syria': http://newskaz.ru/regions/20151119/10269443.html#ixzz3sRum3Mny.

Despite illegal content being monitored and blocked, radical Internet propaganda remains a major problem in the fight against terrorism and religious extremism. This is also confirmed by NSC RK deputy chairman Nurgali Bilisbekov:

> There is still a high level of extremist and terrorist propaganda, which could facilitate the radicalisation of Kazakhstani society. This and other factors dictate the necessity of further improving the nationwide system of fighting against terrorism and religious extremism.[43]

The country's authorities are taking preventative measures to counteract the further departure of nationals to zones of military conflict. According to data from the Anti-Terrorist Centre of the NSC, '70,000 instances of spreading extremist content online are neutralised every month'.[44]

Kazakh radicals in Syria

To date, dozens of generalised portraits of radicals have been made. A range of social drivers, including religious fanaticism, prompted the decision to leave for Syria and join radical groups. The general characteristics of Kazakhstanis who left for Syria can be summed up as follows: relatively young; lacking religious education; leaving with their families. A preliminary social analysis of the personal data of the identified members of radical groups reveals the following picture:

---

43. 'Vice Chairperson of NSC – "Level of propaganda for religious extremism and terrorism in Kazakhstan remains high"':
http://antiterrortoday.com/geografiya-terrorizma/proyavleniya-terrorizma-i-ekstremizma-po-stranam/s-n-g/tsentralnaya-aziya/kazakhstan/15746-uroven-propagandy-religioznogo-ekstremizma-i-terrorizma-v-kazakhstane-ostaetsya-vysokim-zampred-knb.
44. '57 radicals sentenced in Kazakhstan since the beginning of 2016 – NSC': https://tengrinews.kz/kazakhstan_news/57-radikalov-osudili-v-kazahstane-s-nachala-2016-goda-knb-301610/.

Age

The ages of those who left for military conflict zones in Syria and Iraq vary between eighteen and forty-five (excluding small children). The average age is twenty-eight.

The youngest member of a radical group was eighteen when he took part in military action. Every other Kazakhstani who left for the Syrian war zone did not reach the age of thirty. Every third male did not live to twenty-five.

Around 56 per cent of the total number of Kazakhstanis who left for Syria were young men aged eighteen to twenty-nine. Around 24 per cent of Kazakhstani militants were aged thirty to thirty-nine when they left for the conflict zone. Those over forty account for 20 per cent.

Demographic Markers (Age)

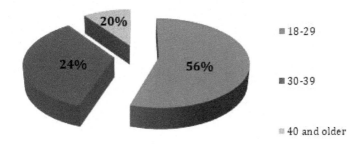

Education, occupation

Around 30 per cent of Kazakhstani fighters had completed secondary or higher vocational education. Moreover, most of them chose occupations that were not connected with military affairs whatsoever. For example, one of the Kazakhstanis who left for Syria worked as a senior specialist in the Zaisan local history museum. Aibek Gubaidullin from West Kazakhstan Oblast was captain of the Akzhaiyk Football Club. Another football player from Ural,

Talgat Tureyev, former defender for the Zhastar Football Club, died in Syria in 2016. One of the '150 Kazakhstanis', Erkebulan Igibayev, worked as an electrical engineer in the Kazkat Factory. Marat Maulenov taught Russian language in a Turkestani school; later, together with his wife and six children, he found himself in Syria. A fifty-year-old resident of Almaty Oblast repatriated during Operation: Jusan had previously worked in law enforcement for several years, later becoming an entrepreneur.

Some men ran private businesses, which allowed their families to live in a third country for an extended period. For example, one prominent businessman from Nur-Sultan sold off several companies with the intention of emigrating to Madinah, but ended up living with his family in the Middle East. One native of Almaty left for Syria from Sweden, where he resided with his wife and children.

The majority of men, however, did not have a stable job at the time of their departure. Some were working as flat renovators, others worked as wardens or security guards, some sold mobile phones in the market, others earned on the side in tyre shops. On the whole, they were engaged in the retail business or were seasonal workers doing odd jobs. These people felt useless and vulnerable and were easy prey for recruiters.

Religious involvement
Future foreign terrorist fighters from Kazakhstan turning to destructive religious movements peaked between 2008 and 2011. Many began performing *namaz* [ritual prayers] at the age of twenty-one. A third of them, however, turned to religion at a relatively mature age, between thirty and thirty-two. According to those convicted for terrorist activities, one of their main reasons for turning to religion was emotional stress and problems in their private lives. Some had lost a child, resulting in the collapse of their family. Others fell gravely ill, which changed their worldview and prompted them to turn to the Qur'an. All in all, people became vulnerable and easily fell into the hands of recruiters from various radical organisations. For example Ruslan, a resident of Almaty

Oblast now serving a sentence for terrorism, was urged by his relatives to turn to religion. On their advice, he began attending friday prayers at the mosque. Lacking solid religious knowledge, he read books bought near the mosque and later began searching for information on the Internet. He began discussing jihad with his friends in 2007–08. Personal tragedy prompted his radicalisation. His daughter died, and then his family collapsed. In 2010, Ruslan decided to leave for Afghanistan but then began considering going to Syria instead. He hit upon the idea of 'joining jihad' some time after seeing a call on the Internet.

For another man, also a resident of the Almaty Oblast, it was emotional stress that served as the trigger for turning to religion – he broke up with the girl he had been living with for three years and had intended to marry. Following his older brother's advice, he developed an interest in religion. He studied by himself, using books sold near the mosque. It was his brother who first showed him banned websites and together they would read radical content. It was also his elder brother who initiated discussions about jihad.

Kamil Abdullin, a resident of Almaty, grew up as a problem child in not the most well-to-do family and, as a teenager, he ran away several times, sometimes of his own accord, although sometimes he was thrown out. At the age of twenty-two, under the influence of close friends, he began performing *namaz*. In 2007, he spent three months in Egypt. He began listening to Said Buryatski's preachings a year later. According to him, local imams and lecturers had very low levels of competence at that time. Kamil became interested in jihad when he and his wife moved to Sweden, where a Chechen man showed him a news website. It was then that he first heard about Syria. Abdullin says those videos impacted strongly on him.

According to information gathered during interviews with him, many people engage in religion through audio and video content and books, sometimes without even knowing who the authors are. As terrorist propaganda spread on the Internet and access became easier, they absorbed everything that was openly accessible, without thinking much about the reliability of the sources. Consequently, the overwhelming majority of Kazakhstani 'jihadis' had no rudimentary or basic knowledge of religion, and only a small proportion had a specialised religious education. A few had studied in Egypt.

Regional specifics

According to interviews with convicts, there were a considerable number of natives from West Kazakhstan Oblast in Syria. But hotbeds of radicalisation were not confined to the west; central Kazakhstan also became one of the main 'providers' of new recruits for international terrorist organisations; we have already mentioned Zhezkazgan and Satpayev. According to local residents, around 250–300 people left from these two towns – in other words, they accounted for a third of the total number of emigrée. Almaty and the Turkestan Oblast also became hubs for the spread of religious extremism. From the Maktaaral district of the Turkestan Oblast alone, fifty people left for Syria. The majority of emigrated Kazakhstani nationals were from urban, not rural areas.

In order to better understand the reasons behind their departure, a series of interviews were held with men who had returned. They were tried upon their return to Kazakhstan and are currently serving prison sentences. All of them were ex-fighters who had, to a greater or lesser extent, taken part in military action on Syrian territory in the ranks of various terrorist organisations. Most are serving six-to-seven-year sentences in general penal colonies.

By analysing the interviews, we can highlight several factors that contributed to the radicalisation of these people.

First. As mentioned above, virtually all interviewees had been in a state of psychological crisis and under severe emotional stress when they became involved in religion (losing loved ones, illness, family collapse, or financial problems).

Second. The main motive behind the decision to leave for Syria for jihad was the desire to help 'brothers in faith'. Violent video footage and appeals for help elicited sympathy and shame for their own inaction, for their peaceful life. They sincerely believed that Muslims in Syria were subject to severe persecution, tortured and mercilessly killed. Video footage showing violence against women and young children elicited particularly strong emotions in the majority of respondents.

Third. One reason why future fighters joined non-traditional Islamic movements was the ineptitude of local imams. According to the respondents, imams in official mosques could not reply to some of their direct questions. Many convicts were unhappy with how they were treated in the mosques, as well as with the lack of conditions for receiving education on religious matters. That is why they began searching for answers to their questions in religious books, even when they did not know who wrote them.

Fourth. Cyberspace became a key factor in transforming individuals into radical Islamists ready to sacrifice themselves and their loved ones in the name of religion. They compensated for their lack of basic religious knowledge by watching radical content on the Internet. In particular, some respondents watched jihadi content on the Kavkaz Centre forum – *sharshsunna.org*.

Fifth. According to data from the interviews, virtually all respondents were members of non-traditional religious groups – jamaats – when they committed crimes. For example, some were followers of the extremist organisation Tablighi Jamaat. Discussions about joining jihad would begin among friends, acquaintances, brothers and jamaats. Consequently, most of the convicts entered the radical path under the influence of close relatives or friends.

During the interviews, respondents spoke of the situation of Kazakhstanis and other nationals in Syria. It should be noted that the interviewees had been in the Syrian conflict zone at various times, but mainly in 2013. How long they stayed in Syria also varied – from several years to four to seven days. As a result, figures for the general number of Kazakhstanis in Syria also vary. For example, one of the convicts reported that there were only a few Kazakhstanis still in Syria, around thirty to forty people. Other interviewees suggested a figure of 100–300. According to information gained from returnees, the average age of Kazakhstanis in Syria was twenty-three to twenty-seven, and most of the fighters were from western regions of the country; they also noted that there were quite a few who arrived from Almaty and Shymkent.

Replying to the question 'who and what was the fight in Syria for?', one of the convicts tentatively divided those who fought in Syria into five groups. However, as the interviewee himself remarked, he himself passed through all of these stages.

Sincere ones. These die first and genuinely believe they are doing something to please Allah. 'They are wild. The emirs know that if they see injustice, they will turn their guns on them.' That is why 'the sincere ones' are first to be sent to 'hotspots'.

Thrill-seekers. Those who came in search of thrills, wanted to 'have fun'. This category normally has a sponsor in Turkey who supports their families. They come to Syria to shoot, take photos with military trophies, and then go back. 'He returned from jihad, he needs to rest up for six months,' they say.

Businessmen. Their aim is to make money. 'Let's say there is a small jamaat of about twenty people. You know that there are 1,000 bucks in the jamaat's safe. And that tomorrow fifteen people are leaving for a military operation. The five that remain are no problem. You can come in at night, grab the money, as well as weapons that can be sold on,' they say.

Fanatics. 'Not of Islam as a whole, but of a particular jamaat.' These people submit not to Sharia law but to the instructions of the leader of their community. 'It's like [Hitler] and his SS. There is no other [authority for them]. The personal guard is taken from these guys. It's from these guys that they prepare returnees who will work back in their homeland.'

Lost souls. This is the smallest category. They really didn't and don't know how they ended up in Syria. Usually, they don't stay in the conflict zone for long. Many want to go away, and manage to do so. But those who don't, remain.

As this tentative classification shows, the circumstances that lead people to join radical groups in Syria can differ. Nevertheless, many returnee fighters share the conviction that it is, in the end, *somebody else's war.* Virtually all interviewees said that what is happening in Syria is not jihad but a big political game between government forces, the opposition and ISIS; also between Russia and the US.

Here are some excerpts from interviews with returnees:

'... I saw everything. I saw NATO weapons with erased numbers. I saw how weapons were brought from Turkey. I saw American instructors.'

'... I just overheard conversations that Russia is going to pump gas through. And so that somehow affects the decision in Europe. Through America, Europe makes deals with the Middle East so that gas would go through Syria, Turkey and into Europe. But since Syria and Russia are friends, they don't allow European interests here.'

'... It's a civil war. It's politics. Oil. Money. Butting their heads against each other. It means that brothers are fighting against brothers. Brother killing brother... It's just a pointless war.'

Another reason why some Kazakhstanis began doubting the 'sincerity of jihad' in Syria was their disillusionment with the religiosity of the Arabs themselves. According to interviewees, they were surprised that not all Arab fighters adhered to religious practices, in particular, performing mandatory *namaz* five times a day. Some of them drank alcohol, smoked, etc. One of the respondents noted: 'They didn't fight in that war on religious grounds.' As history has shown, for Kazakhstani Islamic extremists, jihad is first and foremost the war against infidels in other countries, a war that is meant to help Muslims. They asked themselves the rhetorical question and replied themselves.

'How can I not commiserate? Muslims are being killed in so many ways. Bombed by [Bashar al-]Assad or by Americans, or by ISIS explosions, the result is the same – Muslims perish. Nowadays, the cheapest blood is the blood of Muslims. In Iraq, Egypt, Tunisia, Yemen, Afghanistan and Syria.'

Describing their life in Syria, all convicts reported they were given food and lodging. In the initial stages, people were broken into small 'jamaats' with around eighteen to twenty people per house, and an average of four to five people per room. Food and accommodation were paid for by the 'jamaat' commander. When fighters were moved to larger groups such as ISIS or al-Nusra Front, they were not only provided with food and accommodation but also received 'monthly salaries'. Some received $50 US dollars and were given $150 US dollars to support their family. One of the interviewees noted that, after joining ISIS, they had a stable supply of money, distributed to each house.

'It wasn't in a safe but just lying in a cupboard. You take 6,000, go and buy food, bring it back, write down a list of what you bought and how much for, give it to Abu Khanifa, and he would give it to HQ. The next day, Abu Khanifa pops in and I'm saying: "Only 2,000 left, give me some money," and he replies: "I'll go to HQ now." He goes to HQ, gets money again. So long as I give him a receipt of how much I bought, and the price. Otherwise, there's no problem, "If you want to spend all the money in one day, that's your business." That's what he said.'

According to the interviewees, even if there were weapons, they were not handed out to everyone. Those who were in Syria for less than a month were advised to buy weapons in a special shop. The average price for a Kalashnikov varied between $800 to $2,500. In the larger groups, weapons were given for free. One of the convicts said he helped transport the wounded and prepare food for them. Others just guarded the territory in *ribats* (border posts constructed on the borders of the Muslim world with hostile, non-Muslim states).[45] However, many had to undergo training and practise handling weapons. So, if they did not work or were not sent somewhere, they were free all day to do as they pleased.

Information on the linguistic specifics of Kazakhstanis in Syria was compiled during the interviews. According to the data, the majority of militants were Russian speakers, and only a minority spoke Kazakh. The Russian language became the main facilitating tool for bonding Kazakhstanis with other nationals from the post-Soviet states. According to information from foreign experts, the Russian language became the third official language of the ISIS terrorist group, after Arabic and English. This underlines once again the presence of a significant contingent of fighters from CIS countries.

Broadly speaking, the problem of Kazakhstani jihadis in Syria can be tentatively examined from two standpoints. The first suggests an evaluation of the influence of external factors on Kazakhstanis, while the second focuses on internal cause-and-effect connections within this phenomenon. The dramatic events in the Middle East triggered further geopolitical shifts in the rest of the world. The war transcended the confines of regional conflict, and tensions between various power structures paved the way for new radical groups. The terrorist acts that took place in Paris in January and November 2015 demonstrated that the threat developing from this conflict had become global, and that any person on the planet could become a target, irrespective of their passport or the security systems the authorities had put in place in their country. In this sense, unfortunately, Kazakhstan is no exception.

As for domestic causes prompting radicalisation, we must look at factors that determine the status and prosperity of a person in their own country. According to research and data from experts, Kazakhstani radicals generally come from socially disadvantaged regions. As I have already mentioned, several factors contribute to

---

45. Encyclopaedic dictionary: http://dic.academic.ru/dic.nsf/islam/653/Рибат.

a person's susceptibility to recruitment – poor religious literacy or low emotional state. However, we should not forget socio-economic factors that render a person vulnerable: unemployment, ineffective social policies for youth, problems in education and upbringing. These are problems facing many young, active people and, failing to find a solution, they instead find support and understanding in radical groups.[46] A growing sense of being an outsider in their own country plays into the recruiters' hands. A report by the International Crisis Group also talks about the role that a weak state and poor religious education can play for those predisposed to feeling alienated. Despite the absence of a generalised portrait of the Central Asian militant, there is one factor common to all those who left the region: socio-political fatigue.[47]

These challenges remain current, as do the problems demanding our attention. Despite the fall of the ISIS caliphate, the group itself – now called IS – and its ideology still pose a threat to the world, due primarily to the strengthening and widening of its underground network. Pentagon Principal Deputy Inspector General Glenn Fine stated in his report 'This quarter, IS continued its transition from a territory-holding force to an insurgency in Syria, and it has intensified its insurgency in Iraq.'[48] This highlights that numbers of rebels in the terrorist group in Iraq and Syria may be as high as 14,000–18,000. At the same time, UN data shows that several Central Asian groups associated with al-Qaeda are active in Badakhshan Province (Afghanistan), including about fifty fighters from the Brigade of Imam Bukhari, 100 fighters from the Islamic Movement of Uzbekistan, and fifty fighters from the Islamic Jihad Union. According to UN evaluations, the Islamic Movement of Eastern Turkestan accounts

---

46. 'Fighter calls for jihad in the Kazakh language': https://tengrinews.kz/crime/boevik-prizval-k-djihadu-v-sirii-na-kazahskom-yazyike-238086/.
47. 'Experts talk of growing IS threat to Central Asia': http://rus.azattyq.org/a/icg-ugrozy-bezopasnosti-ig-centralnaya-azia/26805103.html.
48. 'Report: ISIS has been rebuilding as US troops withdraw from Syria': https://www.militarytimes.com/news/your-military/2019/08/06/report-isis-has-been-rebuilding-as-us-troops-withdraw-from-syria/.

for around 350 fighters and Jamaat Ansarullah for around thirty Tajikistan nationals. The number of fighters from Central Asia in the local ISIS branch in Afghanistan headed by the Tajikistan national Saivali Shafiyev accounts for around 200.

Thus, we can say that the deterioration of the situation in Syria and the expansion of radical groups in Afghanistan will exert serious pressure on the security system not only in Kazakhstan but in Central Asia as a whole. As demonstrated by the 2016 terrorist acts in Aktobe and Almaty and the terrorist act near the Chinese Embassy in Bishkek, Central Asian militants fighting in Syria never lost hope of returning to their region in order to fulfil so-called jihad. And this means that terrorism remains a serious threat.

II

THE FEMALE FACE OF RADICALISATION

International terrorism continues to expand, drawing increasingly large numbers of new adepts into its network. The tendency for the active involvement of children and minors in terrorist and extremist activities is of growing concern. However, until now, research has mainly focused on chronicling the radicalisation of thousands of male fighters. Many social portraits have been drawn to show the characteristic of the modern radical, taking into account regional and ethnic specifics as well as what motivated the adult male who deliberately chose this path. For a long time it was thought that jihad was 'a male business'; other, unwitting participants in the radicalisation process – women and minors – were overlooked. Today, studies analysing their motivation still lag behind studies examining the reasons underlying the radicalisation of men.

Nevertheless, this problem is now being discussed more frequently on both a regional and a global level. The trend towards the feminisation of extremism can be observed all over the world, partly because of the widening of the Syrian conflict. To some extent the war in Syria led to women with weapons being seen as heroes. The image of an armed woman was used in both ISIS propaganda and in their opponents' counter-propaganda – for example, in Kurdish brigades.

The UN study 'Women and Violent Extremism in Europe and Central Asia' provides the following data: from 2012 onwards, the flow of foreign terrorist fighters and ISIS supporters leaving for Syria and Iraq became significantly more 'female'.[1] The research focused on several countries, including two Central Asian republics – Kyrgyzstan and Tajikistan. According to this data, worldwide, 15–20 per cent of those attracted by violent extremism were women, and this figure was up to 30 per cent in some countries.[2] It has recently been noted that women recruited to terrorist groups pose no less a danger than their male counterparts. From 2015–17, the number of terrorist crimes committed by women grew by 23 per cent.[3] For example, in Kyrgyzstan, every fifth person convicted of criminal acts of a terrorist or extremist nature is a woman.[4] According to the Ministry of Internal Affairs of Kyrgyzstan, in 2005 the proportion of women involved in extremist crimes was 1.1 per cent, whereas it had increased to 25 per cent in 2015. From 2010 to 2016, 863 Kyrgyzstani nationals joined international terrorist organisations in Syria and Iraq, 188 – or 23.8 per cent – of whom were women.[5]

According to information from official sources in Tajikistan, 1,940 citizens left their country and joined ISIS between 2012 and 2016, including 125–200 women.[6]

---

1. 'Women and Violent Extremism in Europe and Central Asia': http://eca.unwomen.org/en/digital-library/publications/2017/10/women-and-violent-extremism-in-europe-and-central-asia.

2. 'Women and extremism: How many Tajik women went to Syria?': https://news.tj/ru/news/centralasia/20180125/zhentshini-i-ekstremizm-issledovanie-oon-po-tsentralnoi-azii.

3. 'Swiss Jihad': https://www.fondsk.ru/news/2018/06/18/shvejcarskij-dzhihad-46319.html

4. 'The increasingly female face of extremism in Kirgizia': https://www.ritmeurasia.org/new.s--2018-02-08--ekstremizm-v-kirgizii-vse-bolshe-priobretaet-zhenskoe-lico-34846.

5. Ibid.

6. 'Women and extremism': https://news.tj/ru/news/centralasia/20180125/zhentshini-i-ekstremizm-issledovanie-oon-po-tsentralnoi-azii.

According to a report from the International Centre for Radicalisation Studies, of the 41,490 foreign nationals who joined ISIS in Iraq and Syria between April and June 2018, 4,761 (13 per cent) were women and 4,640 (12 per cent) were minors.[7] According to other data, at some point there were 680 women from Western Europe, mostly from France (320), Germany (190) and Great Britain (100) in the ranks of ISIS.[8] According to the words of Kheda Saratova, a member of the Human Rights Council under the President of the Chechen Republic: 'There are 7,000 Russian widows in Idlib alone. Including 3,000–3,500 women from the North Caucasus, and they each have four to five children.'[9] In 2018, twenty-one Russian women in Iraq were sentenced to life in prison, with fifty-seven more still awaiting trial in prison.[10] There are no precise data regarding the number of foreign women in conflict zones; the trend is obvious nonetheless.

Why are women being radicalised? What is behind the growing number of terrorist acts perpetrated by women? And how does this widespread involvement of women in terrorist activity impact on their children's choices? The reasons differ from case to case. According to Kyrgyz experts, one factor behind this radicalisation is the decrease in women's economic activity. In his research, Asel Murzakulova (of the Polis Asia Analytical Centre) concludes that, in 1991, almost 90 per cent of women in Kyrgyzstan were considered economically active. By 2013, this marker was down to 41 per cent. Unemployment was 20 per cent higher among women than among men. Moreover,

---

7. 'Number of women and children joining ISIS significantly underestimated': https://www.theguardian.com/world/2018/jul/23/number-of-women-and-children-joining-isis-significantly-underestimated.
8. 'Swiss Jihad': https://www.fondsk.ru/news/2018/06/18/shvejcarskij-dzhihad-46319.html.
9. '7,000 widows ask to be allowed back into Russia': https://www.kommersant.ru/doc/3798924 .
10. 'From ISIS to Russia: why Moscow halted the programme to repatriate women with children who fled to Iraq': https://www.currenttime.tv/a/29368391.html.

70 per cent of those employed in the shadow labour market were women.[11] Finding themselves in critical circumstances, women easily fell prey to extremist groups. These groups offered help and assistance in the form of social support: paying off debts, providing foodstuffs and medical services. Low levels of education and a general decrease in literacy among women also played a role.

According to Kazakhstani researchers, a tangled web of everyday troubles and mental problems prompts the radicalisation of women. Historian Gulnaz Razdykova, director of the Centre for the Analysis and Development of Inter-Confessional Relations in the Pavlodar Oblast, comments on the situation as follows:

The majority of women experienced a lack of parental love, loneliness, a negative attitude from those around them, and felt misunderstood. In other words, they did not have an emotional outlet. Religious illiteracy coupled with neglected psychological problems – this is the cocktail for the radicalisation of women. Many experienced grief and crisis in the family: the death of loved ones, loss of employment, divorce, or financial difficulties…[12]

According to Anne Speckhard, professor at the Georgetown University School of Medicine (USA) and head of the International Center for the Study of Violent Extremism, we should not differentiate the reasons for radicalisation according to sex or gender alone:

There are not so many differences between men and women who decide to become terrorists. They are influenced by the same factors, only the characteristics of personal vulnerability may differ slightly. At the same time, it is not so easy to get used to the thought that women are capable of violence. But sometimes

11. 'The increasingly female face of extremism in Kirgizia': https://www.ritmeurasia.org/news--2018-02-08--ekstremizm-v-kirgizii-vse-bolshe-priobretaet-zhenskoe-lico-34846.
12. 'Five reasons why Kazakh women become extremists': https://365info.kz/2018/06/5-prichin-po-kotorym-kazashki-stanovyatsya-ekstremistkami/.

circumstances are such that they, too, want revenge. And because they cannot become full-blown fighters wielding weapons, they are ready to don suicide belts.[13]

As for the Syrian case, the majority of married women and their children had practically no say in whether they went to Syria or not. The decision on the family's exodus for jihad was usually taken by men, and the majority of women just followed their husbands. This could be explained by the secondary role wives and women play in radical ideology and religious outlook: 'a wife must follow her husband'. In this case, children are also deprived of the right to choose. However, we should not completely rule out the power a woman has over her destiny. It is not uncommon for women remaining in the territories of Syria and Iraq to remarry several times, considering this normal practice.

Of course, fighters' widows were forced to remain in the conflict zone, and adapted to a reality where there was little choice – follow the rules or die. For example, according to ISIS rules, women whose husbands had died were allowed to return home only if they left their children behind, because militants' children became ISIS property, and they would be trained as a new generation of fighters.[14] On the other hand, there were cases when, mistakenly believing in a better life in the so-called Caliphate, some women went to combat zones in Syria and Iraq by themselves, where they married and obtained certain social status. In some cases, women supported their fighter-husbands and took on the role of recruiters. The story of Samantha Lewthwaite is a clear example of this. She was nicknamed the 'White Widow' after the death of her husband, a suicide bomber who took part in the London attack on 7 July 2005.

According to the *Daily Mail*, Lewthwaite is the most wanted woman in the world, and the search for her has been going on for almost ten

---

13. 'Women and extremism': http://nashagazeta.ch/news/politique/zhenshchiny-i-terrorizm. (Citation paraphrased; translator's note.)
14. 'Wives of ISIS fighters envious of houris': http://rus.azattyq.org/a/ig-zhenschiny-tema-guriy/27154080.html.

years. She is a thirty-six-year-old British citizen with four children. Her name is linked to terrorist groups in Somalia and Kenya.[15] The British intelligence agencies believe that the 'White Widow' recruits women suicide bombers for attacks on resorts all over the world. The Islamic chapter of Samantha Lewthwaite, who attended the University of London, began when her parents divorced. This was a severe blow for her, and she grew close to her Muslim neighbours, converting to Islam when she was seventeen. After the death of her first husband, who blew himself up on the London Underground, various sources maintain she left for Somalia, where she joined radical Islamists, and married one.

According to British intelligence, Samantha Lewthwaite is responsible for the deaths of 400 people[16]

One of the Kazakhstani women returned during Operation: Jusan left for Syria in 2013. She began practising Islam at the age of seventeen, and as early as eighteen decided she must join the cause of jihad.

---

15. 'British spies close the net on British "White Widow" terrorist Samantha Lewthwaite with the world's most wanted woman "in hiding in Yemen"': https://www.dailymail.co.uk/news/article-6539627/British-spies-close-British-White-Widow-terrorist-Samantha-Lewthwaite-Yemen.html.
16. 'British spies close the net on British "White Widow" terrorist Samantha Lewthwaite with the world's most wanted woman "in hiding in Yemen"': https://www.dailymail.co.uk/news/article-6539627/British-spies-close-British-White-Widow-terrorist-Samantha-Lewthwaite-Yemen.html.

She left for Syria via Turkey, where she married an ISIS fighter. Her husband was a native of the North Caucasus. It took her only a year to complete the journey from 'secular life' to the moment when she found herself voluntarily in the combat zone and under ISIS influence. Just one year to undergo all these stages of radicalisation: unfortunately, this is not an isolated case.

A report from the International Centre for the Study of Radicalisation states that the role of female ISIS supporters was not limited to the 'jihadi bride'. They actively recruited other women into the ranks of radical groups, spreading propaganda and gathering funds for the needs of the Caliphate. In Canada, women recruiters from Edmonton offered online Qur'an courses to those interested and, as a result, at least one girl fell under their influence and went to Syria. In the Spanish town of Ceuta, two friends headed a group that recruited other women for Iraqi and Syrian ISIS, before they left for the Middle East themselves.[17] There are even more horrendous cases of women who, either under pressure or following their fanatical beliefs, became direct participants in shocking acts of terrorism. One such incident happened in July 2017, in the Iraqi city of Mosul. A woman blew herself up; she was holding a baby, and that is why she did not arouse suspicion. As a result, she, the baby and two soldiers died.

As for women from Central Asia, many are currently still in temporary camps in various provinces in Syria and Iraq, some of which are under the UN Refugee Office. Others are in prisons. The majority of the women found themselves in Syria because of their husbands and did not particularly try to understand what was happening there. After their husbands died or were arrested, women with children found themselves in extremely hard living conditions.

---

17. 'How many women and children joined ISIS': https://nv.ua/world/geopolitics/ne-tolko-nevesty-eksperty-schitajut-chto-kolichestvo-zhenshchin-i-detej-podderzhivajushchikh-ihil-znachitelno-nedootsenili-2484297.html.

The woman with a baby several seconds before the blast[18]

Such families can be tentatively divided into three categories:

First category: If a killed militant's family remained in Syria after his death, sometimes his children were taken from their mothers and sent to training camps or children's brigades, where they were taught from an early age to handle weapons and carry out executions. The problem of radicals' family members, widows and children being abandoned to the whims of fate after their death is particularly pertinent for natives of Central Asia, because it was predominantly from this region that militants took their families with them to Syria. Some managed to return to the homeland by themselves; others were executed for attempting to leave the Islamic State.

Second category: Families who settled in a third country, for example, in Turkey or Egypt, after their fighter husbands or

---

18. 'Chilling footage captures female suicide bomber cradling baby moments before she blows them both up': https://www.independent.co.uk/news/world/female-suicide-bomber-jihadist-bride-isis-iraq-fall-of-mosul-a7832276.html#r3z-addoor.

relatives were killed or arrested, were killed or arrested. These people also find themselves in difficult conditions, without access to healthcare or education, and are socially unprotected. In 2016, reports began appearing that 'human rights lawyers encountered a new phenomenon – wives and girlfriends of fighters left in third countries began approaching them, seeking help from persecution by secret services who want to return them to the homeland, to Central Asian countries'.[19] Nadeja Atayeva, leader of the Association for Human Rights in Central Asia (AHRCA), stated the following in an interview:

> In the last few months alone (2016), we received seven applications from persons who had previously resided in Tajikistan, Uzbekistan, southern Kyrgyzstan and southern Kazakhstan. We put them into a special category because these people are linked to the Islamic State to differing degrees. Do they fall into the category of refugees, or are they in fact in the category of so-called special circumstances, under which they cannot receive international defence within the framework of the relevant UN convention?[20]

The complex socio-economic conditions in which women who have been deprived of their husbands' care find themselves, as well as fear of criminal prosecution, make them vulnerable to a second wave of radicalisation. It is not surprising, then, that radical groups often recruit suicide terrorists from among these widows.

Third category: Owing to the changed military situation in Syria and Iraq today, many women and children find themselves in temporary camps, and continue to expect their native states to intervene. Unfortunately, despite being moved to such camps after the collapse of the Islamic Caliphate, some of the women are still

---

19. 'Defending the rights of IS fighters' wives: a dilemma for human rights lawyers': https://www.dw.com.
20. Ibid.

under the influence of ISIS ideological convictions. Numerous press interviews show them proclaiming radical slogans and declaring they will raise their children as a new generation of fighters for the Islamic State. There are also cases of women committing crimes instigated by religious disagreements. For example, in summer 2019 the administration of the al-Hawl refugee camp reported the murder of an Indonesian national who expressed her displeasure at other women promoting religious propaganda.[21] The murdered woman was six months pregnant and left behind three children. According to the UN Office for the Coordination of Humanitarian Affairs (OCHA), 128 tents in that camp were burnt down in the first three weeks of September 2019 alone.[22]

The situation in Iraq differs from that in Syria. There, the authorities announced that all foreigners, including women and minors, would be sentenced. Only children under nine years old can be reclaimed by their country of origin.[23] Thus, dozens of women and children from Central Asian states remain in Iraqi prisons today. In February 2019, five Tajikistani women were given life sentences in Iraq, charged with membership of the ISIS terrorist organisation. Forty-three women native to Tajikistan were given sentences of varying lengths (from sixteen years to life) on charges of terrorism.[24] A third of these women do not want to part with their children, although the state is ready to evacuate the latter (in total, ninety-five children are registered for repatriation from Iraq to Tajikistan).

---

21. https://vk.com/kurdistananurani?w=wall-26399191_414272.
22. Aaron Zelin: 'Wilayat al-Hawl: "Remaining" and Incubating the Next Islamic State Generation': https://www.washingtoninstitute.org/policy-analysis/wilayat-al-hawl-remaining-and-incubating-next-islamic-state-generation.
23. 'Nadim Hauri: "I saw women and children from Kyrgyzstan in Syrian camps"': https://rus.azattyk.org.
24. 'In Iraq 5 Tajikistani women sentenced for life for terrorism': https://tajikta.tj/ru/news/v-irake-za-terrorizm-osuzhdeny-pozhiznenno-pyat-tadzhikistanok-?sphrase_id=4521507.

Some countries have already carried out a series of covert humanitarian operations to repatriate women and children from camps controlled by Kurdish military brigades in the northeast of Syria. In the first half of 2019, Kazakhstan, Uzbekistan, Kosovo, Indonesia, Algeria and France repatriated their nationals from one camp alone – al-Hawl. Several European states insist that these women and children be stripped of citizenship and demand the establishment of an international tribunal in Syria.

Women in camps for displaced persons in Syria believe they must bring up the next generation of ISIS[25]

Worsening socio-economic status, leaving for a third country, stripping of citizenship and ongoing uncertainty all contribute to women believing that they are the wives of martyrs, and actively seeking to promote this status. This represents a new stage in the radicalisation of women and their further involvement in terrorist activity. Women who left for conflict zones are much less likely to return home than men. According to data provided by Michèle Coninsx, Assistant Secretary General of the UN, only 5 per cent of all women who found themselves in Iraq and Syria returned. Women accounted for only 4 per cent of all registered foreigners who returned home from military conflict zones.[26]

25. https://vk.com/video-26399191_456244280.

26. 'UN: "Terrorists who return home are a big problem…:"' https://kursiv.kz/news/obschestvo/2019-02/oon-vernuvshiesya-na-rodinu-terroristy-bolshaya-problema.

Jihad and the changing role of women

The most dangerous trend in the radicalisation of women is that international terrorist organisations are drastically changing their attitude to the role of women within their hierarchy. In 2014, female police (military) or religious enforcement units were formed within the structure of ISIS.[27] These units are designed to police morality. One of the most famous is the al-Khansaa Brigade, named after an Arabian poetess of the early Islamic period. An official representative of the group announced the brigade as created '...to raise awareness of our religion among women and to punish women who do not abide by the law. Jihad is not only a man's duty; women have to play their part, too.'[28] The al-Khansaa Brigade resorts to torturing or murdering women who do not conform to ISIS social rules. If a woman tried to run away, she would receive sixty lashes when arrested. Women from the brigade were also engaged in active propaganda and recruitment on social networks. According to the British *Daily Mirror*, they managed brothels of abducted girls frequented by fighters. Women who escaped reported that they were forced to have sex with 100 different men in the space of a few weeks.[29]

Owing to a deterioration in its situation, in autumn 2017 ISIS began actively calling women to take up arms, declaring 'it is their duty to perform physical jihad'.[30] Radical preachers proclaimed that women had fought in the golden age of Islam and appeared as active supporters of the Prophet Muhammad. In February 2018, the group

---

27. 'Fatal Attraction: Western Muslimas and ISIS': http://www.terrorismanalysts.com/pt/index.php/pot/article/view/427/html.

28. 'In Raqqa, an all-female ISIS brigade cracks down on local women': https://www.newsdeeply.com/syria/articles/2014/07/15/in-raqqa-an-all-female-isis-brigade-cracks-down-on-local-women.

29. 'ISIS "female Gestapo" leading campaign of terror against own sex – and 60 arc British': https://www.mirror.co.uk/news/world-news/isis-female-gestapo-leading-campaign-6046944.

30. 'Isis calls on women to fight and launch terror attacks for first time': https://www.independent.co.uk/news/world/middle-east/isis-war-syria-iraq-women-call-to-arms-islamic-state-terror-attacks-propaganda-change-ban-frontline-a7986986.html#r3z-addoor.

published a video presenting around five women as a 'daredevil military brigade' fighting alongside men for the first time.[31] Initially, ISIS had peddled other rhetoric, mainly calling for women to support militants, marry them, follow the Caliphate's ideas, promote them, and bring up their children as a future generation of mujahids.

Members of the al-Khansa Brigade[32]

Women fighting with ISIS[33]

A 2017 UN study on Kyrgyzstan highlighted 'the active role of some women attracted by the idea that ISIS is the real Caliphate'. The study notes that 'gender-oriented extremist propaganda promises women

31. 'Isis propaganda video shows women fighting for first time amid "desperation" to bolster ranks': https://www.independent.co.uk/news/world/middle-east/isis-video-women-jihadis-female-fighters-recruitment-syria-iraq-islamic-state-propaganda-a8200621.html.
32. 'Official of Khansa Brigade escapes, IS alerts its members in Mosul': https://www.iraqinews.com/iraq-war/official-khansa-brigade-escapes-alerts-members-mosul/.
33. 'Isis propaganda video shows women fighting for first time amid "desperation" to bolster ranks': https://www.independent.co.uk/news/world/middle-east/isis-video-women-jihadis-female-fighters-recruitment-syria-iraq-islamic-state-propaganda-a8200621.html.

high status when they join the Islamic police, as well as financial incentives.[34] It was this reasoning which prompted many young women to become fighters. New narratives about the extension of rights and opportunities for women in ISIS played a significant propaganda role in many countries throughout the world. In one infamous case, for instance, four schoolgirls from a Muslim community in Bethnal Green (East London) left for Syria in 2015 to marry ISIS fighters. One of them, Shamima Begum, now wants to come back home, but at the same time she has spoken of her day-to-day life in Syria with no regrets. 'It was like a normal life. [...] Every now and then there are bombs and stuff. But other than that... when I saw a severed head in a bin [...] it didn't faze me at all. [...] It was from a captured fighter seized on the battlefield, an enemy of Islam,' she stated.[35]

Today, following military pressure from various international powers, the ISIS situation remains unclear. As UN experts noted, 'ISIS continues to transform into a terrorist organisation with a flat hierarchy in which cells and affiliates act with increasing independence and autonomy.' As a result, radical networks are spreading all around the world. But the Islamic State continues to recruit fighters, including women. In March 2018, it transpired that, in Afghanistan, around twenty female military instructors were training female brigades in ISIS. According to information from the chief of police of the Darzab region in the Afghan province of Jawzjan (bordering Turkmenistan), instructors train two groups of sixty women each. He says: 'Military training is conducted by twenty foreign instructors who arrived in Darzab about twenty days ago from the eastern province of Nangarhar. They train twice a week. On other days, women are instructed on the rules of conduct for women as per the ideology of the Islamic State.'[36]

---

34. 'Women and extremism: how many Tajik women left for Syria?': https://news.tj/ru/news/centralasia/20180125/zhentshini-i-ekstremizm-issledovanie-oon-po-tsentralnoi-azii.

35. 'Jihadist's wife wants to come home. Will Britain let her?': https://www.bbc.com/russian/features-47242727.

36. 'IS fighters have begun recruiting women in the Afghan Province of Jowjzan': http://www.fergananews.com/news/28915.

Women in ISIS have gone from being passive observers to a taking on a new role. In particular, in January 2019, when ISIS fighters were defending their last stronghold in the east of Syria – al-Baghuz Fawqani – they involved women in military fighting. Having ended up in temporary camps, these women with extreme radical views pose a threat to the security of the countries to which they return. And this is regardless of whether ISIS will lose its main resources or will grow stronger.

This trend towards a change in the role and status of women can be observed in other terrorist groups, too. In August 2017, the Islamic fighter group Tehrik-i-Taliban Pakistan published its first magazine exclusively for women, *Sunnat e Khola*, targeting potential women jihadis. The magazine is named after a seventh-century female Muslim warrior known as Khola.[37] The magazine contains an appeal to women to organise their own clandestine groups and training classes, and to prepare for 'martyr's actions'. An editorial in this publication openly states that this group aims to facilitate women joining the ranks of male fighters.

The Sunnat e Khola magazine[38]

---

37. 'As the caliphate crumbles, Taliban steals ISIS' tactics to target women': https://edition.cnn.com/2017/08/28/middleeast/taliban-womens-magazine/index.html.
38. https://azelin.files.wordpress.com/2017/08/tehcca3ricc84k-icc84-tcca3acc84libacc84n-pacc84kistacc84n-22sunnat-khawlah-issue-122.pdf.

In contrast, the terrorist organisation al-Qaeda continues to uphold more stringent rules regarding women, considering that the latter's lot is to stay at home and support their husband-fighters. *The Economist* quotes Elisabeth Kendall of Oxford University: 'Al-Qaeda is concerned that the conflict made women's voices heard, made them more active, and empowered them.'[39] However, this was not always the case. During the US military operation in Iraq in 2003, al-Qaeda used women as *shahids* for the first time. In 2004, al-Qaeda leader Abu Musab al-Zarqawi published a message titled 'Join the Caravan' in which he announced:

> The war has broken out and the caller to Jihad has called for it, and the doors of the heavens have opened, if you don't want to be [one] of the knights, then make room for the women to commence, and take the eyeliner, O you women with turbans and beards, if not then to the horses and here are the reins and shackles.[40]

He pointed out that jihad – in this case, defensive – is the duty of both women and men.

After American forces withdrew from Iraq, the use of female suicide bombers became a less common practice. Al-Qaeda continues to adhere to an ideology that does not see women as active participants in jihad but where they play the role of wives and mothers instead. Since the end of 2017, the group has published a monthly magazine, *Beituki* ('Your House' in Arabic) for English-speaking Muslim women; it instructs on how to be a good wife to an al-Qaeda fighter.

---

39. 'Terrorist organization Al-Qaeda publishes a women's magazine called "Bеituki", and you have to see it': https://www.cheatsheet.com/culture/al-qaeda-magazine.html/.

40. 'The changing roles of women in violent Islamist groups': https://extremism.gwu.edu/sites/g/files/zaxdzs2191/f/Perspectives%20on%20the%20Future%20of%20Women%2C%20Gender%20and%20Violent%20Extremism.pdf.

Screenshot of the al-Qaeda magazine Beituki[41]

But, at the same time, even conservative al-Qaeda understands the importance of the gender component and is gradually introducing certain corrections into its propaganda activities. In September 2018, the media outlet International Khayr Ummah Foundation (IKAF), which also published an al-Qaeda magazine for women, released a new video message, 'Empowered Women',[42] which shows a small detachment of armed women.

Al-Qaeda women in the video 'Empowered Women'[43]

Another radical group, the Turkestan Islamic Party (TIP), which is affiliated with al-Qaeda and is active in both Afghanistan and Syria, has long since had a clear idea about the role of women in its hierarchy. In 2012–13, TIP published propaganda videos about training women for

41. 'Terrorist organization Al-Qaeda publishes a women's magazine called "Beituki", and you have to see it': https://www.cheatsheet.com/culture/al-qaeda-magazine.html/.
42. 'New video message from Khayr Ummah Foundation: "Empowered Women"':https://jihadology.net/2018/09/04/new-video-message-from-khayr-ummah-foundation-empowered-women/.
43. Ibid.

jihad. One recording shows five women learning to use pistols, sniper rifles, machine guns and rocket launchers.[44] The American website Long War Journal notes that this video shows the growing tendency within TIP to attract women to jihad. According to this journal, before 2010, not a single attack by female terrorist suicide bombers was recorded in the region where TIP was active (Afghanistan and Pakistan).[45] Since 2010, however, women increasingly commit or participate in acts of violence.

TIP video 'The Sisters in the Way of God' about women training, October 2012[46]

The above-mentioned facts and videos form only a part of the general picture, but even they suggest that the role and activities of women in terrorist organisations are considerably underestimated. So far, the

44. 'Turkistan Islamic Party trains women for jihad': https://www. longwarjournal.org/archives/2013/07/turkistan_islamic_pa_4.php.
45. 'Turkistan Islamic Party trains women for jihad': https://www. longwarjournal.org/archives/2013/07/turkistan_islamic_pa_4.php.
46. 'Ṣawt al-Islām presents a new video message from Ḥizb al-Islāmī al-Turkistānī [Turkistan Islamic Party]: "The Sisters in the Way of God"': https:// jihadology.net/2012/10/23/%E1%B9%A3awt-al-islam-presents-a-new-video-message-from-%E1%B8%A5izb-al-islami-al-turkistani-turkistan-islamic-party-the-sisters-in-the-way-of-god/.

perception of a woman as a full-blown active participant in radical groups is in its infancy; and this, coupled with conflicting stereotypes portrayed in the media, creates a dilemma: should women involved in the activities of extremist organisations be helped to return home, or do they pose a threat?

Despite the oft-cited stereotype of a woman as the 'jihadist's wife' who plays a more passive role and entered this path under a man's influence, we should not lose sight of other facts. Women are also active recruiters and propagandists who attract new recruits. This demands closer, in-depth scrutiny. Analytical forecasts raise the question of the high percentage of radicalisation among militants' wives and widows. In the mid-term, these women can pose a real threat, partly also because the radical groups are changing their ideological approach to the role of women in global terrorism.

Female suicide bombers

One of the main and most disastrous consequences of the radicalisation of women is the increasing use of females in suicide bombing missions and violent attacks. Radical groups in the Middle East used women as 'live bombs' long before the rise of religious extremism. For example, during the Israeli occupation of southern Lebanon, which lasted eighteen years and ended in 2000, women carried out several terrorist attacks against the Israeli military. It was women belonging to leftist groups who blew themselves up.[47] The early 2000s saw the appearance of 'black widows' in Russia. These were mainly widows or female relatives of dead fighters from the Northern Caucasus. *Shahid* women blew themselves up in various regions of Russia. According to calculations by the online news site Caucasian Knot, eighty-six terrorist acts have been committed on Russian territory since 2000, with 132 suicide attackers involved. At least fifty-two (39.9 per cent) were women.[48]

---

47. 'Female suicide assassins in history': https://inosmi.ru/social/201511 25/234558952.html.
48. 'Terrorist attacks committed by suicide bombers on the territory of RF': http://www.kavkaz-uzel.eu/articles/224438/.

Other countries were soon facing this phenomenon, too. In November 2005, a thirty-eight-year-old native of Belgium, Muriel Degauque,[49] became the first so-called 'white' terrorist suicide bomber from Europe in the Iraq war. She tried to blow up an American military convoy near Baghdad and died as a result.

In November 2015, during a French covert operation in the Paris suburb of Saint-Denis, a female suicide bomber blew herself up.

In 2015, in Turkey, a pregnant suicide bomber blew herself up in Istanbul old town; two policemen were wounded.

The following year, women carried out several terrorist attacks in Turkey. For example, on 28 April 2016, a twenty-five-year-old suicide bomber blew herself up in the Turkish city of Bursa.

In October 2016, ten women were arrested in Morocco for planning a terrorist attack involving women *shahids* during parliamentary elections. Four of them had married ISIS fighters through the Internet.

The activities of the Boko Haram terrorist group in Nigeria demand serious study. Female members of Boko Haram were responsible for 1,225 deaths in the period 2014–17 alone. They account for about two thirds of all group members who blew themselves up.[50] Between 2014 and 2018, a total of over 450 women and girls were involved in organising terrorist activities. At least one third of them were teenagers and young girls.[51]

One of the most recent terrorist attacks, which involved a whole family, took place in Indonesia. In May 2018, a man committed a terrorist act at the gates of St Mary's Catholic Church in the city of Surabaya. At the same time in the same city, his wife and two daughters, aged nine and twelve, blew themselves up in a Protestant church, while two of his sons, aged sixteen and eighteen, blew themselves up

---

49. 'Islamists suffered because of a female European suicide bomber': https://www.kommersant.ru/doc/841713
50. 'Made-up to look beautiful. Sent out to die: the young women sent into crowds to blow themselves up: https://www.bbc.co.uk/news/resources/idt-sh/made_up_to_look_beautiful_sent_out_to_die.
51. Ibid.

in yet another church.[52] According to some, this was the bloodiest act of terror in Indonesia since 2005. ISIS claimed responsibility.

At the end of 2018, several terrorist acts involving women were carried out simultaneously. On 29 October, a female suicide bomber blew herself up in the centre of Tunis. According to the media,

> [...] a thirty-year-old woman, dressed in relatively modern clothes rather than 'Sharia' dress, suddenly came out of the crowd, approached a group of policemen, and blew herself up. Nine people were wounded (two seriously), eight of whom were police officers. Only the suicide bomber herself died.[53]

Responsibility was claimed by al-Qaeda.

On 17 November 2018, a twenty-five-year-old native of Adygea, Karina Spiridonova, blew herself up at a checkpoint in the city of Grozny in the Chechen Republic. There were no casualties apart from the woman herself. ISIS claimed responsibility for this violent act.

Meanwhile, according to several Chechen women who returned from Syria, in particular Zalina Gabibullayeva and Zagidat Abakarova, the goal of this terrorist act was to prevent the repatriation of women and children from the active combat zone in Syria and Iraq.[54] The process of repatriating Russian women – but not children – has now been paused.

Unfortunately, fatalities in terrorist acts involving women are generally higher. According to one study of violent acts perpetrated by five different radical groups, there are 8.4 casualties in terrorist acts

---

52. 'Family act of terror: in Indonesia members of the same family attack 3 churches': http://9tv.co.il/news/2018/05/13/257499.html.
53. 'Authorities confirm the terrorist nature of suicide bomber's attack in Tunis': https://topwar.ru/149262-vlasti-podtverdili-terroristicheskij-harakter-samopodryva-zhenschiny-v-stolice-tunisa.html.
54. 'Women returned from Syria: terrorist act in Chechnya is aimed at preventing the repatriation of Russian citizens from combat zones': https://www.kavkazr.com/a/29606148.html.

committed by female suicide bombers, compared with 5.3 in those committed by men.[55]

Experts tentatively assign women who decided to commit acts of terrorism to three groups:

> Ideological *shahids*: These women are fanatical believers in the dogma of radical ideology, and they are motivated by the desire to obtain eternal life and rid themselves of sufferings of this life. Another motivation is the desire for recognition. Such girls and women are emotional and easily succumb to suggestion. According to Yoram Schweitzer, an Israeli expert on international terrorism, 'Women *shahids* are not so clever or "advanced" as their handlers.' He points out that '[d]uring interviews immediately following their detention, they first speak of private matters, and you only hear them mention something about patriotism or Allah afterwards.'[56]

> Coerced female suicide bombers: These women are subjected to violence as a result of which they cannot bear such pressure and decide to resort to desperate means (in some cases under the influence of psychotropic substances). An expert bomb defuser said that explosive devices on suicide belts could be detonated remotely: the terrorists attach bombs to the bodies of captive women and send them to death.[57] The Boko Haram group resorts to this tactic more often than other groups; they not only abduct young girls and small children, but also actively use them as suicide bombers. Since June 2014, fighters from the group have used over 100 women and girls as 'live bombs'.[58]

---

55. 'What's special about female suicide terrorism?': https://pdfs.semantic scholar.org/b4b6/358a1230375668374c4fecf8624f15db1f97.pdf?_ga =2.7900274.1585184926.1566809284-1808057843.1566809284.

56. 'The female face of terrorism. The spectre of paradise for shahid women': https://paruskg.info/glavnaya/40609-40609.html

57. 'Female suicide assassins in history': https://inosmi.ru/social/201511 25/234558952.html.

58. 'Over 100 female suicide bombers used in West Africa since June 2014': http://www.longwarjournal.org/archives/2016/02/over-100-female-suicide-bombers-used-in-west-africa.php.

Involvement of Women in Terrorist Activities

2018

Country	Period	Goal	Number of victims	Group
Nigeria	17 February	Three women committed suicide at a market 15 miles from Maiduguri administrative centre in the northeast of the country.	Around 18 dead, over 20 wounded (most of whom were women and children).	Boko Haram
Nigeria	21 April	A man and a woman blew themselves up in a mosque in the settlement of Bama in Borno State in the northeast of the country.	About 4 people died, 9 others were wounded.	Boko Haram
Indonesia, island of Java	13 May	A series of terrorist attacks aimed at Christian churches were carried out by a family of 6, including wife and 2 daughters, aged 9 and 12.	Over 30 people died, 40 were wounded.	ISIS
Niger	5 June	Three women blew themselves up in a mosque in the southeast city of Diffa.	10 people died	Boko Haram
Great Britain	August	In London, 44-year-old Mina Dich and her two daughters Safaa Boular (18) and Rizlaine (22) were planning a terrorist attack in the British Museum. The youngest exchanged messages via Telegram with an IS fighter and intended to go to Syria and marry him. However, when she learnt of his death, she decided to commit an act of terror involving her closest female relatives. She was sentenced to life in prison.	-	IS

2018

Country	Period	Goal	Number of victims	Group
Germany	October	A married couple who joined IS in Syria in 2015 were to play the main role in a terrorist act at a music festival. In particular, a female German national who converted to Islam tried to find brides for fighters as a means of getting them into the country. It is said that the radicals' plans were frustrated by German intelligence agencies as well as by the weakening of the group itself.	-	IS
Tunis	29 October	A woman attacked a group of policemen on an embankment in the Tunis capital. She was wearing a suicide belt with a small amount of explosives. Ten policemen and 5 bystanders were affected.		Al-Qaeda
Chechen Republic, Russian Federation	17 November	A girl blew herself up during an attempt to detain her in the Staropromyslovsky district of Grozny. There were no casualties among the law enforcement officers or local residents.	No law enforcement officers or local residents were killed or wounded.	IS

'Avengers': The psychology of revenge prompted the widows, mothers and sisters of dead militants to play an active role in mass terrorist attacks. In Russia, 'black widows' took part in the hostage-taking in Moscow's Dubrovka Theatre in 2002. In 2010, seventy-year-old Dzhanet (Dzhennet) Abdurakhmanova, widow of the leader of the Dagestani fighters, blew herself up in the Moscow Metro, killing over forty people. We should, of course, note that female suicide bombers from the North Caucasus were most probably motivated by a somewhat different psychological mechanism, namely ethnic consolidation and reaction. Nevertheless, it is precisely the widows and wives of radicals who could pose a serious threat in the future.

Using female *shahids* generally makes it easier for radical groups to organise and implement terrorist acts. First, women and children arouse fewer suspicions. Second, it is easier for them to bring in explosives because they are searched less frequently owing to cultural mores. Consequently, according to data from Israel's Institute for National Security Studies, in 2017 alone, 137 of 623 active terrorists were women.[59]

The facts and statistics available confirm that we are seeing a new and worrying trend – women are becoming a dangerous tool not only for radical propaganda but also for direct acts of violence.

---

59. 'On the frontline: women and terrorism': https://www.global governmentforum.com/frontline-women-terrorism/.

III

'CUBS OF THE CALIPHATE'

In a foreign war for foreign interests, innocent children die alongside grown men. Even though involving people younger than fifteen in military activities is considered a war crime (per the 1998 Rome Statute of the International Criminal Court), today around 500,000 children are involved in various military conflicts worldwide.[1] Every tenth child on the African continent is a soldier. For example, minors make up 80 per cent of the Somalian group al-Shabaab (which translates as Youth).[2] In southern Sudan, 119 children, including forty-eight girls, were freed from armed groups in February 2019. With the help of UNICEF, a total of 3,100 underage 'fighters' have been demobilised since the beginning of the conflict.[3] In Uganda, the extremist organisation Lord's Resistance Army (LRA) abducted tens of thousands of children, turning them into its weapons. According to

1. 'Child Prisoners in War': https://papers.ssrn.com/sol3/papers.cfm?abstract_id=1321546.
2. 'Deadly games': https://focus.ua/ukraine/201991/.
3. 'In southern Sudan 119 children recruited by fighters were liberated': https://ca-news.org/news:1495546.

a UNICEF study, from 1986–2005 this organisation abducted at least 66,000 children.[4]

The war in Syria also mercilessly mangles children's lives. In 2017 alone, no fewer than 900 children took part in military action in Syria, a quarter of whom were younger than fifteen; 244 children were detained.[5]

In any military conflict, especially a prolonged one, children are the most vulnerable victims. Having lost their parents, many of them are forced to take up arms to survive in an active combat zone. In 2012, the number of minors imprisoned for participating in conflicts all over the world grew fivefold.[6]

The problem of the radicalisation of children already existed, but it caught the media's attention owing to military action in Syria and Iraq. Most known terrorist groups have military training camps where they train children from all over the world and prepare 'young terrorists'. They are bringing up a new generation of criminals who see an atmosphere of killing and violence as the norm, because they know nothing else as they grow up. From an early age they are indoctrinated with radical ideas, and hatred and the desire to kill are instilled in their minds. From infancy, these children are growing up in a different reality, a reality where the secular part of life, including such conventional practices as studying in a school, are traits of the enemy's lifestyle.

Experts note that all terrorist groups pay close attention to and spend significant resources on this kind of upbringing, as, in the future, it is this new generation that will increase their chances of survival.[7] Some estimates suggest that in Syria and Iraq alone, around 3,000 teenagers were studying in such camps before the active phase of

---

4. 'The Lord's Resistance Army, an organisation everyone is turning a blind eye to': https://inosmi.ru/social/20160317/235746639.html.

5. 'All sides in the Syrian conflict use children': https://www.dw.com.

6. 'Some child soldiers get rehabilitation, others get prison': https://www.atlanticcouncil.org/blogs/new-atlanticist/some-child-soldiers-get-rehabilitation-others-get-prison.

7. 'You are not born a terrorist': https://www.gazeta.ru/science/2015/11/19_a_7900949.shtml?updated.

the antiterrorist operation.[8] Since 2016, reports by Europol (European Union Agency for Law Enforcement Cooperation) on terrorist trends state that children who are being prepared as a new generation of fighters 'can become a future threat to security'.[9]

Staff at the international humanitarian agency Save the Children have studied the psychological effects the Syrian conflict has on children. These children, after all, are faced with the imminent task of building a new country and a post-war society in the future. The researchers spoke with 458 children, teenagers and adults (teachers, parents, psychologists and staff from humanitarian missions) in seven out of fourteen Syrian *muhafazahs* (regions). This work is considered one of the most far-reaching studies examining the psychological health of children in the Syrian conflict. As a result, the following picture emerges:

- 89 per cent of interviewees said that children's behaviour is becoming increasingly neurotic as the war continues; they develop a sense of constant fear.
- 80 per cent noted increasing aggression among children and teenagers.
- 71 per cent said that children are increasingly suffering from bedwetting and involuntary urination, symptoms of so-called toxic stress and post-traumatic stress disorder.
- 51 per cent of teenagers interviewed admitted to taking drugs to manage stress.
- 48 per cent of adults interviewed encountered children who either lost the ability to speak or developed a speech defect since the beginning of the war.
- 59 per cent of adults reported they knew children or teenagers who ended up in armed groups.[10]

---

8. 'Tajikistani children – a new generation of fighters in the Middle East': http://ca-snj.com/bezopasnost/tadzhikskie-deti-novoe-pokolenie-boevikov-na-blizhnem-vostoke.html.
9. 'ISIS actively bringing up a new generation of violent fighters': http://inosmi.ru/politic/20170405/239047377.html.
10. 'They only know war': https://www.svoboda.org/a/28369363.html.

To date, we do not know for certain how many minors are in terrorist training camps. We do know, however, that they took different routes to get there. According to experts, children are recruited in several ways:

- Via free educational programmes;
- Via family practices, whereby parents deliver their children to specialised training camps;
- Institutional practices, whereby children orphaned when their parents die in combat are sent to military training camps;
- Children join terrorist groups voluntarily of their own accord, either because of ideological motivation or to be paid.

For example, according to the testimonies of former members of the Boko Haram terrorist organisation, children in Nigeria joined its ranks not only when they were abducted, but for other reasons, too, including financial motivation, peer pressure, and the influence of their relatives. Parents sent their children to the terrorists themselves, to make money. We know that in Maiduguri (a city in the northeast of Nigeria, the administrative centre of Borno federal state), two religious schools deliberately lured children who dropped out of other schools, acting as major recruitment bases until 2014.[11] According to information from Lebanese expert Marwan Abou-Taam, the first thing recruiters try to do is create a new, hermetic environment for immature recruits.

[They] isolate children from their usual social contacts: asking teenagers to stop communicating with parents and children because they are allegedly far removed from Islamic ideas, demand that children give up hobbies they enjoy. Once all the students' social ties are cut, they mould them into radical fanatics.[12]

---

11. 'Annual Report of the General Secretary on Children and Armed Conflicts in Nigeria', UN, April 2017.
12. 'Three years of Caliphate: how ISIS recruited 40,000 people': https://snob.ru/selected/entry/126336.

For adults, there are usually only two possible scenarios leading to involvement in extremist activities: either forced, or voluntary. In the case of children, they never have a choice as such; they are coerced into terrorism, the path of violence and death, chosen for them by adults. In November 2015, the media reported that ISIS fighters executed a dozen children for attempting to escape a camp in Iraq. According to a representative of the Kurdistan Democratic Party, 'at least twelve children were killed by Islamic State radicals. The children were being trained in a military camp and were caught trying to escape. The executed children were aged between twelve and sixteen.'[13] There are cases of the children of killed fighters being killed so that their organs could be removed and sold. In other cases, they were used as slaves or subjected to sexual violence. Today, neither age nor nationality makes any difference; children from all over the world become instruments of violence in the hands of adults.

The widespread radicalisation of children has changed the way we think about security issues, and altered our understanding of what lies at the heart of terrorism. Whereas previously we had a generalised portrait of a radical in terms of age and social standing – an idea of the categories of people who took part in terrorist activities – children found in terrorist organisations complicate the issue. Today, the threat of terrorism and religious extremism can come from anyone, be it a baby in the arms of a *shahid* mother, or a trained teenager. That is why deradicalisation and the ongoing rehabilitation of children who came into contact with terrorism calls for a serious and detailed approach from the state.

Children used in ISIS propaganda

On 13 January 2015, ISIS released a propaganda video in which a ten-year-old boy carries out an 'execution'; the video claims the victims were 'two agents of the Russian Federal Security Service'. The seven-minute video shows two men being interrogated about the reason for

---

13. 'IS fighters execute 12 children for trying to escape a camp in Iraq': http://lenta.ru/news/2015/11/01/kids/.

their presence in Syria. It then shows their murder. Everyone in the video speaks Russian. There are subtitles in Arabic and English. It is important to note that the boy who 'carried out the execution' had previously given an interview in another video about Kazakhs fighting in Syria (November 2014). He was also present in the very first video about Kazakhstani nationals in Syria, released in October 2013.

Underage boy participates in the 'execution of FSS agents'

This is one of the first instances of using children in terrorist propaganda content, when it is a child who carries out violence of such magnitude against other people. According to experts, however, the video is staged, partly with the intention of intimidating secret service agents and also to 'promote' the Caliphate's young generation. Nevertheless, specialists also note that the boy in the video is holding the gun correctly and confidently, so this is probably not the first time he is holding one. The video caused a stir; media all over the world reported on this incident. The ISIS promoters achieved their goal – to deliver their message.

Relishing their success, Islamic State exploited the image of this so-called 'little executioner' for a long time. The boy's photo was published on the cover of an ISIS magazine. Moreover, this sensational story has a sequel. That same year, Kazakhstani intelligence agencies thwarted an attempt by an underage schoolgirl from Almaty to go to

Syria. She met a recruiter on the VK social platform and, following his instructions, she reached Shymkent by herself by bus. The girl intended to go to Syria via Turkey. As it transpired later, she heard about the video with the boy taking part in an execution in the news and then came across it on a social network. She liked the look of the 'little executioner' and decided to meet him.

This example clearly shows that videos with child fighters do not only intimidate adults but can impact on children's psyches, lowering their sensitivity threshold to violence. The schoolgirl from Almaty was not deterred by the fact that the hero of her dreams is shown killing people and that he is a member of one of the most dangerous terrorist groups in the world. The girl was attracted by his looks, and her teenage mind turned him into a hero.

It was precisely ISIS that made widespread use of children as fighter units and streamlined the production of bloody promotional videos starring minors. The group is known to have had several training camps for children. According to verified UN data, in one such camp alone near the city of Raqqa, there were 350 five-year-olds.[14]

Minors studying in ISIS camps

14. 'UN: ISIS turns five- to six-year-olds into fighters': http://www.gpclub. ru/6982.htm.l

Researchers from Quilliam, a British counter-extremism think tank, discovered 254 events or announcements using images of children in ISIS propaganda from 1 August 2015 to 9 February 2016.[15] In 2017, ISIS distributed several more videos featuring children. In January of the same year, a video showed three minors from the Cubs of the Caliphate brigade executing 'infidels' – two boys aged between nine and thirteen beheaded their victims. Another four-year-old child was shown shooting a captive in the head, after which he pronounces *Takbir* (the phrase 'Allahu Akbar!').[16] In July 2017, the Wilayah Khorasan ISIS cell in Afghanistan released a ten-minute video showing two boys executing two young people. Dressed in black, children aged seven to twelve stand behind the captives, holding pistols.

Children in the Wilayah Khorasan propaganda video[17]

According to reports by Telegram-channel Directorate 4,[18] which covers and analyses terrorist activities, in February 2018 ISIS published photos from the Yarmuk training camp to the south of Damascus, noting that the training centre for children does not differ much from the one for adults. 'Children are taught to handle weapons,

15. 'Report on the state of children in "Islamic State"': translation from *The Guardian*: https://tjournal.ru/24345-doklad-o-sostoyanii-detey-v-islamskom-gosudarstve-perevod-the-guardian.
16. '"Lion Cubs of the Caliphate": how ISIS fighters train their successors': https://nahnews.org/988736-lvyata-halifata-kak-boeviki-igil-podgotavlivayut-svoih-posledovatelei.
17. 'New "Wilayaht Khorasan" video: children execute children': http://central.asia-news.com/ru/articles/cnmi_ca/features/2017/07/31/feature-02.
18. https://t.me/directorate4/1407.

there are lessons in the shooting range, and they take physical training tests. On the photo you can see children armed with a Kalashnikov machine gun and Kalashnikov assault rifles manufactured in China and Hungary.'[19] This information about the ISIS children's training camp near Damascus was later confirmed by the Syrian military.

Children in the ISIS training camp, Damascus

Virtually all sides in the conflict in Syria use children in military actions. Turkish media accused militias of the Kurdish Supreme Committee/YPG of training children aged between eleven and sixteen in military training camps in Syria.[20]

Minors in YPG brigades[21]

Today, unfortunately, radical extremist groups use children as a terrorist propaganda tool. This problem is particularly pertinent for

19. Ibid.
20. (Kurdish) Yekîneyên Parastina Gel – People's Self-Defence brigade which formed the main bulk of the Kurdish-Arabic opposition alliance Syrian Democratic Forces since 2015.
21. 'TYPG terrorist acknowledged that children participate in military combat': https://www.aa.com.tr/ru/.

Central Asian countries. In terms of numbers of children involved, radical groups with Central Asian members are not at the bottom of the list of organisations using children in propaganda and military actions. Here are a few instances that have been widely discussed in the mass media.

In summer 2013, the Turkestan Islamic Party (TIP) published a video about five-year-old children being trained in a camp in northern Waziristan (Pakistan).

Military training of children in TIP, 2013

The Syrian branch of TIP also actively uses children in its propaganda videos, including girls and children of various ages.

Children in the TIP, 2016[22]

_____

22. 'Turkistan Islamic Party in Syria shows more "little jihadists"': https://www.longwarjournal.org/archives/2016/09/turkistan-islamic-party-in-syria-shows-more-little-jihadists.php.

Another Central Asian group, the Islamic Movement of Uzbekistan (IMU), which had been active earlier, also prepared young children for future involvement in terrorism.

Sixteen- to seventeen-year-olds in an IMU training camp, November 2013

In April 2014, the Uzbek Khatiba Imam al-Bukhari (KIB), which was formed and active in Syria and later in Afghanistan, published a video recording of a message from an Uzbek 'fighter', a teenager who looked no older than thirteen or fourteen, who called for continuing violence in Syria until victory was complete.

Still from a video message from the group Khatiba Imam al-Bukhari[23]

In their next video, released in December 2015, the KIB demonstrated how they prepare the new generation of jihadis.

---

23. 'Uzbek children's jihad': http://postskriptum.org/2014/04/27/bukhari/.

Children in a KIB training camp[24]

The most horrifying factor about involving children in terrorist activity is that it is often their parents' choice. Parents take their children to a training camp themselves, put photos of them holding weapons on social media, and thus promote violence. The children simply have to believe what their parents believe.

On their social media pages, parents of the new 'young generation of radicals' posted photos of their children against the backdrop of symbols of terrorist groups

In December 2014, an Italian woman recognised her three-year-old son in one of the ISIS fighters' propaganda videos. He had disappeared and, according to her, at the end of 2013 the boy's father took him to Syria, where he joined the terrorists. Reportedly, the man was killed.

---

24. 'Uzbek group in Syria trains children for jihad': https://www.longwarjournal.org/archives/2015/12/uzbek-group-in-syria-trains-children-for-jihad.php.

ISIS propaganda photos

As Anne Speckhard, director of the International Centre for the Study of Violent Extremism (Washington) says: 'We spoke to children in Iraqi prisons. Some had been forced to take part in executions. Or their parents encouraged them. Sometimes their mother took them to Caliphate camps, from where there was no escape.'[25]

Researchers at the British think tank Quilliam state: 'Before, children were used in war despite their age, but now they are used in war precisely because of their age.'[26] The involvement of children in radical activity, their way of life, distorted perception of violence, exposure to death from an early age – all this minimises the child's chances of future rehabilitation. Moreover, methods and measures used for adult radicals cannot be used for children. That is why, today, not only experts in terrorism studies but also psychologists and sociologists are faced with the task of finding a way to prevent similar situations and rehabilitate such children.

---

25. 'Underage ISIS fighters: how "Lion Cubs of the Caliphate" are being trained in Syria and Iraq': http://www.ntv.ru/novosti/1826518/. (Citation paraphrased; translator's note.)

26. 'ISIS actively preparing a new generation of cruel fighters': http://inosmi.ru/politic/20170405/239047377.htm. (Citation paraphrased; translator's note.)

Training young militants

The path of a child radical in ISIS begins in special classes organised by extremists for the ideological education of a new generation. In his research published in 2016, Nikita Malik, director of the Centre on Radicalisation and Terrorism, described this education system, focusing particularly on the ISIS group:

> Extremist content within the education system was a crucial tool in the group's indoctrination of children, and in shaping the hearts and minds of the next generation. Rules were determined and regularly released by the *Diwan al-Ta'aleem*, the Ministry of Education, and school attendance was compulsory for all children. Subjects such as drawing, music, nationalism, history, philosophy and social studies were removed. Instead, they were replaced with memorization of the Quran, tawheed (monotheism), fiqh (jurisprudence), salat (prayer), aqeeda (creed), Hadith and Sura (life of Prophet Muhammad). Some subjects were purposefully limited – one Geography textbook, for example, only named continents, and a History textbook only taught Islamic History. Physical education was renamed 'Jihadist Training', and included workout routines and lessons on the assembly, firing, cleaning, and storage of light weapons. Children who refused to conform to the orders of Islamic State were flogged, tortured or raped.[27]

Such training led to a dangerous trend whereby minors are used by terrorist groups not only as a propaganda tool but also as independent combat units and *shahids*. In 2016 alone, the number of child suicide bombers in ISIS doubled. In eighty-nine cases of children blowing themselves up, 39 per cent died in mined cars and trucks, and another 33 per cent in active combat.[28] A research team from the American

---

27. 'What can be done about the children who return from Islamic State?': https://www.forbes.com/sites/nikitamalik/2018/09/14/what-can-be-done-about-the-children-who-return-from-islamic-state/#4a7683bc45a5.
28. 'ISIS is counting on child suicide bombers': https://iz.ru/news/604758.

Georgia State University followed the fates of 300 children who sources claim were used as suicide bombers by ISIS.[29]

Children in an ISIS training camp[30]

In autumn 2017, the Swedish newspaper *Expressen* published an article titled 'Defected field commander: ISIS training an army of children for future missions to the West'. The article explains how ISIS's army of child soldiers works. In particular, according to an ISIS ex-field commander, 'In Raqqa alone, there are fifteen training camps of Ashbal al-Khalifa (Cubs of the Caliphate): such camps are set up in all cities, villages and communities controlled by ISIS. Every camp takes around 600–800 children. They live there for around six months, completely cut off from the world or any contact with their parents. They are trained to be soldiers, not for current military operations but for the future, a kind of reserve army.'[31]

According to UN experts, ISIS 'like no other group used children in such a systematic and organised way, instilling in them a radical

---

29. 'ISIS actively preparing a new generation of cruel fighters': http://inosmi.ru/politic/20170405/239047377.html.

30. 'Report on the condition of children in "Islamic State"', translation from *The Guardian*: https://tjournal.ru/24345-doklad-o-sostoyanii-detey-v-islamskom-gosudarstve-perevod-the-guardian. (Citation paraphrased; translator's note.)

31. 'Cubs of the Caliphate: defected filed commander talks about ISIS child soldiers': https://riafan.ru/986142-lvyata-halifata-beglyi-polevoi-komandir-rasskazal-o-detyah-soldatah-igil.

and extremist interpretation of Sharia law'.[32] In June 2018, the French newspaper *Le Monde* published an interview with 'ex-jihadi' Jonathan Geffroy. According to media reports, he worked with the Clain Brothers, French citizens holding high positions within ISIS. Geffroy said: 'In the future, external operations [outside the Syrian conflict zone] will be conducted with the help of children who grew up within the [conflict] zone and who will be sent to the West – to Europe, to France – when they are to be used as suicide bombers.'[33]

According to Geffroy, bringing up children in ISIS involves instilling in them the ideology of hatred. That is why they are ready to become a weapon against the West. This 'project' for raising a new generation of *shahids* is a long-term plan, and therein lies the main danger. Unfortunately, ISIS has plenty of scope for this; many children are orphaned after the deaths of their parents and have no right to choose another life.

In summer 2018, Syrian military reported the liberation of the Yarmuk region to the south of Damascus and the defeat of ISIS groups active there. After the liberation of this region, the presence of a functioning training camp for children was confirmed. A representative of the Syrian Ministry of Defence stated that children up to the age of thirteen underwent compulsory training at the school, which prepared fighters and suicide bombers. They were taught to use explosives, and firearms of various kinds. They were also subject to ideological brainwashing. All walls in the building are painted with scenes of Paradise, as imagined by the fighters of hardcore armed groups, and numerous Islamist materials were used.[34]

---

32. '"IS" exploits children in Syria and Iraq': http://www.rg.ru/2014/11/24/deti-site.html.

33. 'Enfants kamikazes: le projet secret du groupe Etat islamique': https://www.lemonde.fr/societe/article/2018/06/26/enfants-kamikazes-le-projet-secret-du-groupe-etat-islamique_5321204_3224.html?xtmc=les_enfants&xtcr=33.

34. 'School for preparing child terrorists was active in Yarmuk district of Damascus': https://tass.ru/mezhdunarodnaya-panorama/5261083.

However, children did not only become tools for terrorists in extremist groups' camps. In August 2018, youths aged between eleven and eighteen took part in a series of attacks against police officers in Chechnya. One of them blew himself up; the others were killed. ISIS took responsibility for this act by publishing a video of the four teenagers swearing an oath to the group leader.

Due to actively involving children in radical activities, in 2017 alone, the number of minors used as suicide bombers in Nigeria increased dramatically. In particular, in regions where militants of the Boko Haram radical group are active, there were 135 reported cases of minors used as *shahids* that year, a fivefold increase from 2016.[35] According to UNICEF, there were four such crimes [with the use of child suicide bombers] in Nigeria, Cameroon, Chad and Niger in 2014, and forty-four in 2015.[36] Another dreadful statistic: 75 per cent of all suicide bombers in this region are girls. From 2009 to 2016, the group recruited and used at least 8,000 children.[37]

Children in the Boko Haram training camp, 2015[38]

35. '"Boko Haram" fighters increasingly use children as suicide bombers': http://www.un.org/russian/news/story.asp?NewsID=29175#.WlwlJ65l-Uk.
36. 'UNICEF alarmed by use of children as suicide bombers in Nigeria and neighbouring countries': https://azertag.az/ru/xeber/V_YUNISEF_vstrevozheny_ispolzovaniem_detei_v_kachestve_terroristov_smertnikov_v_Nigerii_i_v_sosednih_stranah-942675.
37. 'Secretary General's Report on the issue of children and armed conflict in Nigeria', Security Council, April 2017.
38. 'Cameroon must act to protect its children from Boko Haram': https://theadvocatespost.org/2016/08/23/cameroon-must-act-to-protect-its-children-from-boko-haram/.

Radical groups do not stop at using children as suicide bombers; they also use them in mass show executions of captives, forcing them to act as executioners. Data from French intelligence agencies alone show that at least three underage French nationals took part in such murders. In a video from March 2015, under the guidance of his father-in-law, twelve-year-old Rayan A. kills a captive with a shot to the head; in another video, released in May 2016, two sons of another French jihadi engage in a similar scene. One boy is twelve, the other eight years old.[39]

Children also took on the role of scouts, lookouts, and spies, played a part in armed attacks, committed arson, and planted explosive devices.

Today, several countries are already looking into the question of including minors in their lists of terrorists. In 2016, the media published information that the Dutch Intelligence and Security Service intended to create a separate terrorist list for children from the age of nine:[40] specifically, minors on territory controlled by foreign fighters in Syria who presented a threat to The Netherlands. At the beginning of 2016, seventy such children were identified. Human Rights Watch reported that children as young as nine were liable for prosecution in Iraq, facing up to five years' imprisonment for participating in ISIS activities, and up to fifteen for acts of violence.

As we have already mentioned, in contrast to other foreign fighters, Central Asian nationals usually left for the active combat zone with their whole family. Moreover, many of the men already had several wives and young children. That is why children from Central Asia were also used in the jihadi propaganda machine. According to data from some experts, in 2013–18, around fifty-five video, audio and text materials in Arabic, Uighur, Russian,

---

39. 'Lioncubs of the Caliphate: ISIS prepares attacks by child kamikaze in Europe': http://www.dsnews.ua/world/-lvyata-halifata-igil-gotovit-ataki-detey-kamikadze-v-27062018201300.
40. 'Netherlands adding child soldiers as young as 9 to terrorism list': https://nltimes.nl/2016/05/04/netherlands-adding-child-soldiers-young-9-terrorism-list.

Kyrgyz and Tajik languages featured children from Central Asia. From 2013, al-Qaeda released more than thirty such materials featuring children from Central Asia.[41] In addition, various Central Asian groups opened their own study centres and madrasas in Afghanistan and Syria.

In October 2015, during an anti-terrorist raid in Istanbul, fifty Tajikistani and Uzbekistani nationals were detained, including twenty-four minors. It was reported that 'IS agents were training children younger than eighteen as fighters in cellars of homes in the Pendik and Bashakshekhir districts.'[42]

Governments must realise that children with this kind of social experience can later turn to violence and terror. This raises the complex but logical question: how to deal with the many women and their children still trapped in camps for displaced ISIS people in northern Syria? Should they be left there or returned to their country of origin? Should attempts be made to change their mindset and resocialise them? After all, these children think and feel along completely different lines – they did not attend conventional school, they do not know the secular celebrations, many have no idea about their birthday. And some of them were brought up on the ideology of violence when they were in training camps. They know nothing but war, some simply because they were born during the war. We cannot rule out the risk that tomorrow some of them may commit terrorist acts in a third country (not necessarily their own) or that their ethnicity may become a manipulative information tool.

Nor should the propaganda effect be underestimated. 'Young Warriors of Jihad' can become serious role models, especially for children who grow up in a disadvantaged social or emigrant environment. In 2016 in Germany alone, three out of five Islamist

---

41. 'How al-Qaeda and ISIS teach Central Asian children – different methods, common goals': https://moderndiplomacy.eu/2018/12/11/how-alqaeda-and-isisteach-central-asian-children-different-methods-common-goals/.
42. 'Mass Media: IS created centres for turning children into fighters in Istanbul': http://tass.ru/mezhdunarodnaya-panorama/2359283.

attacks were committed by minors.[43] As pressure from propaganda increases among teenagers, this indicator may go up. Forced child terrorism is one of the most serious consequences of the Syrian conflict that any state may face today.

This dilemma has yet to be resolved on the international level. But it is already obvious that, for radical groups, minors are as much a military resource as adult recruits, and so thousands of children from the families of ISIS fighters can eventually resupply ISIS or other radical groups.

43. 'Germany: security services on high alert': https://news-front.info/2018/01/09/germaniya-sluzhby-bezopasnosti-v-polnoj-gotovnosti/.

IV

DETAILS OF THE OPERATION

The fates of the 'Caliphate's' women and children: a dispute

Before discussing Operation: Jusan itself, I would like to give readers an overview of the whole puzzle. Besides being an unprecedented action that demanded huge efforts on all levels, this operation would not have been possible without first answering the main question. A key decision had to be made: to repatriate our citizens from Syria or not? The question surrounding the future fate of minors still in the active combat zone, including those in terrorist training camps, is probably not as acute as the question of repatriating their fathers or the problem of deradicalising their mothers. Nevertheless, this question triggered debate about the necessity of repatriating the children. The crucial issue in the current situation is: which poses a higher risk to their own country? Is the risk of them becoming a threat to their own countries higher if they are left in a destructive environment, or if they are brought home? As yet, there is no clear answer. Nor is there a unified international approach regarding the minors found in terrorist groups. Only certain countries have declared that the state has a duty to protect the rights of these children. We will examine some of these cases below.

The question of repatriating family members of former fighters did not arise immediately. While several countries and international organisations tried to form a unified approach to dealing with the phenomenon of 'foreign fighters' in the conflict zone, a significant contingent of families of radicals who flocked to Syria from all corners of the globe gathered in the conflict zone itself. After ISIS began losing its positions in 2017–18, not only fighters but also their family members were captured, especially after the fall of the Islamic Caliphate's two capitals – Mosul in Iraq and Raqqa in Syria.

Initially, many countries simply ignored this situation. However, the number of detained foreign nationals continued to grow. At a press conference in Brussels in November 2018, official representatives of the self-governing Kurdish administration in the northeast of Syria called on foreign states to collect their citizens. At the conference, the speakers announced that they were holding '790 foreign ISIS fighters, 584 women and over 1,248 children from 46 different countries'.[1] The appeal was mainly addressed to European governments that had shown no desire to decide the fate of their citizens. The Kurdish authorities insisted this was not just their problem, but was also a problem for the countries of origin, and stated that the territory where women and minors were being held was not 100 per cent secure.

Philippe Vansteenkiste, a representative of the association for victims of terrorism V-Europe, also spoke at the press conference after having visited the Kurdish camps. He said: 'The longer women and children remain in the camps, the higher the risk of them becoming radicalised and wanting revenge.'[2] While various countries put off finding a solution to this matter, the number of women and children in Syrian camps rose sharply. According to some sources, by the

---

1. 'Syrian Kurds call on the EU to repatriate women and children of IS fighters': http://riataza.com/2018/11/01/siriyskie-kurdyi-prizyivayut-es-zabrat-v-svoi-stranyi-zhen-i-detey-boevikov-ig/.
2. Ibid.

beginning of 2019 Kurdish groups were holding 13,500 foreign women and children detained in three temporary camps in the northeast of Syria (al-Hawl, al-Roj and Ayn Issa).[3]

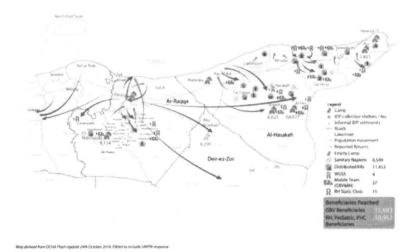

Figure 1. *ISIS prisoners and families in camps in the northeast of Syria.*

According to various international organisations, the population of the al-Hawl camp alone was 68,744 at the time, 94 per cent of them being women and children. At the same time, 20,000 of the minors were aged five or under. Of the foreigners detained in this camp, 7,000 were children, 65 per cent under the age of twelve, and 25 per cent were five or younger.[4] In May, a Kurdish information network reported that the population of al-Hawl was 73,000, out of which 11,500 were women and children from ISIS.[5] These numbers let us imagine the

---

3. Jean-Pierre Keller: 'ISIS after the US repositioning in the Northeast of Syria: camps, women and children, and leadership revival': https://dam.gcsp. ch/files/images/Syria-Transition-Challenges-Project-Discussion-Paper-6. (Citation paraphrased; translator's note.)

4. Ibid.

5. Twitter account @RojavaIC, 1 May, 2019.

scale of the problem which governments of various countries were finding it increasingly hard to ignore.

This issue became even more pressing after US President Donald Trump warned, on 17 February 2019, that ISIS fighters and their families detained in camps in the northeast of Syria would be released if the governments of their countries of origins failed to take appropriate measures. The US president's warning was mainly addressed to EU leaders. At the time, around 800 EU citizens were being held jointly by Kurds and the international coalition headed by the US. In autumn 2019, a similar threat was voiced by Turkey, which declared they would be forced to let go of ISIS fighters detained by the Turkish military as they would not be able to hold so many radicals in their prisons. But, in reality, it is the autonomous Kurdish administration that found itself in the most difficult situation, as it was left to hold tens of thousands of fighters' family members in camps in the northeast of Syria. According to a Human Rights Watch report, 'Most countries ignored calls by the autonomous administration to repatriate their citizens, citing the security threat they posed and the difficulty of verifying the citizenship of children without documents or who were born in ISIS-controlled regions. They took only small numbers of people, mainly orphans.'[6]

Discussion of the fates of ISIS women and children mainly centred on legal aspects and security issues. In particular, there were disagreements regarding the legal status of the detainees – on the one hand, they were not counted as prisoners of war and were not terrorists, but on the other hand they saw themselves as part of Islamic State, which is in effect a terrorist group. The question of children also came up repeatedly: how should their citizenship be ascertained, since many had been born on the territory of Syria or Iraq, had no documents and, more often than not, their parents held different citizenships? The main question concerning everyone was how to evaluate the risks associated with repatriating these people. None of the governments wanted to take so many people who, just yesterday, had fought for or

---

6. 'Syria: dire conditions for ISIS suspects families': www.hrw.org/news/2019/07/23/syria-dire-conditions-isis-suspects-families.

lived in ISIS. As a result, thousands of women and children remained hostage to a difficult and complex situation – on the one hand, they were not under arrest, yet on the other hand, they could not leave the camps, and were forced to survive on humanitarian aid from various organisations.

ISIS or home? The experience of other countries

In Europe, a serious debate unfolded about repatriating families of ISIS fighters. In this instance, European countries usually sensitive to human rights issues took a predominantly negative stance or applied a series of limitations to returnee citizens. For example, Belgium intended to allow all children aged ten or under to enter the country,[7] but only on the condition that a DNA analysis confirmed they were indeed the children of Belgian nationals. As for their mothers, in February 2019 Belgium won a court of appeal case regarding the repatriation of two wives of ISIS militants. The court had previously ordered the state to accept the two Belgian women and six of their children fathered by members of the terrorist group. The court of appeal ruled that the Belgian authorities 'are not obliged to assist repatriation' of terrorists' wives in any way.[8] Nevertheless, in June 2019, seven children were returned to the country.[9]

In January 2018, news broke that the German government was preparing to repatriate over 100 babies and children.[10] They explained that the decision was prompted by humanitarian considerations, due to the state's obligation of care for its citizens. When making the

---

7. 'The heavy legacy of the "Islamic State"': https://www.dw.com/ru/42 136821.

8. 'Take it or leave it? SI Europe ready to repatriate "their" ISIS terrorists from Syria?': https://riafan.ru/1156860-zabrat-nelzya-ostavit-gotova-li-evropa-vernut-iz-sirii-svoikh-terroristov-igil.

9. 'Syria: dire conditions for ISIS suspects' families': https://www.hrw.org/news/2019/07/23/syria-dire-conditions-isis-suspects-families.

10. 'Germany: security services completely ready': https://news-front.info/2018/01/09/germaniya-sluzhby-bezopasnosti-v-polnoj-gotovnosti/.

decision, the German authorities took security issues into account, too, of course. German security services do not consider repatriating pre-school children as problematic.[11] However, according to Hans-Georg Maaβen of the Federal Office for the Protection of the Constitution, teenagers who lived with their parents among jihadis were socially conditioned accordingly and could to some extent have adopted ISIS ideology. And so, by repatriating them, Germany 'could bring up a generation of domestic jihadis'. Nevertheless, in August 2019, over 100 children as well as dozens of women and men were evacuated from the camps.[12] The authorities had previously estimated that 117 children with German citizenship were being held in prisons and camps in Syria and Iraq, along with a further twenty-one children who, although not German citizens, nevertheless had some connection to Germany.[13]

According to the latest figures, sixty-eight children aged between eight and thirteen have been returned to France,[14] where a new programme to fight Islamic radicalisation has been adopted: in contrast to the previous three programmes implemented between 2014 and 2016, this plan foregrounds psychological support for minors. In summer 2019, France evacuated twelve orphans. According to statistics from an international human rights organisation, a further 400 French nationals are being held under guard in northeast Syria, at least half of whom are children.[15]

---

11. 'Berlin intent on returning children of German Jihadis from Iraq': https://www.dw.com/ru/41498304.

12. 'Germany to repatriate over 100 ISIS-linked children, adults from Syria: monitor': https://www.rudaw.net/english/middleeast/syria/180820191.

13. 'German authorities lost track of over 160 Islamists who left for Syria and Iraq': https://www.dw.com.

14. 'Prevent and protect: France unveils anti-radicalisation plan': https://ria.ru/world/20180223/1515197713.html.

15. Letta Tayler: 'Western Europe must repatriate its ISIS fighters and families': https//www.hrw.org/news/2019/06/21/western-europe-must-repatriate-its-isis-fighters-and-families.

Most European countries have not yet regulated the mechanism for repatriating citizens held in camps in Syria and Iraq, and the process is rather selective. The repatriation of minors is no different. Governments return children from Syria in small groups, and, even when they do, the process of repatriation drags for several months. In March 2019, Sweden initially refused to accept thirty to forty children of Swedish nationals from Syria;[16] but, in summer 2019, seven were repatriated. The Netherlands and Norway also evacuated a small group of children.[17] That is precisely why human rights organisations criticise the European governments. According to Human Rights Watch experts,

> Countries including France, the United Kingdom, and the Netherlands insist that logistical challenges and security risks make it practically impossible for them to help their citizens accused of membership in the Islamic State of Iraq and the Levant (also known as ISIL). But others, like Kosovo, Turkey, Russia, and especially Central Asian countries are showing that where there is a will to bring citizens home, there is a way. [...] In stark contrast, repatriations by Western European countries have been piecemeal, despite far greater resources and, in many cases, fewer numbers of ISIL-linked detainees.[18]

Public opinion in European countries still does not back the repatriation of ex-fighters' family members. Research carried out by an American analytical centre, The Center for Global Policy, states that:

> [D]omestic concerns over security and broadly hostile public opinion to repatriation have meant that Western governments

16. 'USA threatens to send terrorists to Europe': https://lenta.ru/news/2019/08/02/isis_europe/.
17. Letta Tayler: 'Western Europe must repatriate its ISIS fighters and families': https//www.hrw.org/news/2019/06/21/western-europe-must-repatriate-its-isis-fighters-and-families.
18. Ibid.

have so far failed to repatriate all but a small number of children from among these citizens. Public opinion polling shows strong opposition to repatriating ISIS members and affiliates; one poll last year showed that 89 percent of French respondents were worried about the prospect of ISIS members being returned to France, and 67 percent objected to the return of children.[19]

American authorities who criticised other Western countries for refusing to repatriate their own citizens have repatriated sixteen adults and children since July 2018, including – since the beginning of 2019 – a woman and four children in February and two women and six children in June.[20] The US campaigns actively for returning citizens to their country of origin and is calling on governments to take responsibility for them.

In July 2019, Australia adopted new changes in legislation that ruled out repatriating citizens as young as fourteen for two years if they are suspected of having acted as foreign fighters abroad.[21]

Russia is very actively engaged in the repatriation of minors. In August 2017 – in close coordination with the Presidential Commissioner for Children's Rights and with the aid of the Ministry of Defence, EMERCOM, the Ministry of Health, and other relevant bodies – the Ministry of Foreign Affairs began the complex task of repatriating Russian citizens from conflict zones. At the same time, under the Human Rights Council, a commission was set up to return Russian children from Iraq and Syria.

It is thought that the issue came to public attention at the beginning of 2017 when Chechen leader Ramzan Kadyrov published a video on Instagram shot by Russia Today correspondents in an orphanage

---

19. 'The Children of ISIS Detainees: Europe's dilemma: https://cgpolicy.org/briefs/the-children-of-isis-detainees-europes-dilemma/.

20. 'U.S. repatriating 8 women and children with ties to ISIS, Kurdish officials say': https://www.cbc.ca/news/world/isis-women-children-us-1.5162893.

21. 'Syria: dire conditions for ISIS suspects families: https://www.hrw.org/news/2019/07/23/syria-dire-conditions-isis-suspects-families.

in Baghdad. The video shows Russian children whose parents had joined ISIS and who were later abandoned after the liberation of the Iraqi city of Mosul. According to data from the Children's Rights Commissioner Office, around 350 children were taken from Russia to the active conflict zone,[22] most of whom had been born in Dagestan and Chechnya. In addition, an unspecified number of children born into Russian families in the Middle East later lost their families after the latter joined the militants. The statistics were under constant review. In March 2019, Kheda Saratova, a member of the Human Rights Council under the Leader of Chechnya, reported that over 1,000 children had been taken to Syria and Iraq from Russia, with 643 in Syria and 536 in Iraq.[23]

According to Human Rights Watch, from August–December 2017, the state helped twenty-three women and sixty-eight children return to Russia.[24] As Kheda Saratova explains, the Iraqi side allegedly demands too high a price for the Russian citizens. 'The Russian Ministry of Foreign Affairs told us that the Iraqi side is asking $6,000 per child to pay for the expenses incurred keeping them in orphanages for six months,' said Saratova at a meeting of the relatives of women still in Iraq.[25]

In August 2018, Ramzan Kadyrov noted on his VK page that 'Chechen authorities are working on repatriating 117 Russian children to Russia, and 300 still remain in camps controlled by the western

---

22. '100s of women ask the UN to return their daughters and grandchildren from Iraq and Syria': https://www.miloserdie.ru/news/sotni-materej-prosyat-oon-vernut-iz-iraka-sirii-ih-docherej-vnukov-iz/.

23. 'Chechnya reports about Russian children remaining in Syria': https//ria.ru/20190307/1551627467.html.

24. '"From ISIS to Russia." Why Moscow paused the programme to repatriate women and children who had fled to Iraq with their children': https://www.currenttime.tv/a/29368391.html.

25. '"We won't help you." Why aren't children being returned from Iraq?': https://www.kavkazr.com/a/pochemu-ne-vozvrashchayut-detey-iz-iraka/29405104.html.

coalition.'[26] On 30 December 2018, a further thirty young Russian children were returned from Iraq.[27]

In February 2019, Russia repatriated a further twenty-seven children from Iraq, whose mothers were in Iraqi prisons accused of ISIS membership.[28]

In June 2019, Kadyrov stated on his Telegram channel that five children native to Chechnya whose parents had died during the conflict in the Middle East had been brought from Syria to Moscow. Overall, since summer 2017, 158 people – 137 children and twenty-one women – have been returned from Syria and Iraq.[29] On 18 November, the Russian Ministry of Foreign Affairs announced that all minors found to date – 122 Russians aged one to fifteen – had been evacuated from Iraq. Most of the Russian children were evacuated from Iraq at the time when thousands more minors and their mothers remained in camps in neighbouring Syria. Nevertheless, Russia did a great job in repatriating its citizens and was one of the first to show a responsible approach towards the fate of its women and children.

As for Central Asian countries, it is worth noting that Kazakhstan, Tajikistan and Uzbekistan are consistently engaged in the repatriation of women and children. At the beginning of 2019, Central Asian countries began actively repatriating their citizens from combat zones in Syria and Iraq. Kazakhstan was one of the first in the region to undertake a large-scale humanitarian operation – Jusan – to evacuate women and children.

Following Kazakhstan's example, Tajikistan also began working to repatriate its children. In April 2018, four Tajik children were

---

26. 'Qadirov: plans to return over 100 to Russia from Syria': https://tass.ru/obschestvo/5504108.

27. 'On repatriating underage Russian citizens from Iraq': http://www.mid.ru/foreign_policy/news/-/asset_publisher/cKNonkJE02Bw/content/id/3469378.

28. 'Moscow returns 27 children of Russian fighters from Iraq': https://rus.azattyq.org/a/29762983.html.

29. 'Five Russian children brought back from Syria': https://www.kavkaz-uzel.eu/articles/337041/.

returned from Iraq, including nine-year-old Abdullo and Mariam, seven-year-old Fotima, and three-year-old Muhammad, who had been living in an orphanage.[30] On 30 April 2019, eighty-four children were transferred from Iraq to Tajikstan's capital, Dushanbe. They were the children of Tajik fighters from extremist groups. According to an announcement from the Department of Information of the Ministry for Foreign Affairs of Tajikistan,[31] the evacuees had been held in camps or prisons in Iraq.

The returnees included children aged from eighteen months to fifteen years. Most are girls, many of whom only speak Arabic. According to official data, eighty-six women and 468 children from Tajikistan remain in refugee camps in Syria. A further forty-three women and one child are held in Iraqi prisons.[32] The government also created a commission to oversee the repatriation of forty-eight women who are serving sentences in Syrian and Iraqi prisons. In October 2019, it was announced that the Tajikistani authorities were preparing to conduct yet another operation, to return more than 575 Tajik women and children from Syria. The group includes around ninety women, over 200 girls, and 240 boys. The children are aged from one to seventeen, and 134 were born during the past two years. The majority are orphans who have lost both parents. [33]

Uzbekistan became the third Central Asian country to repatriate citizens from the Middle East who had left to establish a Caliphate in the military conflict zone.

---

30. 'Tajik families evacuated from ISIS enclave in Syria': https:// tj.sputniknews.ru/country/20190225/1028373661/tajikskie-semji-evakuacia-igil-syria.html.

31. 'Tajik children returned from Iraq to Dushanbe': https://news.tj/ ru/news/tajikistan/society/20190501/tadzhikskie-deti-vozvratsheni-iz-iraka-v-dushanbe.

32. 'Around 600 wives and children of Tajik fighters still in Syria and Iraq': https://www.fergana.agency/news/109574/.

33. 'Tajikistan prepares to take 500 women and children from Syria': http:// www.news-asia.ru/view/tj/topical/12913.

Tajik children whose fathers either joined ISIS, were killed,
or disappeared without a trace, and whose mothers are held
in Baghdad prisons[34]

On 30 May 2019, Uzbekistan carried out a humanitarian covert operation known as 'Merh', which means 'goodness' in Uzbek. This operation saw the repatriation of 156 Uzbek nationals, including 106 children and forty-eight women.[35] According to official data from Kurdish authorities, a total of 300 Uzbeks were prepared for departure.[36] In October 2019, within the framework of the next covert operation, Merh II, Uzbek authorities returned sixty-four children from Iraq – thirty-nine boys and twenty-five girls, fourteen under the

34. 'Tajik children returned from Iraq to Dushanbe': https://news.tj/ru/news/tajikistan/society/20190501/tadzhikskie-deti-vozvratsheni-iz-iraka-v-dushanbe.

35. 'In Uzbekistan the rehabilitation of "victims of deception" who arrived from Syria begins': http://central.asia-news.com/ru/articles/cnmi_ca/features/2019/06/11/feature-01.

36. 'Syria Kurds say repatriating 148 Uzbek ISIS women, children': http://english.alarabiya.net/en/News/2019/05/30/Syria-Kurds-say-repatriating-148-Uzbek-ISIS-women-children.html.

age of three, and two orphans.[37] As noted above, a special working group conducted talks with women from Uzbekistan sentenced to long (ten to twenty years) or life imprisonment for participating in international terrorist organisations, and received their permission to repatriate their children.[38] The Uzbek authorities should be congratulated for involving experts from various international organisations to implement this complex rehabilitation programme.

As this book is being prepared, around 3,000 Uzbekistani nationals remain in the Middle East according to the chairman of the Muslim Board of the Republic,[39] with 150-500 Uzbek nationals in the northeast Syrian camp of al-Hawl alone.

Women and children returning from Syria to Uzbekistan[40]

---

37. '64 children brought from Iraq to Uzbekistan': https://www.gazeta.uz/ru/2019/10/10/mehr2/.

38. Ibid.

39. 'Mufti of Uzbekistan: "3,000 Uzbeks are fighting in the Middle East"': https://eadaily.com/ru/news/2019/06/10/muftiy-uzbekistana-na-blizhnem-vostoke-voyuyut-okolo-3-tys-uzbekov.

40. 'Uzbekistan returns 156 women and children from the active combat zone in the Middle East': https://fergana.agency/news/107844/.

In February 2019, Kyrgyzstan authorities announced that they were also working on repatriating their citizens from Syria and Iraq and taking steps to verify their identities. In June 2019, the country's Ministry of Foreign Affairs reported that, in collaboration with Iraqi authorities, they had completed the identification of Kyrgyzstani citizens[41] remaining in Iraq. The question of their repatriation is under government review. Similar work is being carried out in Syria.

Mapping out Operation: Jusan

The special operation for returning Kazakhstani nationals from Syria was code-named *Jusan*, the Kazakh name for wormwood – a plant traditionally associated with the homeland in Kazakh literature and cinema. 'If he does not respond to the song, tie up a bunch of *jusan* from the steppe and give it to him, and then he will return,' advises a figure in the steppe legend about a man who forgot his homeland. His brother sends a messenger with instructions to remind him of his home in this way. One whiff of the tangy aroma of wormwood reminds the man of the Great Steppe, and his fatherland. It is symbolic that the return of children to their historical homeland from the outback of the Middle East was given this sacral name. The name of the mission highlights the fact that it is first and foremost a humanitarian operation, and only then a political, diplomatic and military one.

We must point out that, as early as 2017, the Anti-Terrorism Centre (ATC) of the National Security Committee (NSC) of the Republic of Kazakhstan predicted the repatriation of fighters' family members to Kazakhstan, two years ahead of the full defeat of ISIS. In particular, in September 2017, the matter of beginning preparations for the above-mentioned operation was raised at a session of ATC. The leader of ATC, NSC Chairman Karim Massimov, approved corresponding protocol measures for state departments, including measures on the creation of social projects for the rehabilitation of women and children returning from the conflict zones.

---

41. 'KR working on repatriating its children from Syria and Iraq': https://rus.azattyk.org/a/kyrgyzstan-syria-return-citizen/29981217.html.

The development stage of Operation: Jusan began in May–June 2018. But a lot of work had already been done.

First, the NSC received information from operational sources about Kazakhstani nationals belonging to ISIS who were being held on Syrian territory by other groups. Files were then transferred to foreign intelligence agencies for validation and verification.

Second, during special operations conducted by the NSC Anti-Terrorist Centre, a significant proportion of Kazakhstanis in the conflict zone were persuaded to surrender.

Third, the task at this time was not to allow fighters and their families to slip through the net, and to prevent them committing terrorist acts against Kazakhstan. Maintaining the principle that punishment was inevitable for criminals was of utmost importance, as was the socialisation of citizens who had been subject to radical influences. And that is how the idea of evacuation was born. After reaching an agreement with foreign partners, the decision was taken to carry out this humanitarian operation to repatriate Kazakhstani nationals.

It took months of painstaking work to coordinate all the necessary procedures, both at home and abroad. The preparation stage required the involvement of other state departments, including the Ministries of Defence and Foreign Affairs, as well as of other executive bodies. However, not all participants in this process agreed with the basic concept of repatriating those who had spent a long time in the active combat zone. Some argued that these people may further promote terrorist ideology in Kazakhstan. Tough closed discussions continued for two months, and the matter was also discussed in the Security Council.

The discussions were ended by the First President of Kazakhstan, Nursultan Nazarbayev, who sanctioned the implementation of Operation: Jusan in September 2018. It is worth noting that, even before the go-ahead had been received, Kazakhstani intelligence agencies collaborated with other state bodies to develop and test the child rehabilitation programme. The Ministry of Education and Science of the Republic of Kazakhstan was tasked with implementing this programme. In other words, besides the operative capabilities of the intelligence agencies, the readiness of civic departments to work with the people who were to return from the active combat zone had to be considered. In total, around 425 representatives from ten government bodies participated in this operation at various stages:

- National Security Committee (Department for Combating Terrorism, territorial divisions, Headquarters of the Anti-Terrorism Centre, Arystan Special Forces Service, Academy of the National Security Committee);
- Ministry of Health;
- Ministry of Education and Science;
- Ministry of Internal Affairs (Migration Service Committee, Members of the National Guard, Department of the Interior and Department of Emergency Situations of the Mangystau Oblast);
- Ministry of Information and Social Development;
- Ministry of Foreign Affairs;
- Defence Department;
- Akimat of Mangystau Oblast;
- General Prosecutor's Office;
- Security Council.

Non-governmental organisations were also given an important role in implementing the rehabilitation programme. In particular, staff of the Pravo Public Foundation experienced with working with so-called difficult teenagers, and theologians from the Akniet and ANSAR organisations, were involved in organising the adaptation centre's activities.

The active preparation stage of the special operation began at the end of August 2018. The NSC RK operational Department for Combating Terrorism acted as initiator, main participants and main coordinator of the whole operation. Agents from this department initiated a broad spectrum of measures, from outlining to planning all the details of the operation (establishing and maintaining contact with foreign intelligence agencies, and Kurdish military brigades; coordinating the work of state bodies and organising training) to procuring essential items for the evacuees and developing a modus operandi for rehabilitation centres.

To successfully effect the repatriation of our citizens, NSC case officers had to resolve complex logistical problems on-site, at the evacuation point itself, since the operation was not simply about coming and collecting our citizens. First, their precise location in the various camps in northeast Syria had to be established. Temporary camps and prisons holding captured ISIS fighters and families were located on territory controlled by the Kurdish SDF (Syrian Democratic Forces), an umbrella organisation composed of various Kurdish and Arab armed brigades. It was also necessary to liaise with various groups and clarify information about the location of our citizens within the various camps. At that point, there were three temporary camps in the northeast: al-Hawl, al-Roj and Ayn Issa, as well as two so-called Centres for the Detention of Foreign Terrorist Fighters (al-Malikiyah and Gerevana prisons) plus several small prisons holding captured ISIS members.

Our citizens had to be found among tens of thousands of people detained in these camps and prisons. Once their location had been established, they had to be identified rigorously: was that person really our citizen, or were there some people who tried to pass themselves off as Kazakhstani by using someone else's personal details? We could not rule out that radical groups, in particular ISIS, would try to embed active supporters, including fighters from different countries, into the evacuation of our citizens. Furthermore, this situation could have been used by foreign intelligence agencies for their own interests.

Moreover, the Turkish army's military actions in northeast Syria at the beginning of 2019 forced large numbers of people to leave their houses, and some found refuge in temporary camps. As of 9 October 2019, a total of 710,000 people displaced from earlier conflict zones found themselves in northeast Syria, and 91,000 were in camps presumed to contain Kazakhstani nationals (al-Hawl, al-Roj, Mahmoudi and Areesha).[42] Kazakhstani intelligence agency case officers identified individuals *in situ*, in collaboration with local

42. Syrian Arab Republic: North East Syria Displacement (28 October 2019): https//reliefweb.int/sites/reliefweb.int/files/resources/Syrian_arab_republic_north-east-syria-displacement-28october-2019.

Kurdish groups. Meanwhile, in the capital, a commission was set up at the Ministry of Information and Social Development involving parents of citizens who had left for conflict zones to compile and confirm a general list of wanted people and members of their families. All this data was checked and rechecked many times to rule out any errors.

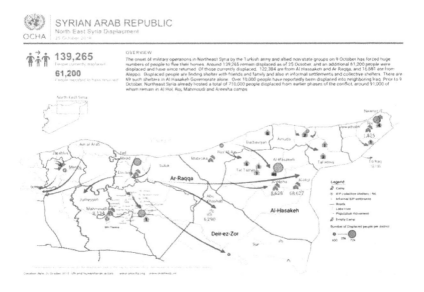

The Arystan Special Forces Service became another important player in the operation. Arystan agents ensured the safety of our citizens during transfer and arrival, providing physical protection and escorting former ISIS members. Since most of the evacuees were female, female Arystan agents were involved in the operation, particularly for body-searching women.

Many problems had to be addressed – transport and logistics, for instance. Because the planned evacuation was to take place from active combat zones, it was decided to use military planes rather than civil aviation thanks to their ability to take off and land on airstrips with dirt runways. To this end, air force defence planes of the RK armed forces were used. In particular, the Spanish-made turboprop transport aircraft of the RK Air Force – CASA C-295 (*speed: 482 km/h; range 4,500 km; altitude ceiling 7,620 m; crew 2, can accommodate up to*

60 people on board) were used.[43] Highly qualified military medics were also involved in providing first aid during the evacuation.

Military transport plane CASA C-295
used to repatriate Kazakhstani nationals[44]

Considering that the destination was located in an active combat zone, as well as the absence of necessary aeronautical support there, it was decided to secretly dispatch experienced military pilots to the evacuation site in advance. Following the tragic event involving a Malaysian aircraft that went down over Ukraine in summer 2014, international airlines no longer fly civil aircraft over northern Syria, to avoid similar incidents. It is known that medium- and long-range civil aircraft generally fly at an altitude of 9,000–11,000 metres, while the military planes used in Operation: Jusan could fly at an altitude of 7,000 m. It is worth noting that all planes had armed NSC RK

43. '"Artemisia", or simply "Jusan" or some thoughts on an operation by Kazakh commanders': http://kazanalytics.kz/artemisia.
44. 'Special operation for repatriating Kazakhstanis from Syria': https://www.youtube.com/watch?v=ZLpi4tyKC4M.

and Arystan Special Forces agents on board. They also carried tents, baby food, clothes, medical and other specialised equipment. For this reason, the planes could not stay long at maximum altitude. As a result, there was some risk even for military aircraft.

On the eve of the first Operation: Jusan, 18 September 2018, the Russian Ministry of Defence reported the loss of the Russian military plane Il-20 in Syria. All fifteen military personnel on board died. It later became clear that the plane had been shot down by a Syrian anti-aircraft rocket by mistake. The rocket was aimed at Israeli F-16 fighter planes that were targeting Syrian objects in Latakia Province. However, the system mistakenly locked onto the Russian Il-20 that was returning to the Khmeimim airbase in the same province. That is why, before Operation: Jusan, a group of secret service agents together with military pilots visited the evacuation point and calculated landing and take-off *in situ* there. To pre-empt possible unforeseen circumstances, a special landing technique, 'the Afghan approach', was tested; this had been used by military pilots in the Afghan war and consists of an almost vertical landing that is executed when there is a high risk of ground fire.[45]

Kazakhstan's foreign service also played an important role in Operation: Jusan. Representatives of the Ministry of Foreign Affairs had to resolve extremely complex procedural issues with several countries, such as the legal framework for the transfer of Kazakhstani citizens, including ISIS fighters. In addition, the flight path had to be agreed on and an air corridor for our planes had to be established over other states' territories. The process was complicated by the fact that the planes were military transport planes, not civil aircraft. Moreover, the route took them over the territories of countries with which Kazakhstan had rather complicated relations. For example, our aircraft, with ex-ISIS fighters' families aboard, had to take off from a military airfield on Kurdish territory controlled by American military, and fly over Iranian territory. This is just one of the complicated episodes of Operation: Jusan.

---

45. "'The Afghan Approach" in Syrian Khmeimim': http://www.sovross.ru/articles/1668/38404.

The plan was for special military planes to take off from the city of Aktau and then fly over countries with which an agreement had been made, and collect our citizens in at predetermined points in northeast Syria. Aktau, in the west of Kazakhstan, had been deliberately chosen as the main base for the planes' departure, and also as the main place for lodging the evacuees. Geographically, this city represented the closest point for those returning within the framework of this operation. Furthermore, 30 km from the city, an adaptation centre had been established with various specialists involved: psychologists, theologians, and medical staff.

Owing to the time difference with Syria (plus five hours), the aircraft were scheduled to leave Aktau early in the morning; there was just a two-hour window to collect our citizens at the evacuation point. After 120 minutes, our partners' security guarantees would expire. Therefore, it was critical to meet this deadline. To achieve this, a few weeks before the operation, all those who would take part in extracting Kazakhstani citizens at the presumed point of evacuation spent several days practising the operational procedures at the military aerodrome in Nur-Sultan. Following the training, the initial plan was adjusted; some elements had to be trimmed or removed to ensure everything could be successfully completed in the two-hour window.

The intelligence agencies conducted drills covering the whole process – our citizens had to be identified at the point of evacuation, their data had to be checked, and men and women also had to be searched for security reasons. Several tents would be put up for these searches. Each stage of the operation was timed: taxiing military aircraft to the parking bay; offloading equipment; pitching tents; receiving our citizens; first aid; refuelling the planes; boarding, etc. Groups trained on the clock for several days until full coordination was achieved.

Similar work was underway in Aktau, too. Collaborating with agents from the Mangystau Oblast Department of Internal Affairs, a special group of NSC and Arystan Special Forces Service staff worked out a plan for receiving Kazakhstani returnees: receiving the planes in Aktau city airport; rechecking identity; issuing documents; loading into vehicles; departure to the adaptation centre in convoy with a police patrol. All this was done in top secrecy for reasons of security.

First attempt and *force majeure*

In order to understand the difficult conditions when the attempt to return our citizens home was made, we first need to understand what had been happening in Syria over the past eight years.

Civil war has been raging in Syria since 2011. Since fighting began, Syria's terrorist map has been significantly enriched by the appearance of new groups, including both large and small extremist organisations. According to Alain Rodier, senior associate researcher at the Centre Français de Recherche sur le Renseignement (CF2R), there are hundreds of such groups in Syria: '… but in most cases they are very small. They act within the framework of individual villages, urban districts or small territories. Their goals do not extend beyond the local level.'[46]

The emergence of ISIS in Syria became a major tragic consequence of the crisis in the Middle East. The organisation was formed in October 2006 by a merger of ten radical Islamist groups headed by an al-Qaeda subdivision in Iraq. The cell's ideological inspiration came from Abu Musab al-Zarqawi (liquidated in 2006), a notorious international terrorist who had previously fought in Afghanistan.

From 2010 the organisation was led by Abu Bakr al-Baghdadi, and a new epoch in the story of ISIS began. In April 2013, al-Baghdadi announced the group would broaden its activities. Its members were already fighting on Syrian territory. He also announced that the organisation would rename itself the Islamic State of Iraq and the Levant. A year later, on 29 June 2014, the group announced the creation of the 'Islamic Caliphate' on seized territories in Iraq and Syria, and al-Baghdadi was proclaimed Caliph. ISIS's war strategy and tactics meant that this previously unknown cell could not only leave al-Qaeda but also demand that al-Qaeda's leader, Ayman al-Zawahiri, swear allegiance to them. The idea of 'global jihad' became a reality and acquired subjectivity in the form of the declared quasi-state. The world had to respond to the illegal activities of this group that had announced itself so loudly.

---

46. 'Seven major Islamist groups in Syria': http://inosmi.ru/world/2015 1109/231232545.html.

On 8 August 2014, US President Barack Obama sanctioned military attacks on ISIS camps in Iraq to protect American personnel in the Iraqi city of Erbil and to save Kurdish Yazidi civilians stranded in the Sinjar mountains. On 11 September 2014, Obama announced his plan to combat the terrorist group. An international coalition against ISIS headed by the US was created. It was joined by over fifty countries and several international organisations. On 23 September 2014, the US began military operations against ISIS militants in Syria. Bahrain, Jordan, the United Arab Emirates, Qatar and Saudi Arabia took part in air strikes against ISIS fighters in the territories of Iraq and Syria. They were later joined by Great Britain, France, Canada, Australia and Turkey. In addition, in January 2016, the US president gave the Pentagon permission to carry out air strikes on ISIS positions in Afghanistan. In turn, from September 2015, Russia began conducting air strikes in Syria at the request of the country's president, Bashar al-Assad.

The eight-year-long military campaign by Russia and the international coalition headed by the US finally led to the fall of the ISIS Caliphate.

Whereas in January 2015 the fighters controlled 90,800 km², by January 2017 they controlled less than 60,400 km², and by the beginning of July, just 32,600 km².[47] In October 2017, the international coalition confirmed that Raqqa, the official ISIS capital, had been liberated from the terrorists. The Iraqi city of Mosul, captured by ISIS in summer 2014, was liberated several months earlier. In December 2017, the full liberation of Iraqi territory was announced. From that moment on, the group began rapidly losing its positions and territories in Syria. By September 2018, ISIS was active only in northeast Syria and, according to then US Defence Minister James Mattis, occupied around 2 per cent of the total Syrian territory it had controlled in 2014.[48]

---

47. 'ISIS is more dangerous dead than alive': http://svpressa.ru/war21/article/176735/.
48. 'Is ISIS defeated?': https://www.diplomatie.gouv.fr/ru/politique-etrangere/securite-desarmement-et-non-proliferation/terrorisme-l-action-internationale-de-la-france/daech-est-il-vaincu/.

Territories controlled by ISIS in Syria (black), September 2018[49]

I must point out that most Kazakhstani nationals who left for the Middle East with their families to live there under Sharia law did not plan to return. However, the military situation in ISIS-controlled territories was deteriorating every day, forcing people to leave for 'quieter' places. In these circumstances, they grasped at the hope of being able to survive and escape. At the same time, several women with children made their own way to Kurdish outposts and surrendered, after which they contacted their relatives so that the state could assist in their return home.

As we have seen, planning Operation: Jusan took several months. After prolonged and complex negotiations at the inter-state level, the decision was made to conduct a humanitarian mission in October 2018 to repatriate women and children who had asked for state help. The preparations lasted several weeks. In September, the overall plan as well as the full details of the operation were agreed upon. On 9 October 2018, at 3 p.m., three military transport planes belonging to Kazakhstan's air force took off from the military aerodrome in Nur-Sultan and headed for Aktau. They were carrying agents of the Arystan Special Forces Service and military medics. In the evening, they landed in Aktau and, early the next morning, 10 October, they should

49. 'Syria's war: Who controls what?': https://www.aljazeera.com/indepth/interactive/2015/05/syria-country-divided-150529144229467.html.

have flown to Syria. However, a sudden worsening of the military and political situation in the evacuation zone, coupled with the absence of security guarantees, led to one of the international partners suddenly refusing to provide an air corridor.

The situation in Syria began deteriorating rapidly just before the operation. The conflict started escalating on 17 September, after Syrian anti-aircraft defence shot down a Russian Il-20 by mistake. Let me repeat that the Russian side accused Israeli fighter planes that had been conducting raids in Latakia Province to have 'set up' the Il-20 to be shot. At the end of that month, Russia delivered three S-300 air defence systems 'to increase their fighting capabilities', as they said, within a range of 200 km. Israel responded, saying that its air force would continue air raids in Syria. These actions elicited concern from the US and Turkey, whose military positions in Syria were also within the range of the Russian rockets.

That same month, Russia and Turkey reached an agreement on creating a de-escalation zone in the Syrian province of Idlib. According to this agreement, large military groups facing off the Syrian government's army had to withdraw heavy artillery within their territories. In the beginning of October, however, heavy fighting broke out between these groups, who wanted to strengthen their positions as much as possible before the deadline of 20 October when the de-escalation zone was due to be implemented. At the same time, a Kurdish detachment of the Syrian Democratic Forces (SDF) began advancing on ISIS positions around the city of Hajin. The offence brought no substantial tactical advantage for the Kurdish militia.

The sharp, all-round deterioration of the situation in Syria thwarted the Kazakh intelligence agencies' plans. The working group in Aktau began devising an alternative safe route. At the same time, in Nur-Sultan, the leadership of the Ministry of Foreign Affairs and the NSC were collaborating with foreign partners on a new plan. It took about a week to agree on a potential new route, but, in the end it was decided to cancel the special operation owing to the unforeseen circumstances that had arisen.

After a week of waiting on stand-by, the military transport plans and Arystan agents left from Aktau for their main bases in other cities. The first attempt to return women and children had failed. The operation was postponed for a week at a time, and so several months passed. It was not until December 2018 that the new plan for Operation: Jusan was finally agreed on, as a result of which around 600 Kazakhstani nationals were repatriated.

Operation: Jusan in action

Although it is generally assumed that Operation: Jusan was realised in three main stages, in fact there were five. The general public knows much less about the last two stages. In this chapter, I will cover them in more detail. But the Kazakhstani mission did not stop with the Operation: Jusan evacuation; several more of our compatriots returned home from Iraq under an operation code-named 'Rusafa'.

But, for now, let us return to statistics. In recent years, more than half of those who left Kazakhstan for active combat zones were women and children. According to official data from Kazakhstani intelligence agencies, from 2015–17 alone, 255 people from Kazakhstan joined international terrorist organisations.

Left	2015	2016	2017
Women	83	26	
Children	64	35	No data
Total	186	69	
Returned	2015	2016	2017
Women	6	2	15
Children	13	4	26
Total	19	6	41

On 12 September 2018, several domestic mass media outlets reported that seven women and sixteen children, all Kazakhstani citizens, had been held in a refugee camp in Syria for eight months. One of the women, who introduced herself as Sabira Moldabekova, contacted the Khabar 24 news agency. She said she had gone to Syria four years previously

to fetch her daughter and grandchildren, whose father had been killed there. She was now with other Kazakhstanis in a refugee camp on territory controlled by Kurdish militias on the border with Turkey. The conversation with Moldabekova revealed that the Kazakhstani nationals were from Uralsk, Aktobe, Almaty and Zhezkazgan.[50] In the interview, she complained that the Kazakhstani authorities were apparently in no hurry to take their children out of Syria.

As later became clear, this was in fact a leak organised by Kazakhstani women in the Syrian camp who of course knew that Kazakhstan was preparing a special operation to repatriate them. With this appeal, they wanted to exert pressure on the Kazakhstani authorities and thereby speed up their liberation from the Kurdish camp. In this way, several women tried to present themselves as innocent citizens who ended up in Syria not of their own volition. Later, these women were returned to Kazakhstan during the first stage of the humanitarian Operation: Jusan in January 2019.

However, at that time, any information about the planned evacuation could create risks for the women themselves, as well as for the operation. ISIS had its own informants among women in the Kurdish camp, via whom they gathered information about citizens who expressed an active desire to return to their homeland and who collaborated with intelligence agencies. There were instances of ISIS including those who collaborated with intelligence agencies in the list for prisoner exchanges with Kurdish brigades, with a view to staging a show execution when they were returned. There were other risks, connected with possible sabotage or terrorist acts against the evacuation team, and disruption of the planned evacuation. That is why the publication of similar information regarding the planned operation was later suppressed. And indeed, our intelligence agencies did later discover a woman in the group of evacuees who passed information on to ISIS.

---

50. '7 Kazakhstani women and 16 children remain in Syria: RK Ministry of Foreign Affairs is working on repatriating them': https://newtimes. kz/obshchestvo/77749-sem-kazakhstanskikh-zhenshchin-i-16-detej-nakhodyatsya-v-sirii-mid-rk-rabotaet-nad-ikh-vozvrashcheniem.

To date, Kazakhstan has become one of the first countries in the world to conduct a large-scale covert mission to repatriate its citizens from active combat zones in Syria. It was carried out in three main stages, with two additional ones.

'Jusan-1'

After the first failed attempt in October 2018, Kazakhstani intelligence agencies postponed the operation week on week. However, no agreement could be reached with foreign partners in either October or November on the extraction date for family members of ex-ISIS fighters. In the end, one international partner refused to collaborate at all, justifying its refusal by citing an inability to provide firm security guarantees to Kazakhstani planes. The real reason for the refusal was that the Kazakhstani intelligence agencies managed to reach an agreement with the Kurdish militia about the transfer of captive fighters and their family members held in the camp without the mediation of third parties.

Nevertheless, Kazakhstan authorities forged an agreement regarding Operation: Jusan with almost all sides directly or indirectly involved in the Syrian conflict. Kazakhstan foreign policy, aimed at building balanced relations with the key players in international politics, played its role in this diplomatic success. By and large, Kazakhstan has forged trusting relations with Middle Eastern countries. This was also facilitated by Kazakhstan's having previously provided a platform for multilateral negotiations to resolve the situation in Syria. During the 'Astana Process', mechanisms for reaching agreement on the creation of de-escalation zones and reducing the level of military confrontation in Syria were developed. The mediatory role Kazakhstan played in negotiations in Syria was acknowledged by practically all sides. That is why the Kazakhstani authorities finally succeeded in reaching an agreement with many countries on the mission plan, although the main phase of the operation was conducted in collaboration with the US.

The American military was not just an ally of the Syrian Kurds, it was also the main power directly coordinating the military situation in northeast Syria. Consequently, to achieve anything in that part of Syria, it was necessary to negotiate with America. The final agreement with the US military on implementing the mission was reached at the end of December 2018. The first stage of the operation was scheduled for 10 January 2019.

However, in the first days of January, foreign partners approached the Kazakhstani side, proposing to bring the operation forward by several days. So as not to miss this opportunity – the military and political situation in Syria was changing every day – Kazakhstani intelligence agencies managed to mobilise all the resources in the shortest possible time, and confirmed their readiness to bring the starting date forward. As a result, on 5 January 2019, at 6 a.m., three Kazakhstani air force military aircraft took off simultaneously from the international airport in Aktau. The light turboprop C-295 planes were loaded with foodstuffs, medical equipment, and other specialised equipment. NSC RK and Arystan operatives as well as military medics were also on board. Other NSC RK case officers and staff of the consulate service of the Ministry of Foreign Affairs were waiting at the evacuation point. Around eighty professionals took part in the first phase of the operation.

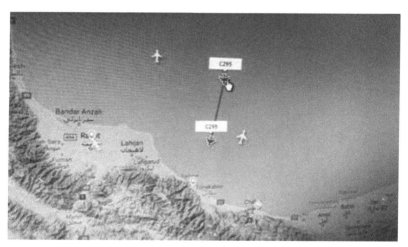

Screenshot of the Flightradar24 app showing the flight path of Kazakhstani C-295 military planes, 5 January 2019

The planes arrived at the evacuation zone on time. The evacuees were identified and searched within the two-hour window. The decision had been taken earlier that Kazakhstani ISIS fighters captured by Kurds would be taken as well as women and children. They boarded a separate plane under reinforced escort, while the women and children were transported in two other planes. The American military provided protection at the external perimeter of the territory where the handover was taking place. Kazakhstani paramilitary protected the aircraft, conducted a thorough search of all evacuees, and acted as their armed escort. The women and children were given food immediately, and some were given first aid. The children were also given toys and books prepared in advance. Later, on arrival, everyone was given winter clothes.

This phase of the operation in the evacuation zone went according to plan, minute to minute, with no delays. However, before take-off, it had taken a long time to reach an agreement regarding the flight path, and this in turn created new risks. This was because the Kazakhstani planes had to transit the air corridor provided by one of the countries by 00.00 hours on 6 January. The delay before take-off, coupled with headwinds and the planes being loaded to maximum weight capacity, reduced the likelihood of them managing to transit this air corridor in the time allotted. Deviation from the agreed flight path could create additional difficulties, possibly even a forced landing on the territory of a third country. The intelligence agencies were ready for this scenario, so the planes were kitted with special communication equipment and all other necessities for such an eventuality.

However, all pilots managed to make the time frame, and the first Kazakhstanis evacuated from Syria were brought to Aktau in the early morning of 6 January 2019. Upon arrival, they were all given temporary ID documents. Border control guards carried out the necessary procedures, and the people were then taken to the adaptation centre near the city of Aktau, escorted by police and ambulances. Because the women and children had been kept in unsanitary conditions in the Syrian camps, and also to avoid the spread of infectious diseases, they were placed under quarantine in the adaptation centre under medical observation. Social service staff from the Akimat of the Mangystau Oblast worked with the women and children alongside medical staff, psychologists and theologians.

As a result, during the first stage of Operation: Jusan, on 6 January 2019, forty-seven Kazakhstanis (six men, eleven women and thirty children) were repatriated. The men, ex-fighters, were immediately transferred to the territorial subdivisions of the NSC. They were taken by special planes to the regions where they had lived before leaving for Syria, where they were investigated and later given sentences of various lengths by the courts for their involvement in terrorist activities.

From 7–8 January, some foreign media outlets published the first information about the repatriation of former ISIS fighters and members of their families to Kazakhstan, although Kazakhstan maintained confidentiality in the interests of security for all those involved in the programme. The operation was conducted on Saturday 5 January 2019. Two days later, on Monday 7 January, the press centre of the Kurdish-led SDF published an official announcement about the completed operation, stating that: 'the democratic self-administration in the northeast of Syria, with the attendence of SDF commanders, handed over five terrorists, eleven women and thirty children of ISIS-arrested members who have Kazakhstani nationality to their country's government; the process took place via US mediation.'

The announcement also mentions the many months of negotiations with the Kazakhstani side: 'A few months ago, during a meeting between SDF and Kazakhstani anti-terrorism forces in northeast of Syria, an agreement was held to hand over the arrested Kazakhstani causalities [sic] who participated in the ISIS terrorist organisation, and who are arrested by SDF, to their country's government; the meeting included the discussion about the mechanism of transferring them home. [...] However, the reason that made the handing over of those people late was technical, however, [sic] the agreement was applied on 5 Jan 2019, when they were formally handed over to their country with American mediation.'[51]

---

51. 'The Self-Administration handed over the arrested Kazakhstani ISIS members to their country': http://sdf-press.com/en/2019/01/

SDF press centre announcement regarding the transfer of ex-ISIS members and members of their families to Kazakhstani authorities

Following this, information appeared on other media outlets affiliated with Kurdish groups. The sources stated that the ISIS members were transferred to Kazakhstan with the mediation of the US.[52]

the-self-administration-handed-over-the-arrested-kazakhstani-isis-members-to-their-country. (English editor's note: some changes made to punctuation, etc, for clarity.)

52. '5 ISIS militants, families returned to Kazakhstan with US mediation: SDF': https://www.rudaw.net/English/middleeast/Syria/070120193.

A report about the operation appeared on the social media accounts of American information agents working in the Middle East.

 Bassem Mroue ....مـسـاب ✔ · 07.01.2019 ⌄
The main U.S.-backed group in Syria says it has handed over IS fighters and civilians from #Kazakhstan to their country. #SDF said in a statement that those handed over to authorities in their country are five fighters, 11 women and 30 children. #Syria #ISIS

  ♡1

Screenshot of correspondent Associated Press correspondent for the Middle East Bassem Mroue's Twitter account

American mass media, however, did not highlight the US's mediating role, only reporting that US military 'supported the return of foreign terrorist fighters from Syrian Democratic Forces (SDF) custody to Kazakhstan'.

 Ryan Browne ✔ @rabro... · 08.01.2019 ⌄
The US military "supported the return of foreign terrorist fighters from Syrian Democratic Forces custody to Kazakhstan" Saturday, according to the Pentagon. US defense officials have told CNN that over 700 ISIS foreign fighters are currently being detained by the Kurdish-led SDF

♡ 3 ↺ 14 ♡ 21 ↥

Screenshot of CNN reporter on matters of national security Ryan Browne's Twitter account

Initially, there were no plans to divulge the details of the covert mission since there was a chance it would be extended. However, considering the risk of fostering distorted information and to avoid speculation among the general public, the decision was made to make an official announcement. Thus, on 9 January 2019, the Akorda press agency released a special announcement by the President of the Republic of Kazakhstan, Nursultan Nazarbayev:

> On 6 January this year, as a result of the humanitarian operation conducted on my orders by law enforcement bodies and the Ministry of Foreign Affairs, forty-seven Kazakhstani citizens, including thirty children, were evacuated from Syria.
>
> They had been led into this crisis-stricken country by deceit and remained there as hostages of terrorists from the international terrorist organisation ISIS (banned in Kazakhstan). When they arrived in Kazakhstan, the women and children were given all manner of state support. These innocent people who had found themselves in such a difficult situation were tremendously glad of their salvation. They will continue to undergo adaptation and to receive all necessary medical help in the coming month. The efforts undertaken will contribute to preventing similar cases.
>
> Kazakhstan always supports its citizens, no matter where they find themselves. Our main task is to provide security and protect the country's integrity and unity. We will continue this work of returning children who remain in the active combat zone against their will.[53]

Most of the women who returned home during the initial stage of the covert operation had been in Kurdish custody for about a year. They

---

53. 'Announcement from the Head of State about the completion of the humanitarian mission to evacuate Kazakhstani citizens from Syria': http:// www.akorda.kz/ru/events/akorda_news/akorda_other_events/zayavlenie-glavy-gosudarstva-v-svyazi-s-zaversheniem-gumanitarnoi-operacii-po-evakuacii-grazhdan-kazahstana-iz-sirii.

had found guides and paid them themselves in order to escape ISIS-controlled territory. In preliminary short interviews, they said they constantly wanted to return home. However, their wish was met by hardcore propaganda on the part of ISIS members. The women were threatened and told their children would be taken from them, or that they would be branded as traitors. Here is a quote from an interview with one of the women:

> They were saying different things. First, they said you'd be a traitor [*if you leave ISIS – author's note*]. Then they said you are a traitor and apostate because you are forsaking Islam, you're becoming an infidel, a *kaffir*. We'll put you in prison, take away your children. These children who were born in ISIS and became *shahids*, you won't get them – that's how they pressured us.

The ISIS propaganda was continuous and active. And when women began escaping more fequently from their territories, they started 'warning' about violence on the part of the Kurds.

One of the Kazakhstani women told how she got out. She got to know a local ethnic Arab woman and asked for her help, because she knew that her new acquaintance's son was a guide. She paid $250 US dollars per family member to get into a Kurdish militia camp, where she subsequently spent a year. She said she was afraid of being punished in Kazakhstan, but this fear did not outweigh the dread she felt for her children, who might die in Syria. Later in the interview, the woman said she was glad she had saved her children and brought them back home. In the future, she plans to return to the life she led before she left, and send her children to school and her granddaughter to kindergarten. And she wants to forget everything she experienced in Syria.

'Jusan-2'

The first phase of Operation: Jusan showed Kazakhstanis in Syria that the authorities did not simply want to return and then incarcerate all the women. Consequently, family members of ex-fighters and ex-ISIS fighters themselves began contacting NSC RK through various channels, saying they wanted to return home. The number of people to be evacuated during phase 2 was growing rapidly. But a different approach was needed, because the military situation in the evacuation zone was deteriorating once again. The military ring was tightening around ISIS. As a result, the remains of the group were concentrated in the last population centre under their control – the town of al-Baghuz on the east bank of the Euphrates, on the Syria-Iraq border.

Al-Baghuz, the last village controlled by ISIS

After being on the move for a while, the families of Kazakh radicals and other foreign ISIS members arrived at the same spot: al-Baghuz. At the beginning of February, Kurdish military forces, aided by the US air force, conducted the final 'battle' against remaining ISIS forces in their last military-territorial stronghold. The fighting was so intense that the White House hurried to make announcements regarding the impending victory over ISIS. On 6 February 2019, US President Donald Trump addressed a meeting of representatives from countries of the Global Coalition to Defeat ISIS. He announced that Washington would be able to officially announce complete victory over ISIS as early as the next week.[54] However, it was not possible to retake al-Baghuz immediately, and it was not until 12 February that Trump announced

---

54. 'Watch live: President Donald Trump speaks at global coalition to defeat ISIS'. NBC News: https://www.youtube.com/watch?v=gHEFa84v6mo& feature=youtu.be.

that the US controlled 100 per cent of the territory that had previously belonged to ISIS in Syria.

It was precisely in this difficult period of active combat that tens of thousands of women and children would begin leaving al-Baghuz, according to the agreement reached between the Kurds and ISIS fighters. Kazakhstanis and their young children would be among them. They would all be held in the al-Hawl camp for displaced people, from where they would later be evacuated and returned to their homeland.

Bearing in mind the success of the previous repatriation operation – and trusting Kazakhstan – this time international partners provided their own military planes for the evacuation of Kazakhstani nationals. This simplified the operation from the point of view of transport and logistics. But, as before, success depended on many and varied factors, including the ever-changing geopolitical situation. Once again, the operation was constantly postponed. A special group of secret service agents went to Syria in advance to carry out identification procedures and to prepare for the evacuation. In consideration of the large amount of work to be done, the contingent of the advance party was enlarged.

Once again, they searched for Kazakhstani citizens among the many thousands living in the camp for displaced people, giving them necessary medical help and preparing them to return home. Medical help was needed because some were wounded – women and children remained in the ranks of ISIS until the end and came under heavy fire. In order to give some idea of the scale of work undertaken by our intelligence agencies, I will cite some figures. The population of the al-Hawl camp alone, in northeast Syria, increased from less than 10,000 in December 2018 to over 70,000 in April 2019.[55] In other words, our intelligence agencies had to search tens of thousands of people to find and identify our citizens scattered in various camps and prisons.

Nevertheless, Kazakhstani intelligence agencies managed to quickly agree a new protocol with our partners. As a result, from

---

55. '24th Report of the Analytical Support and Sanctions Monitoring Team, submitted pursuant to resolution 2368 (2017) on ISIL (Daesh), "AlQaeda" and individuals and organisations associated with them': //undocs.org.

7–9 May 2019, 231 people were evacuated to Kazakhstan during the second phase of Operation: Jusan. Early in the morning on 7 May, the first group of our citizens was delivered by military plane to Aktau, escorted by secret service agents. In the space of one and a half hours, all the returned citizens were examined by medical staff, and documented, and the aircraft flew back to Syria. On 9 May, also in the early morning, the same plane brought the second group of women and children. This group included many wounded as well as pregnant women and small children. Taking the large number of refugees into account, the territory of the adaptation centre in Aktau was enlarged.

On 10 May the second President of Kazakhstan, Kassym-Jomart Tokayev, made a special announcement about Jusan-2:

On my orders, on 7 and 9 May, 231 Kazakhstani citizens were evacuated from Syria, including 156 children, mostly of pre-school age, and eighteen of whom are orphans. This large-scale humanitarian mission was the continuation of Operation: Jusan carried out on the orders of the First President, Elbasy Nursultan Nazarbayev, in January this year. State agencies and non-governmental agencies conducted rehabilitation measures for all citizens who arrived home. Medical, psychological, and social assistance were provided. We can already say that this work has been beneficial. The women who returned in January this year have rejected their radical past, found work, and reconnected with their relatives. The children have been accepted into schools and kindergartens. The citizens of Kazakhstan who left for active combat zones made such a rash decision under the influence of the destructive and in fact false propaganda spread by terrorists. Now, they are voluntarily returning to Kazakhstan in the hopes of beginning a new life. Their children should not suffer in a foreign land or be held responsible for the mistakes of their parents. Kazakhstan reaffirms its commitment to combat terrorism as well as to provide comprehensive assistance to citizens who find themselves in difficult situations. The humanitarian mission will continue. None of our people will be left to the whims of fate. I would like to express my gratitude to the employees of the Ministry of Foreign Affairs, the National Security Committee, and also to other state bodies, as well as to our foreign partners who took part in this humanitarian operation.[56]

'Jusan-3'

Our citizens were returned in greatest number as a result of the third phase. They were evacuated following the same protocol, i.e. with the help of international partners, on special foreign military aircraft. As a result of the final third stage, from 28–31 May 2019, 246 Kazakhstanis returned to their homeland from Syria. Following the completion of this large-scale humanitarian mission, on 31 May 2019 the President of the Republic of Kazakhstan, Kassym-Jomart Tokayev, gave a special address:

On my instructions, from 28–31 May, the final third stage of the *Jusan* Special Humanitarian Operation was successfully carried out. Yet another group of our compatriots was repatriated from Syria. Thanks to the well-coordinated work of the state structure of Kazakhstan in close collaboration with foreign partners, 171 children were evacuated from active combat zones. Upon returning to Kazakhstan, they were housed in the special adaptation centre where they are currently being rehabilitated and receiving all necessary help. The humanitarian Operation: Jusan is large-scale action initiated by the First President, Elbasy Nursultan Nazarbayev, and has been continuing since last year. As a result of a range of measures, 357 children have been returned to their homeland from active combat zones. Ensuring the safety of children has become the main goal of Operation: Jusan.

Operation: Jusan has shown our state's ability to effectively solve tasks of the utmost complexity. I thank all those who took part in this operation – intelligence agencies, diplomats, the military – who carried out the mission entrusted to them with honour.

---

56. http://www.akorda.kz/ru/speeches/internal_political_affairs/in_speeches_and_addresses/zayavlenie-prezidenta-respubliki-kazakhstan-kk-tokaeva.

Our repatriated compatriots have been given the chance to begin a new life, and the children now have a peaceful sky over their heads.

We will continue to protect the rights and safety of our citizens.[57]

Statements by the country's leadership are included here for good reason. The authorities approached the task of repatriating citizens very thoroughly, focusing not only on logistical issues but also on delivering correct information. At the completion of every stage, the authorities gave a special address in which they explained to the public the measures they had taken. These statements underlined the main focus of the state's actions. In particular, it was repeatedly stressed that the operation was exclusively humanitarian; the role of the intelligence agencies and military was not brought to the fore. It was immediately pointed out that those repatriated had found themselves in the conflict zone by mistake, that many had been tricked into going there. Each address underlined the state's commitment to help its citizens, even those who make a mistake. All these statements were addressed not only to the returnees, but to the country's population as a whole, to foster a tolerant attitude towards those repatriated and protect them from public condemnation.

For this reason, after the completion of each stage of the operation, officials held special media briefings attended by representatives of the Ministry of Foreign Affairs, the NSC and other government bodies. Parents of citizens who had left for hotspots or the returnees themselves spoke at almost every briefing. The briefing on the first operation was held on 10 January 2019. Government bodies were represented by the Head of NSC Bakhytbek Rakhymberdiyev and Vice Minister of Foreign Affairs Yerzhan Ashykbayev. A member of the parents' committee, Botagoz Makhatova, also took part in the press conference. The briefing on the results of the second operation was held on 14 May 2019. Besides government officials, the parents

---

57. Address by the President of the Republic of Kazakhstan K. K. Tokayev: http://www.akorda.kz/ru/speeches/internal_political_affairs/in_speeches_ and_addresses/zayavlenie-prezidenta-respubliki-kazakhstan-kk-tokaeva-1

of repatriated citizens participated, as well as Ainur Tergeusizova, a woman who had been returned in the first phase.

The media was given the chance to hear real-life stories and find out first-hand what prompted people to leave for Syria and Iraq. This information strategy was also important for Jusan-4 and Jusan-5, which were to begin straight after work on rehabilitating returnees.

'Jusan-4' and 'Jusan-5'

The third stage of Operation: Jusan was officially counted as the final one because the main bulk of Kazakhstanis had been evacuated by that point. However, at the end of June 2019, around forty people were returned, employing the same procedure as was used to repatriate the previous group in May. This was the fourth stage of the operation. As a result, in June, all Kazakhstani women and children were repatriated from camps in northeast Syria. But there was also a fifth stage, which the intelligence agencies did not publicise at all. Nor did they disseminate information about it after its completion.

Operation: Jusan, as it had been conceived, was basically over, but intelligence agencies continued to monitor the situation of individual groups and people and, whenever possible, made attempts to repatriate them. In September 2019, four more women and fourteen children were returned from Syria via Turkey. This operation (Jusan-5) was carried out in a different way. According to Kazakhstani intelligence agencies, three widows of Kazakhstani ISIS fighters and one widow of a fighter from the Hay'at Tahrir al-Sham (hereafter HTS) affiliated with al-Qaeda were among the returnees. These ISIS widows fled the terrorist-controlled territory for north-western Syria in 2018–19, where they were lying low in Idlib Province. They had to hide from both ISIS and other local radical groups hostile to ISIS. It is important to point out here that ISIS was fighting HTS; although both organisations are branches of al-Qaeda, they often attacked each other and staged executions with captives. Should ISIS widows be found by HTS fighters, a worse fate awaited them.

Contact was established with these Kazakhstani women in 2019. They expressed their intention to return to their homeland, and reported their whereabouts in Idlib Province. As these women had no documents, the Kazakhstani side approached the Turkish intelligence agencies and reached an agreement to take the women to Kazakhstan via Turkey. But, for that to happen, the Kazakhstani women had to reach the Syrian-Turkish border. Kazakhstani intelligence agencies were able to secure a safety corridor. For several days, the women were smuggled to the Syrian-Turkish border, by-passing militants' checkpoints. From there, they were taken to the Turkish town of Hatay, where they were temporarily held in a local deportation centre. Later, thanks to the efforts of the Kazakhstani Ministry of Foreign Affairs, they were issued documents for their return and, on 7 September 2019, accompanied by NSC agents, the women and children arrived in Kazakhstan aboard civil airlines.

As a result of Jusan-5, fourteen children were evacuated from Syria. The youngest was just over one year old, the eldest between three and four.

In total, 613 Kazakhstani nationals were repatriated as a result of all stages of Operation: Jusan. This is the largest number of foreign nationals taken from Syria by any foreign state.

Total Number of Citizens Evacuated from Syria in All Stages of Operation: Jusan

Category	Men	Women	Children
Jusan-1	6	11	30
Jusan-2	16	59	156
Jusan-3	8	67	171
Jusan-4	3	19	49
Jusan-5	-	4	14
Total	33	160	420 (32 orphans)

The courts sanctioned the arrest of forty-nine people (thirty-three men and sixteen women) on their return, in connection with ongoing criminal investigation cases for their part in terrorist activities and propaganda.

In this way, practically all Kazakhstani citizens who had been in camps for displaced people in northeast Syria were returned home.

On 6 February 2020 Nurgali Bilisbekov, Deputy Chairman of the National Security Committee, spoke in the Senate of the Parliament of the Republic of Kazakhstan. He stated that all stages of Operation: Jusan for the repatriation of Kazakhstanis from the zone of terrorist activity had been accomplished.

We have completed all stages of Jusan. No further stages are planned because we are taking the appropriate steps regarding our citizens who remain in the conflict zones, and we do not have complete information about them. Preliminary preparatory work and consultations are underway.[58]

According Bilisbekov, over 100 Kazakhstanis remain in terrorist conflict zones, mainly in Syria, where there are thirty-six men and around eighty women. Some of our nationals are also in Iraq and Afghanistan.

Rusafa Operation

Parallel to Operation: Jusan, intelligence agencies were also developing a strategy for rescuing Kazakhstani children from Iraq. Compared with Syria, where Kazakhstani citizens could be evacuated directly from the active combat zone, evacuation from Iraq did not seem difficult from the logistical point of view. But there were legal problems. Kazakhstani minors were being kept in an Iraqi prison with their mothers, who were serving sentences for their involvement in terrorist activities.[59]

---

58. 'NSC: All stages of Jusan Operation complete': knb.gov.kz/ru/article/knb-vse-etapy-operacii-zhusan-zaversheny.
59. 'What is known about the parents of 14 Kazakhstani children returned from Iraq': https://diapazon.kz/news/95363-chto-izvestno-o-roditelyah-vozvrashennih-iz-iraka-14-kazahstanskih-detei-foto.

I must point out here that assisting ISIS is punishable by death in Iraq. That is why ISIS wives in Syria did not go to Iraq but chose to surrender to the Kurds; they knew very well that the Iraqi authorities have very strict measures in place for people connected with ISIS. In February 2018, sixteen Turkish women were sentenced to death in Iraq.[60] In April 2018, news agencies reported that three Azerbaijani women and one woman from Kyrgyzstan were also sentenced to death. All of them were accused of having links with ISIS.[61]

By summer 2018, Iraq had sentenced at least 300 people to death for assisting ISIS, including around 100 foreign women.[62] According to Amnesty International, the number of those executed in Iraq has almost doubled, from fifty-two in 2018 to 120 in 2019.[63] According to an AI report, 'The 92 per cent increase in recorded executions in Iraq is largely attributable to the continued use of the death penalty against individuals accused of being members of, or affiliated to, the armed group calling itself "Islamic State".[64] An Iraqi court sentenced Kazakhstani women to twenty-five years in prison for their involvement in terrorist activities and for assisting ISIS. Had Kazakhstani authorities not intervened on behalf of our women, they could have faced a worse fate.

Negotiations for the return of our citizens from Iraq lasted several months, and the absence of a permanent diplomatic mission of

---

60. '16 Turkish women sentenced to death in Iraq for their connection to IS': https//www.rbc.ru/rbcfreenews/5a92f89a79475e311b136c.

61. 'Capital punishment: Azerbaijani executed in Iraq': https://m/az/ sputniknews.ru/world/20180417/414921840/kazn-irak-azerbajdzhanki-ig. html?mobile_return=no.

62. 'Execution of IS militants has begun in Iraq. Death also hangs over the wives of Russian jihadists': https://www.bbc.com/russian/features-44656489.

63. 'Record numbers executed in Saudi Arabia in 2019 amid falling numbers of worldwide executions': https://m.forbes.kz/process/smertnaya_ kazn_v_2019_v_saudovskoy_aravii_kaznili_rekordnoe_kolichestvo_ lyudey_na_fone_snijeniya_chisla_kazney_vo_vsem_mire/.

64. 'Amnesty International Global Report: Death Sentences and Executions 2019': https://www.amnesty.org/download/Documents/ACT50184720 20ENGLISH.PDF

Kazakhstan in Baghdad was felt. Negotiations were facilitated through the Embassy of the Republic of Kazakhstan in Jordan. Due to the lack of a legal agreement between Kazakhstan and Iraq on the exchange of convicts, the Kazakh authorities had to resolve the issue by returning children without their parents. This required DNA tests.

Kazakhstani children returning from Iraq[65]

Before the humanitarian operation could be implemented, an advance group of Kazakh diplomats held meetings with an Iraqi judge and immigration authorities and agreed on all necessary procedures for handing over children. At the same time, Kazakhstani authorities developed a detailed evacuation plan – dispatching a special charter flight and agreeing the flight path. Besides diplomats, the evacuation team was joined by special medical personnel, including child psychologists. The UN children's foundation UNICEF provided invaluable help in resolving procedural issues by providing specialists from its Baghdad office to accompany the children. In contrast to Operation: Jusan, no military aircraft were required to repatriate the children from Iraq, and Arystan agents were not involved. The government hired a Boeing 757 from SCAT Airlines.

The operation was planned and ready to go, but the internal political situation escalated in Baghdad itself. Riots broke out, leading to armed clashes between protestors and police. Given the unpredictable nature

---

65. 'What do we know about the parents of 14 Kazakhstan children returned from Iraq?': https://diapazon.kz/news/95363-chto-izvestno-o-roditelyah-vozvrashennih-iz-iraka-14-kazahstanskih-detei-foto.

of the development of the situation in the region, the humanitarian operation could not be postponed or delayed. Consequently, despite the difficult situation, Kazakhstani diplomats continued negotiations *in situ* and finally managed to resolve all logistical issues.

As a result of the Rusafa humanitarian operation (named after the Baghdad district where the prison holding Kazakhstani women was located), fourteen Kazakhstani children were evacuated from Iraq to Kazakhstan on 27 November 2019. The oldest was thirteen years old, the youngest one year and ten months old. One orphan boy was among the evacuees. When the returnees arrived in Nur-Sultan, they met with relatives before being accommodated in the Support Centre for Children in Difficult Life Situations, where they were quarantined.

Reactions to Operation: Jusan

When information about Operation: Jusan was made public, heated debates followed. Although the majority of experts as well as the public were generally supportive, concerns were expressed that these women posed a potential threat. There were also those who claimed the information about the covert mission was 'fake news' or a 'propaganda stunt'. For example, one domestic political analyst wrote on his Facebook page that there was no such thing as Operation: Jusan and that women and children had apparently been brought to Kazakhstan by the Russian military. He later deleted his post. Some news outlets even published their own 'investigations', looking into the credibility of the facts surrounding the operation. The authors researched various details – the types of military aircraft and military equipment used, and even the vegetation around the aerodrome. They used all this as 'evidence' that Kazakhstani women and children had been put on the plane at one of the military airfields in southern Russia.[66] Doubts were expressed about the state's ability to carry out such a complex, large-scale operation.

Nevertheless, the public generally welcomed reports about the repatriation of citizens from Syria. Most people understood that

66. 'Jusan: a bitter whiff of PR?': https://youtu.be/VAMXR1kZddbw.

the operation was conducted primarily for the sake of repatriating children without the right to choose. The dilemma surrounding the repatriation of minors was not so acute in the minds of the public. Moreover, many countries have also spoken out about the protection and repatriation of the most vulnerable group: children.

Screenshots of posts from Kazakhstani Facebook users about Operation: Jusan (9–11 January 2019)

However, the main beneficiaries of this operation were the parents of the young people who had left for Syria and Iraq. It is common knowledge that, long before the operation was implemented by the Ministry of Information and Social Development [at the very beginning of this process, this department was called Ministry of Civil Society and Religious Affairs], a parents' committee was created where relatives of citizens who had emigrated to Syria collaborated with government bodies to compile and verify lists, check incoming data and photographs, and help carry out the checks necessary to identify people. Hence, the parents and relatives of returnees were privy to this large, complex mission the state was undertaking. When the first stage of the covert mission was complete, they wrote a letter expressing their thanks to all who had played a part in this huge task. Here is a quotation from the letter:

> From 7–9 May, Kazakhstani intelligence agencies carried out yet another humanitarian mission to repatriate our children and grandchildren from Syria, special operation Jusan-2. We, parents, grandmothers and grandfathers, wish to express our deep gratitude to the leadership of our country, namely the First President of the Republic of Kazakhstan, Elbasy Nursultan Nazarbayev and President Kassym-Jomart Tokayev as well as the Ministry of Foreign Affairs, the National Security Committee, and other state bodies which assisted in this noble task.
>
> Our daughters-in-law and grandchildren are among them. Unfortunately, many of our errant sons did not live to see this happy day; they perished in a foreign land, in a foreign war, having fallen into the clutches of recruiters for international terrorist organisations. This covert mission was truly unprecedented in scale and, thanks to it, dozens of women and 156 children were evacuated from the active combat zone. It is all but impossible to look at the little children who were brought to Kazakhstan in a grave condition without shedding tears, children who were wounded during the fighting. Our children and grandchildren, who found themselves in Syria and Iraq against their will, experienced hunger, cold, disease, deprivation and fear. They know the harm planes can do, they know war, blood, and death… They experienced all these horrors because of their parents who stumbled, lost their way, and fell victim to ISIS.
>
> We thank the government for the comprehensive help they gave our children and grandchildren, who are now in a specialised quarantine centre under the supervision of doctors and psychologists, and receiving medical, mental and social support in a rehabilitation programme provided by government agencies and NGOs. We hope that we will soon see our fully rehabilitated children get jobs and restore ties with relatives, and that our grandchildren will attend schools and kindergartens.

We fully agree with President Tokayev and his words, that 'The citizens of Kazakhstan who left for active combat zones made such a rash decision under the influence of the destructive and in fact false propaganda spread by terrorists. Now they are voluntarily returning to Kazakhstan in the hopes of beginning a new life. Their children should not suffer in a foreign land or be held responsible for the mistakes of their parents.' We are glad that this humanitarian mission will continue and that, as our President has said, 'none of our citizens will be abandoned to the whims of fate'.

May peace and tranquillity always prevail in our country! May there always be well-being and prosperity in our country! May our children never again find themselves in such situations, may they never again fall into the web of destructive, extremist and terrorist organisations![67]

Public figures in Kazakhstan also supported this decision. After the return of such a significant number of citizens was announced, members of the lower chamber of the Kazakhstan Parliament proposed making a feature film titled *The Jusan*, about this large-scale humanitarian mission. In particular, Kuanysh Sultanov, member of the lower chamber, declared that the operation 'may well serve as an excellent plot for the creation of highly artistic films…'[68] A well-known Kazakhstani political analyst, Aidos Sarym, noted:

This was the realest operation. There were lots of official – and even more unofficial – flights and negotiations. Our aircraft were banned by a country we least expected it from. I believe that now you can write a book and a screenplay. We can really be proud of

67. 'Kazakhstani parents: we rejoice that the Jusan humanitarian mission will continue': https://kaz.zakon.kz/4969495-kazahstanskie-roditeli-my-rady-chto.html.
68. 'MPs suggest shooting a film about Operation: Jusan': https://24.kz/ru/news/social/item/290493-deputaty-predlozhili-snyat-film-ob-operatsii-zhusan.

this! But there are new challenges, too. People, especially adults, are strongly indoctrinated.[69]

Kazakhstan's efforts to repatriate its nationals were particularly well-received abroad, by international organisations and experts. Fionnuala Ní Aoláin, UN Special Rapporteur on the promotion and protection of human rights and fundamental freedoms while countering terrorism, called on other states whose nationals are in the conflict zone '...to follow the example of Kazakhstan's humanitarian initiative, because Kazakhstan has illustrated that it is practical and realistic to bring out women and children'. She also noted: '...and the remaining responsibility to do so lies with multiple states. This is a very important humanitarian initiative that safeguards the rights of children and mothers who find themselves in a vulnerable position. This step shows much needed leadership on the critical global issue.'[70]

The International Committee of the Red Cross (ICRC) also welcomed the repatriation of Kazakhstani children from Iraq. The head of the organisation, Peter Maurer, sent a letter to Kassym-Jomart Tokayev in connection with the successful completion of the humanitarian mission to repatriate fourteen Kazakhstani children from Iraq. It reads:

Following on from the success of Operation Jusan, Kazakhstan has set an example to the world on how to handle this challenging issue. [...] The ICRC, under our mandate, can support your government's efforts by carrying out visits, on humanitarian grounds, to people detained in Kazakhstan in relation to their involvement in the conflicts in the Middle East. We would be glad to have further discussions on this matter. Finally, as we have previously suggested, we would be glad to

---

69. https:// t. me/s/ aidossarym? before=91.

70. 'UN Rapporteur cites Kazakhstan as an example for other countries thanks to Jusan Operation': https://liter.kz/1706-dokladchik-oon-postavila-kazahstan-v-primer-drugim-stranam-za-operatsiyu-gusan/. (Citation paraphrased.) https://www.ohchr.org/EN/NewsEvents/Pages/DisplayNews.aspx?NewsID=24620&LangID=E

organize, in Nur-Sultan or Almaty, a meeting with representatives of other countries of the region concerned by the same issue to exchange experiences around this challenging question.[71]

Foreign experts also applauded the actions of the Kazakhstani authorities, greeting them as a positive example for other states contemplating the expediency of returning their citizens. Unlike officials, experts valued not only the very fact of repatriating militants and their family members, but also highlighted the scrupulous approach the Kazakhstani authorities had taken to this mission in general.

Former President of Kazakhstan, Nursultan Nazarbayev, attempted to moderate any public concern regarding the repatriation of 'foreign fighters' by calling Operation: Jusan a humanitarian mission. At the beginning of the mission, he said that those remaining in Syria and Iraq had been deceived by ISIS and other terrorist groups and later detained against their will. The children were clearly identified as victims, which indeed reflects their true status in this conflict, from the point of international law [...] and the United Nations (UN). Religious leaders supported Nazarbayev's narrative, as did his successor, Kassym-Jomart Tokayev.[72]

The US actively welcomed Kazakhstan's decision to repatriate its citizens from Syria. The US State Department's counter-terrorism coordinator, Nathan Sayles, noted Kazakhstan's role in the repatriation of former ISIS fighters from Syria: 'Countries such as Kazakhstan

---

71. 'The International Committee of the Red Cross welcomes the return of Kazakh children from Iraq': http://www.akorda.kz/en/special/events/international_community/telegrammes_and_letters/the-international-committee-of-the-red-cross-welcomes-the-return-of-kazakh-children-from-iraq
72. Sarah Wolfe, Cholpon Orozobekova: 'Lessons learned from Kazakhstan's repatriation and rehabilitation of Foreign fighters': https://bulaninstitute.org/wp-content/uploads/2020/05/lessons-learned-from-Kazakhstans-Experience.pdf.

and Kosovo have been able to repatriate dozens and, in some cases, hundreds of militants and their families.'[73] He also stressed:

> We not only observed this process very carefully but also provided all kinds of assistance. What we saw during this observation inspires enthusiasm. We see that not only the government of Kazakhstan made the best use of all its resources, but so did the private sector and religious authorities, who can stand against false dogma and 'Islamic State', as well as psychologists and medics, who can help those undergoing rehabilitation. We see this as a very holistic approach that the rest of the world can take as a foundation. Kazakhstan is a world leader who took a bold decision to return hundreds of its nationals – several militants and several hundred women and children. On Sunday, I was able to visit one of the rehabilitation centres in Karaganda and saw for myself that religious authorities, child psychology specialists and representatives of the Ministry of Education and Science and of other government agencies were all working [there]. [...] The whole world today should pay attention to what is happening in Kazakhstan, because the lessons learned here will be useful to the whole world.[74]

In January 2020, at a meeting with President of the Republic of Kazakhstan Kassym-Jomart Tokayev, US Secretary of State Mike Pompeo praised Kazakhstan's efforts to repatriate its citizens from the active combat zone in the Middle East under the auspices of

---

73. 'Special Envoy for the Global Coalition to Defeat ISIS Ambassador James F. Jeffrey And Counterterrorism Coordinator Ambassador Nathan A. Sales': https://www.state.gov/special-envoy-for-the-global-coalition-to-defeat-isis-ambassador-james-f-jeffrey-and-counterterrorism-coordinator-ambassador-nathan-a-sales/.
74. 'US State Department speaks about Kazakhstan's Jusan Operation': https://tengrinews.kz/kazakhstan_news/gosdepe-ssha-vyiskazalis-kazahstanskoy-spetsoperatsii-jusan-381070/. (Citation partially paraphrased; translator's note.)

Operation: Jusan.[75] Later, during a joint briefing with the Minister of Foreign Affairs of the Republic of Kazakhstan, Mukhtar Tleuberdi, he called on other countries to follow Kazakhstan's example.

It was not only US officials who watched Operation: Jusan; leading American media outlets did, too. In particular, *The New York Times* ran an article on the women who had been repatriated during Operation: Jusan. The article noted:

> Kazakhstan has sought a larger role in international diplomacy with a variety of initiatives to solve global problems, including once offering to dispose of other countries' nuclear waste on its territory. And to date, it is the only country with a large contingent of citizens in Syria to agree to repatriate all of them — a total of 548, so far.[76]

Operation: Jusan impacted on the nature of state policy itself, further strengthening the humanitarian aspect. The bar was raised in terms of a state's responsibility towards its citizens. In March 2020, a state of emergency and an enhanced quarantine regime were introduced in Kazakhstan, as in other countries, in connection with the COVID-19 pandemic. As a result, international flights were suspended as well as any movement of citizens in or out of the country or population points. This led to thousands of Kazakhstanis finding themselves victims of circumstance, unable to return home. The Ministry of Foreign Affairs was receiving appeals from our citizens in other CIS (Commonwealth of Independent States) countries, the Middle East, South Asia and Europe, asking for assistance in returning to Kazakhstan. The government established an operational HQ that provided the framework with which Kazakhstani diplomats, in

---

75. 'President of Kazakhstan receives US Secretary of State Mike Pompeo': http://www.akorda.kz/ru/events/prezident-kazakhstana-prinyal-gosudarstvennogo-sekretarya-ssha-maikla-pompeo.
76. 'Kazakhstan welcomes women back from the Islamic State, warily: https://www.nytimes.com/2019/08/10/world/europe/kazakhstan-women-islamic-state-deradicalization.html.

cooperation with other state bodies, tackled the issue of bringing our citizens home. In some cases, the resources of Kazakhstan's Ministry of Defence were used.

Evacuation of Kazakhstani citizens from Tajikistan, Kyrgyzstan, and Saudi Arabia during the pandemic (March 2020)

The Kazakhstani authorities facilitated the evacuation of our nationals from various countries following the already well-developed protocol of Operation: Jusan, i.e., on board Kazakhstan's air force planes. In particular, a group of Kazakhstanis with children who were being treated for cerebral palsy in Kyrgyzstan were evacuated on C-295 planes. The children were all taken from Bishkek to the city of Atyrau in compliance with the public health requirements necessitated by the pandemic. Kazakhstanis were evacuated from Saudi Arabia in a similar way. On social networks during those days, every piece of information on the evacuation of our citizens was viewed as a continuation of Operation: Jusan. In other words, Operation: Jusan became a kind of symbol for the state's responsibility of care and solidarity to its citizens.

Kazakhstan's repatriation of its nationals, the family members of former militants, was generally received positively by both domestic and international audiences. Many were impressed by the risks the authorities had taken to complete this mission. The state went to great lengths to repatriate hundreds of citizens from active combat zones. It was a truly successful, large-scale operation, thanks to which dozens of Kazakhstanis were given a second chance and children were given a home and a peaceful life.

Although there are certainly reasons to rejoice, nevertheless both the state and the experts understand that, with this success, we found ourselves facing new challenges.

V

CLOSE-UP: PORTRAITS OF KAZAKHSTANIS REPATRIATED IN OPERATION: JUSAN

'I followed my husband to Syria because I wanted to be with him, and I thought we would find the true Islamic Caliphate there.' These are the words of one of dozens of women returned to Kazakhstan during Operation: Jusan. We heard similar explanations for why they stayed in the conflict zones from most of those with whom we spoke. Similar interviews can be found online, too: it is not the first time that women with children had been returning home from the Middle East. For example, a woman from Uralsk with four children was evacuated in November 2017 during a Russian covert operation. She would later tell that, like many others, her family had been lured there on the promise of a wonderful place for true believers, but, as with everyone else, disappointment awaited her family.

> We were 'tricked' by the propaganda about a better life, and left for Syria. But, in reality, life in Syria wasn't as good as they said it would be. They don't live there according to Sharia law... [They said that] we could just leave if we don't like it for any reason. But

149

that was a lie, too. Nobody would let you leave. Anyone who tried to escape was caught and locked up.[1]

Even before Operation: Jusan, Kazakhstanis disillusioned with the Caliphate would periodically return from the active combat zone. In autumn 2018, four families returned under their own steam to West Kazakhstan Oblast. They are still under the care of outreach workers, including theologians and psychologists. There are reports that lawyers assist such families to get their documents reissued, apply for benefits for the loss of breadwinners, and find work. From 2016–18, ninety-one children and thirty-nine families returned to Kazakhstan from the active combat zone. They were also given assistance. Out of forty parents who returned to Kazakhstan, thirteen have found jobs.[2]

However, Operation: Jusan is the first instance in which Kazakhstan has taken responsibility for organising the repatriation of such large numbers of women and children.

We find a similar rhetoric in each interview the women gave to the media. Most say that this is not how they imagined life in the land of the Caliphate. Once the main phase of Operation: Jusan was completed, we conducted talks and interviews with these women, trying to understand what had driven them to leave for zones of terrorist activity in the Middle East. It is worth noting that all interviews were conducted during the first couple of days of repatriation, before the women had adapted to the new reality.

Let me remind you that during the first stage of the operation (January 2019), eleven men and thirty children were repatriated. They were evacuated from the Kurdish camps they ended up in when they tried to flee ISIS territory, and where they were detained for over a year.

Unlike them, 84 per cent of those repatriated during the Jusan-2 and Jusan-3 special operations had been forced to flee the town of

---

1. 'About life in Daesh – the story of a Kazakhstani woman rescued in Syria': https://tengrinews.kz/kazakhstan_news/o-jizni-v-daish-rasskaz-vyizvolennoy-iz-sirii-kazahstanki-332683/.
2. 'Over 90 Kazakhstani children returned from "hot spots"': https://1tv.kz/bolee-90-kazahstanskih-detey-vernulis-iz-goryachih-tochek/.

al-Baghuz, where fierce fighting broke out from January to March 2019. This was only possible thanks to the agreement reached between Kurdish militias and ISIS radicals. Up until that moment, the women had not attempted to escape, explaining that they feared being raped, sold into slavery, or sent to Iraqi prisons.

The courts sanctioned the arrest of sixteen women on their return to Kazakhstan in connection with ongoing investigations into their involvement with terrorist activities and terrorist propaganda. A further eight women were prosecuted and served with restriction-of-travel orders. Another six Kazakhstani women were sentenced to life imprisonment in Iraq (according to Iraqi law, this equates to twenty-five years in prison).[3]

To study the causes and factors that contributed to whole families emigrating to Syria, interviews were conducted with 125 women who were returned during the special operation. This research provided experts with the following data: socio-demographic indicators; specific regional details; reasons for turning to religion and emigrating to Syria; returning to Kazakhstan and plans for the future.

Socio-demographic indicators

Age

Over 60 per cent of those who returned to Kazakhstan were young women aged between twenty-five and thirty-five. The youngest is fifteen years old. She is a native of Almaty. Her mother took her to Syria when she was just eight years old. At thirteen, the girl married in a war-torn country. Her mother and sister have gone missing.

The oldest of the women returnees is sixty-one. A resident of the Zhambyl Oblast, in October 2015 she left for Syria hoping to come back with two of her daughters who were living out there. But it was only three years later that all three managed to return home, during Operation: Jusan.

---

3. 'Six Kazakhstani women sentenced to long-term prison in Iraq': https://total.kz/ru/news/proisshestviya/shest_kazahstanok_osuzhdeni_na_dlitelnie_sroki_v_irake_date_2019_11_28_18_53_36.

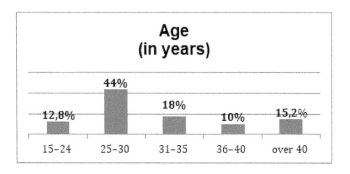

Today, the average age of the female returnees is thirty-two. Fifty-one per cent of the women were under twenty-five when they emigrated. The average age of the emigrée women was twenty-six (by comparison, the average age of the men was twenty-eight).

The majority of Kazakhstanis left for the combat zone between 2013 and 2015, before ISIS had proclaimed it the land of the Islamic Caliphate. Seventy-four per cent of women returnees spent more than five years on the territories of Syria and Iraq. That is not simply a long time – it means that most of these women were present at the moment when the Islamic Caliphate was proclaimed in 2014 right through to its liquidation in 2019. They witnessed all the major stages of ISIS activities.

Education

Most of these women had passed through the standard channels of socialisation. Almost all had attended secondary school (usually Kazakh schools). Some of them had gone to college after ninth year. Others, having graduated after eleventh year, were accepted into institutions of higher education to study for professions such as primary teacher, Kazakh philologist, fashion designer, etc.

Sixty per cent of the women have no specialised education at all. Thirty-five per cent have secondary education; 25 per cent did not complete secondary school. For example: the above-mentioned girl who was taken to Syria at the age of eight completed only two years of secondary school in Kazakhstan. A similar case is a sixteen-year-old girl who was taken to Syria with her mother after completing five years of secondary education in Atyrau. In Syria, she married at the age of fourteen and, at the time of the interview, her daughter was seven months old.

Those girls who joined college often dropped out, for a variety of personal reasons. Some left school after converting to Islam. Many married at an early age.

A thirty-two-year-old woman from Atyrau began attending the mosque when she was fifteen. She then began performing *namaz*, and fasting. For some time, she went to school wearing a head covering, but when the school administration changed, the new director banned it. The same school was attended by some religious boys who also performed *namaz*, and they suggested their own solution to her. They said they could sort out her life, and suggested she marry their 'good brother'. As a result, the fifteen-year-old girl left school, married, and gave up her studies. After her marriage, her husband began influencing and guiding her on matters of faith and religion, feeding her with literature. Under his influence, she began listening to lectures by Daryn Mubarov (in 2017 this ideologue was called to administrative responsibility for conducting illegal missionary activities). And subsequently, the girl found herself in Syria.

Another girl who turned to religion left school when she was in the eighth year, after she, too, married in accordance with Muslim traditions.

Nevertheless, 40 per cent of the women held certificates of education, including twenty-one who had graduated from specialised secondary schools and 19 per cent with higher education.

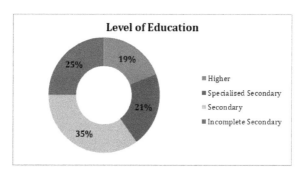

Level of Education

19%
25%
21%
35%

- Higher
- Specialised Secondary
- Secondary
- Incomplete Secondary

Only one of the women has a specialised religious education; she studied in a madrasa in Almaty for one year. Some of the interviewed women had learnt Arabic in Egypt.

Ethnicity
Of the emigrée women, 90 per cent were ethnic Kazakhs. The other 10 per cent belonged to the following ethnic groups:

- *Russian*
- *Uighur*
- *Kyrgyz*
- *Dungan*
- *Talysh*
- *Azerbaijani*
- *German*
- *Tartar*

Seventy-eight per cent of the Kazakh women spoke Kazakh; 22 per cent spoke Russian. This indicator refutes the theory that it is predominantly representatives of the Russian-speaking population who are becoming followers of destructive religious movements. According to that premise, these people were allegedly trying to solve issues of self-identity because they lack the strong ties to tradition inherent in the Kazakh-speaking population.

Professional experience
Eighty-five per cent of the women were housewives when they left for Syria. Just 15 per cent worked after marrying and turning to religion. The women in work were employed in various spheres. One was an editor for a Karaganda-based website. Another was a manager/designer in Almaty. Another worked as a teacher. However, most of the emigrée were involved in the retail sector. Some even had small retail businesses selling children's and Muslim clothes. It is not surprising that some of the women turned to religion under the influence of their shopping centre colleagues. And so, in 2010 a thirty-seven-year-old woman living in Nur-Sultan became acquainted

with an ethnic Ingush woman from the neighbouring boutique in the Artem shopping centre. Her neighbour was a religious woman who performed *namaz*, and she suggested her colleague try and do it 'at least once'. When the girl said she didn't know how to pray, the reply came: 'Just repeat after me.' After the first *namaz*, the 'teacher' told the girl that Allah's punishment awaits those who stop praying. As a result, five days later, the girl was already performing *namaz* by herself, and after a couple of weeks she donned the hijab.

Another woman, a thirty-two-year-old who worked at the Gulzhan shopping centre in Nur-Sultan, had met a woman from the next department when she was in her twenties. The woman was also Ingush, and facilitated her conversion to Islam.

Family model

Many of the women who left for Syria (39 per cent) grew up in broken families. Their relatives either died or divorced. Psychologists find links between loss of family support in childhood and vulnerability to recruitment. When such children grow up, they project the difficulties they experienced within the framework of existing social structures onto adult life.[4] As a result, their sense of alienation engenders the desire to belong to a group and to resolve self-identity issues. The Russian book *The Psychology of Terrorism and Counteracting it in the Modern World* states that: 'around 25 per cent of left-wing terrorists lost one or both parents by the age of fourteen; it was discovered that losing a father was particularly destructive for the personality of the future terrorist.'[5]

In our case, some girls who lost their fathers at a relatively young age (fifteen to sixteen) got married.

There are cases of dysfunctional families, too. One of the women (she is from the city of Satpayev) was abandoned by her mother who

---

4. I. Malkina-Pykh: *Psychology of Victims' Behaviour* ('Психология поведения жертвы'), Moscow: Exmo, 2017.

5. V. Sosnin: *The Psychology of Terrorism and Counteracting it in the Modern World* ('Психология терроризма и противодействие ему в современном мире'), Institute of Psychology of Russian Academy of Sciences, 2016.

left her and two brothers in the care of their alcoholic father. At the time, the girl was in the ninth class. Soon after her mother left the family, the schoolgirl began attending Friday prayers at the mosque and then began performing *namaz*.

Another case is the story of a fifty-year-old woman from the West Kazakhstan Oblast. In her family, one of her daughters was the first to start reciting *namaz*. In 2011, following her daughter's advice, the woman turned to religion in the hope that it would somehow help resolve family problems; her husband was also an alcoholic. The daughter convinced her mother it might help: 'Mama, let's perform *namaz*. It will help us and Papa, too.'

And here is a quote from a returnee girl:

Many women I met ended up in Syria after a row with their parents. When my husband left, I asked my mother not to put pressure on me and at least let me wear the headscarf and perform *namaz*. Our last quarrel was on my birthday, 24 July 2014. Mama and Papa said they don't want to see me in hijab, and if I didn't stop wearing it, they would take my children away from me.[6]

In fact, from the moment girls and women become involved in religion, almost all of them change their social circle; most of their social connections stop functioning working if they were of a secular nature (relatives, friends, colleagues).

Regional specifics

Of the women who emigrated, 77 per cent were from urban regions, mainly from western Kazakhstan: Atyrau, Atkobe, Uralsk, and also from the south: Almaty, Zhezkazgan, Shymkent.

---

6. '"I paid for my mistakes with my son's life": Kazakhstani woman evacuated from Syria speaks about her 5-year ordeal': https://newtimes. kz/eshche/mneniya/93993-za-svoi-oshibki-ya-zaplatila-zhiznyu-syna-evakuirovannaya-iz-sirii-kazakhstanka-rasskazala-o-pyati-godakh-mytarstv.

Western Kazakhstan

Aktau (Zhanaozen - 1)	Aktobe	Atyrau	Uralsk
6	10	19	23
Total – 58 (46.4%)			

Southern Kazakhstan

Almaty	Shymkent	Almaty Oblast	Zhambylsk Oblast	Turkestan Oblast	Kysylordinsk Oblast
13	6	7	7	9	2
Total – 44 (34.4%)					

Central Kazakhstan

Nur-Sultan	Karaganda	Zhezkazgan	Satpayev
4	4	5	6
Total – 19 (15.2%)			

Northern Kazakhstan

Akmola Oblast	Pavlodar Oblast
1	2
Total – 3 (3,2%)	

Eastern Kazakhstan

Zaysan
1 (0,8%)

Eighty-one per cent of women emigrated from western and southern regions of the country, of whom 47 per cent were from the cities of Uralsk, Aktobe, Atyrau and Aktau.

Radical preachers had previously conducted their subversive activities in the Aktobe, Atyrau and Karaganda oblasts. It was these locations that became the main centres for preaching extremist ideas; a significant kernel of followers of non-traditional religious movements is still present there.

The group dynamics factor also became one of the key triggers contributing to the mass emigration of citizens. Close ties in Kazakhstan (relatives, friends, acquaintances) became the 'springboard' for emigrating to the Caliphate. As we have already seen, a resident of the town of Merki in the Zhambyl Oblast followed her daughters. A woman from Zhezkazgan also followed her only son. In Syria, Kazakhstani citizens were roughly divided into three large regional Jamaats: Shymkent, Western Kazakhstan, and Zhezkazgan. Additionally, before emigrating to Syria, 26 per cent of them lived in third countries for some time, including Egypt, the UAE, Turkey, Russia (Chechnya), Austria and Pakistan (Northern Waziristan).

For example, a woman from Almaty followed her mother to Austria after completing her ninth year. There, she studied private entrepreneurship for three years at BFI College. In 2014, she met an ethnic Chechen from Russia online and joined him in Syria. She had lived in Austria for five years.

Religious practice

Research into the causes of religious conversion reveals the following statistic: 41 per cent of women questioned had come to religion of their own accord, from personal interest sparked by problems or the indirect influence of external factors. Below are excerpts from interviews in which the girls and women talk about the problems they tried to resolve by converting to Islam.

> *'There was no peace in my soul. I was always searching. I was drawn to religion. I liked girls who wore hijab.'*

> *'I was drawn to it. I found out how to perform* namaz *and how to study the Qur'an.'*

> *'I liked sisters who "covered themselves", I was always interested in what they were doing, what kind of religion Islam is. By the will of Allah, I met a sister. We got talking. She began telling me about Islam. I liked it. I asked her to teach me how to perform* namaz.'

According to sociological research undertaken in several regions of the country by the Institute of Equal Rights and Opportunities of Kazakhstan, women of different confessions 'usually turn to faith because of difficult personal circumstances – family problems, financial difficulties. They seek salvation and support in the faith [...]. In religion, they see the chance to better themselves and find harmony, a sense of security.'[7]

Thirty-six per cent of women grew up in religious families and converted to Islam under the influence of close relatives. Contrary to popular belief, not all women converted to Islam under the influence of men. Only 23 per cent began performing *namaz* after marriage. Moreover, some women played a significant role in their husbands' conversions.

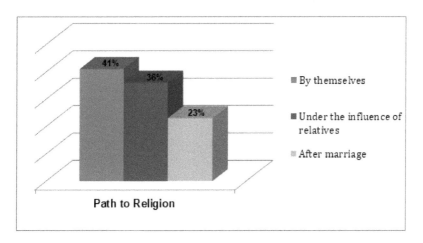

Thirty-seven per cent of women came to religion at an early age – before turning eighteen. And they married soon after. Usually, after marrying, it was the husband who became the main source of religious knowledge in the family. It is interesting to note that,

7. E. Koemets, '80% of religious women had contemplated abandoning religion', Caravan, 11 December 2018: https://www.caravan.kz/gazeta/80-procentov-veruyushhikh-kazakhstanok-zadumyvalis-ob-otkaze-ot-religii-unikalnoe-issledovanie-502523/.

during the interviews, it was the youngest, 'newly converted' women who were the most uncompromising and adamant. Almost all women neophytes began by listening to lectures by Daryn Mubarov, Nazratullah Abu Maryam or Nadir Bukhari, preachers who interpreted jihad for women as 'fighting their *nafs*' (desires) and performing *hijra* (resettlement). Whereas according to their sermons, jihad for men means war against infidels, oppressors of Muslims. Therefore, jihad was perceived by many women as 'war on the path of Allah'. The interviews did not reveal any clear religious identification among the women – when asked what branch or *madhhab* of Islam they professed, the overwhelming majority of interviewees replied evasively, saying only that they are Muslims. At the same time, it was clear that they deliberately avoided such terms as 'Salafism' and 'Wahhabism'. Only a few replied emotionally, in the belief that the interviewers' questions belied society's hostile attitude towards them as 'terrorists'.

All the women declared that, according to Islam, their place is the hearth, their duties are raising children and obedience to their husbands. And although during the interviews most of them stressed their passive role, some did not deny that there were Kazakhstani women who joined training courses and were even ready to become *shahids*. Despite living through tragic events in Syria, many women do not regret emigrating from Kazakhstan, arguing that they 'lived there according to Sharia laws'.

In one interview, a woman said she has no regrets because 'she learned a good lesson. All this was predetermined. Allah doesn't test us beyond what we can bear. This was my test.' During their interviews, some women stated categorically that in the future they 'have no intention of deviating from the norms of Sharia for the sake of society'.

Life in the Caliphate

Seventy-two per cent of women emigrated to the Middle East with their husbands or followed them there; the remaining 28 per cent moved there independently, or accompanied their parents and close relatives (brothers, sisters, sons-in-law).

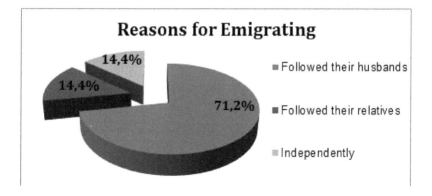

Among those who followed their husbands were also women who had been misled. For example, before emigrating to Syria, one man was always telling his twenty-two-year-old wife from Almaty Oblast that he wanted to move because they 'cannot practise Islam here'. To which she would respond that she could perform *namaz* and don the hijab in Kazakhstan, too, without any problem: 'I do everything a woman has to do.' Her husband's acquaintances, boys from the parallel class, left for Syria and wrote to them from there, encouraging them to follow their example. As the girl said, her husband was always receiving messages from his friends, and they wrote enthusiastically about their life there: 'Oh, I got married, it's cool here, you should come, they give us money – 100 dollars is enough for a month.' The girl told her husband she was against the idea, so there was no more talk about leaving.

According to her, one day at the end of 2013, her husband invited her to the cinema, and there he told her they were going on holiday to Turkey for three days. They drove to the capital of Kyrgyzstan, Bishkek, by car and bought tickets for a plane to Istanbul. The girl said that a man came to pick them up in Turkey and took them to a flat where there were already other people. Men and women were placed in separate rooms. The next day they travelled to the city of Gaziantep, and from there a minibus drove to them to the border. There, the escort ordered them to run. So, the woman ended up in Syria as a result of deception. When she arrived, she was put in women's dormitory – *makar* – and her husband was taken to a *muaskar* militant training camp. They were allowed to see each other only one month later. Her husband died the following year year, and she had to wait another four years before returning to Kazakhstan.

Another case is that of a fifty-two-year-old woman, who left for Syria in 2013 together with her three children, daughters-in-law and grandchildren. Her children decided to emigrate in order to 'live in the lands of the Caliphate'. When she arrived in the Middle East, she lived intermittently with one of her sons, and sometimes with her daughter. The woman said she did not go out in that country, and was practically in seclusion, performing *namaz* and being near her children. A year after arriving in Syria, both her sons were killed, and her daughters-in-law remarried. At the time of the interview, her daughter was still in the al-Hawl temporary camp in Syria. At present, the woman has no definite plan for the future and does not know how or with whom she is going to live. The children sold their house before they emigrated. She says she just wants to live a peaceful life.

For many, emigrating to Syria was a conscious decision.

At least 67 per cent of these women have been married at least twice. There were cases of women marrying nine times, and living with their spouses from one day to several months. After the death of their husband, some of the women lived in so-called 'widows' houses', but most decided to remarry. One woman said she married three times and all three times married natives of the same city, Zhezkazgan. She explained her second and third marriages as 'wanting to be of service to Allah' by being beside men and helping them. In interviews, the women often explained that remarrying was their survival technique, because women did not have the right to lead independent lives on Caliphate territory.

Moreover, their husbands married several women at once. One interviewee said that, as soon as she and her husband arrived in Syria, he married two more women, and told her that religion allowed it: 'They are your sisters and you shouldn't think badly of them.' The three women lived in different houses and he would visit them in turn. In December 2018, he was killed with his third wife when a rocket hit the house.

From conversations with these women, it soon became clear that many agreed to be second or third wives.

During the interviews, many women not only stressed their passive role but also stated that their husbands did not participate in military actions. Only a few openly admitted that their husbands were '*amirs*' or commanders and took part in '*amalia*' (military operations).

Twenty-two per cent of the women lost their children in Syria. The children died for various reasons – gunshot wounds, burial under rubble during bomb raids, or disease, because they lacked access to proper health care. One woman lost all the five children she had taken with her to Syria. They were all together in one place when they came under drone attack.

She commented on this tragedy as follows:

I sometimes feel guilty. When it comes to repentance, no, I don't repent. I look at this primarily from the religious point of view. It was preordained by Allah. I know that if I complain now, it means I am complaining at Allah. Even if they had been together in a car, here, it would have happened anyway, on the same day, at the same time. There is a book of fate, it is true. It can't be denounced.

A twenty-nine-year-old woman from Kyzylorda Oblast lost her child to malnutrition in the al-Hawl camp. When asked if she felt responsible for the death of her daughter in Syria, she replied: 'There is such a thing as fate in Islam. I cannot repent. Everything happens by the will of Allah. In any case, I couldn't order her [the daughter], she had a husband.'

A forty-three-year-old woman from Almaty Oblast shares this opinion about a parent's responsibility for their own child: 'It is the will of Allah. According to religion […] what must happen, happens.' Explaining this premise, the woman noted that religious people in Syria have a different worldview.

When describing their life in the Caliphate, virtually all the women spoke of the daily routine when they first arrived, then about the constant fear for their lives when the mass bombings and air strikes began.

At first, we lived well. We had luxurious villas, we had a good life. We were paid a '*kafal*' [allowance] of $50 per adult and $35 per child. Then intensive air strikes and bombing began, and there wasn't enough food.

Despite the horrors the women described, only a few made any attempt to return, explaining this by the fact that there were no routes, money or trustable local guides.

In the course of their interviews, the women repeatedly stressed that they spent most of their time at home doing daily chores, and emphasised that they tried generally not to socialise with anyone, especially with compatriots. However, some women, especially enterprising ones, opened kindergartens, sold things, and did sewing.

But some also mentioned that there was a *muaskar* – a special training camp, for women in particular – in the Syrian city of Mayadin. One of the interviewees reported that they intended to organise training for women to teach them how to handle weapons, allegedly for self-defence, but for some reason that never happened. During conversations with us, children said there were weapons in every house. Some girls were also taught to handle them by their fathers and brothers.

Many of the interviewed women knew about the existence of a Kazakh Jamaat and spoke about how big it was, but could not or did not want to provide precise numbers. According to them, many Kazakhstanis lived in the city of al-Shaddadah, in al-Hasakah Province in northeast Syria, now controlled by the Kurdish military. Before large-scale fighting broke out, almost all of them lived in Raqqa, a city designated the capital of ISIS by the terrorists. Thus, the vast majority of Kazakhstani citizens lived in ISIS-controlled territory, which automatically implies they were members of the group. The women maintain that many Kazakhstani citizens have already been killed.

When speculating about what is really happening in Syria, nearly all the women stated that war is raging in that Middle Eastern country for resources, territory, power and money. According to one of the women, this is a war of all against all. Some expressed the opinion that the ISIS leader Abu Bakr al-Baghdadi perhaps did not exist at all.

They argued that he had not been seen again after his appearance in a mosque in Mosul in 2014.

Returning to Kazakhstan

Ten quotes, ten women's fates, ten excerpts from the uneasy conversations with women returned home as a result of Operation: Jusan — these pieces fit into a single puzzle and allow us to understand what was happening to Kazakh families in the so-called Islamic Caliphate in Syria and Iraq.

'We started thinking, wondering why Kazakhs are going there… Then you start to understand. When you come to Islam and want to live according to Sharia, you want everybody to be wearing hijabs…'

'We could live according to Sharia law freely there. There was no theft, no violence. For almost a year, it was really like that. After the Caliphate was proclaimed, you couldn't see anyone on the street during designated namaz time except small children running about. You could leave stuff in the bazaar and nobody would touch it. Everybody knew their hand could be cut off if they did. Nobody stole anything. It was nice. For a whole year, we led a wonderful life, and if someone had suggested going back to Kazakhstan then, I probably wouldn't have. Nobody bothered me there, and I hadn't seen anything bad there at that time. Women didn't worry [for their safety]. Nobody bothered us, we walked in peace. The doors and windows were always open in every house…'

'And we were given our own house. Water, electricity, food – everything was free…'

'Everything was fine when my husband was still alive. You don't worry about anything – food, clothes, you have whatever you want. We went to the most beautiful Iraqi city, Mosul, to walk around, we lived in a five-star hotel. While the father of my children was alive, I had no problems at all.'

'My husband used to tell me: "If I am gone, you won't find a better place either for me or for your children. Here you can freely profess your religion. If I am gone, don't even think of returning to Kazakhstan…"'

'Towards the end, when things got really difficult, the roads were blocked. The Kamaz [a Russian manufacturer] *trucks bringing food didn't come any more. It was really difficult, I didn't know what to do, I worried about the children…'*

'There was an attempt to build a state for all Muslims in Syria. But nothing comes easy. […] They used Kazakhs for their own ends…'

'This place has stopped being the place of Islam and has become the land of war…'

'We got used to death…'

'If it were truly an Islamic State, Allah would not let such small children suffer…'

In their interviews, all the women said that, in the end, they did regret their decision to emigrate after all. But each of them needed a different length of time to realise the full scale of the consequences of their decision. Some realised this was not the place they wanted to live as soon as they arrived, but it took others months or even years. The deteriorating situation, military pressure on ISIS, death of loved ones – it was only shocks like these that forced some of them to return home.

At first, many of the emigrées thought they had found their place on this Earth: 'If you know the hadiths [sayings of the Prophet], they often talk about the blessed land of Sham… When we arrived, we thought that's where we were. Everything was really good at that time.'

But after some time, bombing started in Syria: 'We lived quietly for a year, then Russian planes began dropping cluster bombs.' And then the situation turned in such a way that it was no longer heaven but hell: 'On one side, a quiet life, beautiful palm trees, on the other, heads on fences. It was terrible.'

As rumours reached Syria about those who returned home, many women were afraid of criminal prosecution. People said they were sentenced and sent to correctional institutions. I repeat, for most of these women, returning to Kazakhstan was probably a forced move. Many ended up in the al-Hawl camp as a result of a treaty between Kurdish and ISIS radicals. Only a few made several independent attempts to escape from ISIS-controlled territory. There were also those who did not want to return to Kazakhstan because their foreign husbands remained in Syria. There were also some who wanted to emigrate to Turkey. One woman said that this was precisely what she wanted to do, to go to Turkey, but she was captured and detained in a refugee camp from where she was evacuated to Kazakhstan.

Life in the al-Hawl camp also made many women want to return home. While detained there, the captives faced hardships, aggression from others, and other difficulties. This is how one of the girls interviewed describes her disillusionment:

I was always shocked, how could such a society get the power of the Caliphate? But Allah is so wise that he led us out of there. Now it is clear that we didn't see many things while we each lived on our own. But when Allah tested us by making us all live together, with no food, we realised who is who.

In the camp, the women were forced to stand guard themselves, 'keep the *ribat*' ['hold the fort']. They changed shift every two hours, guarding in pairs the tents where they lived. According to the women, the ISIS widows were quite aggressive towards other captive women, blaming them for the deaths of their husbands who remained loyal to ISIS until the end. Widows could take property and money from other detainees. We learnt from the interviews that sometimes it even went as far as murder. There were also Kazakhstani women among the widows. However, the most aggressive and radical, according to the interviewees, were nationals of Tunisia and Russia (Chechnya and Dagestan).

'There was disorder, theft, fighting, murder – no morality at all.' That is how one woman described the situation in the camp.

During the interviews, the women were asked if they were met with negative attitudes towards themselves or their religious practices, or any kind of persecution in Kazakhstan before emigrating to Syria. Some affirmed this, mentioning in particular unkind looks on public transport, especially from older women and men. They said they were afraid that they would not get a job because of the hijab. But the women did not give many specific facts.

Now, many of them are saying that they were afraid of public condemnation and of being labelled a 'terrorist'. Here are the words of one repatriated woman: 'It seems as though there is no future for me here because we have all already been branded as ISIS returnees.'

Another woman (a native of Pavlodar) also remarked that she did not see any prospects for herself back home, but that she wants things to work out better for her children than they did for their parents: 'There is no future, no future for me. Now I have to do my best for the children… […] I ask Allah that they won't become like their father, that they won't break any laws.'

Following the rules established by ISIS, women did not work in Syria. They were given food and money for their personal needs. Their husbands and special ISIS structures (if women lived in a house for widows) provided everything they needed. As a result, now many of them don't know how to provide for themselves and their children. Some, however, have plans for their future. They say that they see themselves in the business sphere: they want to open businesses selling Muslim clothes, or beauty parlours, or engage in online retail. But they still doubt that, with their history and because they wear a hijab, they will be able to find employment. Some of them plan to return to their parents but do not mention any specific intention to take a job or study as yet. Many said that they just want to rest in peace and quiet surrounded by their relatives, and will only start making plans afterwards.

All the returnee women have children, and it is their future that concerns them most of all. They fear they will be stripped of their parental rights because of potential criminal prosecution. They all agree to their children receiving a decent secular education: 'They are street kids, illiterate, they know nothing, saw nothing. You can say they are wild. I want my children to be educated and to know what's what.'

It is worth pointing out that almost none of the women expressed gratitude to the state for returning them home; most saw it as a necessity that became possible because of an agreement between countries. Still, they are glad that they could return after their hard lives in the camp.

One of the women describes her return from Syria as follows: 'You can't find a way out for ages, and then suddenly one day the doors open.' For her, as for many other women, returning home was like waking up from a nightmare. That is why, for many, this was a conscious choice – they really wanted to go home.

The threat of female extremism

Another aspect is the 'rebelliousness' of members belonging to non-traditional religious groups. It takes the form of both male and female group members rejecting some of the social services provided by the state and state institutions. In particular, because of their ideological and at times radical convictions, many decline medical help or vaccination, and refuse to send their children to public schools if they cannot attend in religious dress.

The following picture emerges:

- According to statistics from the Ministry of Health, 35.3 per cent of those in Kazakhstan refusing vaccination for their children do so on religious grounds;
- In Atyrau, around 100 gave birth at home in 2017 because they refused state medical help;
- In Aktobe twenty-two schoolgirls did not move up to the next class in 2018 because they refused to wear their school uniform. That year, seventy-two schoolgirls did not attend school for the same reason.

For these people, social protest becomes a way of interacting with the state. Because of religious illiteracy, many consider themselves victims of secularism. Moreover, they criticise the majority of Kazakhstani Muslims, who profess so-called traditional Islam, in particular the Hanafi *madhhab* (one of the four principle legal schools of Sunnism).

Zholdas Kalmaganbetov, head of the Department of Religion in the Aktobe Oblast, notes in one of his interviews:

> Among the followers of non-traditional forms of religion, there are many illiterate women with neither an education nor a job, and that means they lack a social network, so they have no other source of information. They don't leave home and aren't integrated in society. They are mainly busy with housework and raising children.[8]

Tolganay Mustafina is the executive director of the Public Foundation Centre for the Study and Analysis of Public Processes (she was involved in organising the work of the Republican Information and Outreach Group of Religious Affairs). According to her, there is usually an unofficial leader in women's religious communities:

> In women's religious circles adhering to non-traditional religious views, there are more-dangerous so-called 'women curators' who became authorities for younger female believers. They may have a better education as well as experience of working in the state sector. Such women will never take up arms or become *shahids*, but actively assist in recruiting new people into the ranks of destructive movements. Often, extremist ideology in a given women's social group is based on their support. They instruct on what to study, how to build family and kinship relations, what to say to representatives of the state, and how to disguise themselves as religious women of the traditional Hanafi *madhhab*. In fact, they are the unofficial leaders of the female half of non-traditional jamaats.[9]

---

8. 'Disastrous June 5th: hitherto unknown details of the terrorist act in Aktobe in 2016': https://ru.sputniknews.kz/regions/20180605/5899389/aktobe-terakt-vospominaniya.html.
9. '"To believe does not mean putting yourself at odds with society!" – Tolganay Mustafina talks about the female factor in the radicalisation process': http://www.antiterrortoday.com/antiterror/sistema-mer-borby-s-terrorizmom-po-stranam/at-v-kazakhstane/16837-verit-eto-ne-oznachaet-protivopostavlyat-sebya-obshchestvu-tolganaj-mustafina.

Brief interviews with women returned from Syria revealed a disturbing trend. In their case, it is difficult to recognise familiar radicalising factors that influenced their transformation. We can also say that the repatriation of women and children to Kazakhstan brings new challenges, the most important of which is their rehabilitation. Although the woman spoke openly about their life in Syria during the interviews and were glad to have returned to Kazakhstan, we can already say that there are concerns about how they will reintegrate into society here.

First, many women have reported potential public harassment because of the time they spent in Syria and Iraq.[10] They are already concerned that others see them as 'terrorists'. At the same time, they adamantly insist on their right to don religious dress and ask why others are so against it. Most of them used the expression 'harassment' when speculating about their future in Kazakhstan.

Second, the women said they wanted their children to receive an education, but are worried about how they will adapt socially. Many want their children to study at home for some time first. They raised the subject of segregated education and the possibility of girls being allowed to wear the hijab in school. The oldest of the evacuated girls was fifteen and her mother was concerned about the hijab issue, too. Concerns were also raised about how the local children would relate to 'the Syrians'.

Third, some of the returnee women have absolutely no idea about how they will live from now on. They do not know how to lead an independent life without their husband. They do not have any professional skills and have lost their social network. For example, under her husband's influence, one of the women completely cut ties with her parents. Another example is a twenty-four-year-old who has no other family in Kazakhstan except relatives of her first husband (she was married three times). There are fears that, having followed their husbands once, these women may again fall under someone's influence and join a new wave of radicalisation.

---

10. These interviews were recorded immediately after repatriation, when the women were being held in the adaptation centre in Aktau.

One of the main consequences of the radicalisation of women in Kazakhstan is the current trend to involve their young children in this process. While they themselves came to religion five or six years ago, their children are growing up from infancy in an alternative social reality, where the secular side of life, including school, seems hostile and alien. For example, statistics for Aktobe Oblast 2016 were quite alarming. In the Temir region alone, around 500 secondary school pupils were raised in families adhering to radical views. Three-hundred and forty-eight children did not attend school because their parents forbade it. These children grow up in an atmosphere of social rejection, and a whole generation more radical and hostile towards their peers and compatriots is now being raised.

It should be noted that clothing has been causing serious conflicts between parents and staff of educational institutions for a long time. These disputes often spilled over into courtrooms. The Ministry of Education issued a decree approving unified requirements for school uniforms. The Spiritual Administration of Muslims of Kazakhstan also intervened in this process by issuing a special statement that called for compliance with the country's laws, according to which education in secondary schools is compulsory and is carried out in accordance with the principles of the secular state.

Thanks to the state's firm position on this matter, in the Aktobe Oblast in particular, the number of girls attending school in hijabs has decreased from 530 to thirty. This was announced by the former head of the region, Berdibek Saparbayev, in April 2018, who noted that work on this matter is ongoing:

> We are now working with their parents. We explain to them that all children should come to school looking the same. All children should be dressed in keeping with modern standards, requirements and possibilities. Children should receive an education, play freely and do sports – this is our responsibility as parents.[11]

---

11. 'In Aktobe 500 schoolgirls take off hijab to study': https://ru.sputniknews.kz/society/20180420/5360290/shkola-hidzhab-aktyubinskaya-oblast-saparbayev.html.

According to official reports, contacts are being established with potential radicalisation victims and outreach is being carried out with them, based on the individual psychological portraits that have been compiled of women.

Departments of Religious Affairs engaged in preventative work are active in all regions of the country, but experts note that the country lacks a unified process to determine the indicators for the radicalisation and de-radicalisation of an individual. Ruslan Irzhanov is a teacher at the Academy of the National Security Committee of the Republic of Kazakhstan and a member of the Republican Information and Outreach Group at the Public Accord Committee of the Ministry of Social Development. In his view:

> Often, even in judicial practice, the degree to which a person has been radicalised is determined by an expert's subjective opinion. As of today, the radicalisation barometer has not been sufficiently developed as an algorithm and methodology. This requires the close attention of scientists, experts and designated authorities.[12]

The problems of reintegrating women into society, as well as their further socialisation, are of utmost importance because these women are bringing up children and their role in this process is paramount. Systematic work must be carried out with them, with the involvement of female theologians and psychologists, so that the women do not feel excluded from Kazakhstani society.

The children's view

In June 2019, three children blew themselves up while watching a soccer match at a cinema in the city of Konduga, Nigeria. The

---

12. 'Bias in attention towards pseudo-Islamic trends apparent in Kazakhstan': https://www.kazpravda.kz/news/obshchestvo/v-kazahstane-nabludaetsya-perekos-vnimaniya-v-storonu-psevdoislamskih-techenii--mor-rk.

terrorist attack killed thirty people and injured dozens more.[13] Physical abuse, psychological pressure and sexual exploitation have contributed to thousands of innocent minors becoming the main victims of military conflicts around the world. The children of Kazakhstanis trapped in Syria are no exception. These children became victims of bombing, hunger, violence, and many of them even died in someone else's war.

Women returnees reported cases of paedophilia in ISIS. According to one of them, that was why she did not let her sons go anywhere. Another woman said that, in the same training camp, ISIS instructors often raped their pupils. Older students harassed younger ones. All this was done with the silent encouragement of the militants.[14]

Hundreds of minors who returned to Kazakhstan in 2019 had found themselves in a difficult situation in the Caliphate. Almost all ISIS children were taught to handle weapons. A ten-year-old boy called Hamza said: 'I used to shoot with a Kalashnikov, a sniper rifle, and a machine gun, and once I took part in *amalia* [covert operation]. I prefer the sniper rifle, it has a long range and is precise.'

It was not only boys who were taught how to shoot in the Caliphate; girls also learnt. Ten-year-old twin sisters stated proudly: 'We love shooting. Aga taught us. We used to go to some wasteland and shoot at cans.'

An orphan called Khadidja said: 'I'd like to be given a submachine gun, even if it's only a toy. They won't give me a real one in Kazakhstan. I would shoot into the sky. I like shooting.'

Parents showed their children videos about Muslims being killed. Now, the children believe that, when they grow up, it will be their duty to 'kill infidels'.

In an interview with Kazakhstani media, children also spoke about the fate of boys who had declared in ISIS propaganda videos that they 'would kill kaffirs everywhere'.

---

13. '30 dead in triple suicide bomb blasts in Nigeria': https://edition.cnn.com/2019/06/17/africa/nigeria-triple-bomb-blasts-intl/index.html.
14. 'What Kazakhstani children said when they returned from Syria': https://www.zakon.kz/4979330-chto-rasskazali-kazahstanskie-deti.html.

One of the boys said:

I remember those guys. Abdulla was one. Abdulaziz and Alikozhe were on the video, too. I know that none of them survived. Some were killed when they went to swim in the Euphrates. They were killed by a drone. They were in military fatigues and armed. We often used to hang out around that *muaskar*. The lads there boasted and showed how well they could shoot. They didn't let us shoot, just taught us how to assemble and disassemble pistols and machine guns.[15]

Abdulla and Abdulaziz

These minors, who knew war first-hand, had terrible things to say: for example, they could determine whether a bomb was artillery, aviation, or dropped by a drone just by its sound. Used to death, these children are not afraid of anything that would terrify a normal child – not bombs, not corpses, not weapons. Some boys proudly reported that they participated in military operations on an equal basis with adults.

But, despite this show of bravado, and despite the fact that these children had to grow up fast, many of them could not hold back tears

---

15. 'Prisoners of the "Caliphate"': https://time.kz/articles/risk/2019/07/26/zalozhniki-halifata.

when they remembered their loved ones. A twelve-year-old orphan cried during an interview while talking about the mother he will never see again. Another ten-year-old boy says he has only one dream: to hug his grandmother and never go back to Syria. A fifteen-year-old girl who is already married mourned her mother and little sister who went missing, saying that her only wish is to see them. (She then clarifies that she means her only desire besides the main one for a Muslim woman: Paradise after death.)

Eighteen children evacuated from Syria were completely orphaned there. We spoke to one of the boys. There is no precise information about Alikhan's parents. He was repatriated during the first Operation: Jusan. Initially, his older brother was on the list but, during the pre-evacuation identification process, it turned out that Alikhan had lost his mother and older brother in Syria and so he was orphaned and alone. He is a reserved child, and speaks Arabic and Russian. He is afraid of the hum of planes or loud noises – they remind him of rocket attacks. He talks about his dreams, which are like those of any child. Despite psychological traumas due to choices his parents made, he is thinking about his future. He wants to become a mathematician.

According to one of the teachers who worked with the children during their time in the rehabilitation centre, most of them have a good chance of returning to a normal life. 'The children are very smart. They get good marks in maths. I think if they try, they can catch up with their peers.'[16] The future of these children depends primarily on what sort of social conditions adults create for them, so that Alikhan will be able to realise his dream of becoming a mathematician, for instance.

Like their peers, the children are curious and open. Most of them speak Kazakh, Russian and Arabic. They say they went to school in Syria where they studied the Qur'an, Arabic, and maths in special classes. All the children say that they 'love the Qur'an very much' although they don't know all the surahs [verses].

---

16. 'Kazakhstanis returned from Syria undergo rehab': https://24.kz/ru/news/social/item/290976-vernuvshiesya-iz-sirii-kazakhstantsy-prokhodyat-reabilitatsiyu.

Director of the Pravo Public Foundation, Olga Ryl, notes:

One of the first words or phrases that a two- to three-year-old returnee child says is 'give [something] to me' [*otdai*]. But our children say 'hand it over' [dai]. *Give it to me* – because they need [that thing] to 'survive'. In those conditions, in that situation. For example, children in the first wave [returned during the first Operation: Jusan] didn't speak like that; they had a different vocabulary. They hadn't been bombed or buried under rubble, they hadn't seen people dying. Maybe their sense of security was one degree higher, or maybe they had more opportunities in that situation. Maybe they were lucky that the prolonged bombing raids began after they left.[17]

When thinking about his parents' decision to leave for Syria, a six-year-old boy said that the reason was that girls were banned from wearing the niqab and hijab in Kazakhstan.

When asked about their dreams and desires, the children repeated the religious suggestion 'to go to Paradise'. Some children were asked what they understood by Paradise'. Here is one-year-old boy's answer: 'It's a place near Allah. Everything is there. You can get there by fighting and becoming a *shahid*.' Then he was asked what present he would like, and he replied: 'a toy car'.

None of the children know their birthdays or have any idea that it can be celebrated. They only know how old they are. The only celebration they know is Eid al-Adha or Kurban-bayrami. Their parents gave them presents on that day. And, for many, that was their best and happiest memory.

Specialists at the rehabilitation centres observed that it was easier to work with children from the first wave of Operation: Jusan, and hardest of all to work with children who had been repatriated from Iraq. There is a reason for this. The women and children evacuated during Jusan-1

---

17. "'It's not their fault that their parents fought for DAESH" – expert on the rehabilitation of children returned from Syria': https://bilimdinews. kz/?p=55026.

left ISIS territory long before the collapse of the Islamic Caliphate, whereas the second and third stages mainly evacuated those still in the last ISIS stronghold, the Syrian town of al-Baghuz, which saw the fiercest battles. Children evacuated during the Rusafar Operation had probably lived through much harder times than the others, as they had spent a long time in Iraqi prisons with their mothers and were returned to Kazakhstan without them.

VI

FIRST-HAND ACCOUNTS

We have attempted to analyse the motives and causes that prompted people to leave for active combat zones. Sociological research was carried out and large amounts of data were analysed, and we have given generalised portraits and excerpts from interviews. Perhaps the only things missing so far are personal stories. Below are the stories of girls who went to Syria and returned home. They contain emotions, personal tragedies, disappointments and hopes. These memories describe details of life in war, everyday life before and during the Caliphate, tragic military operations, daily life in the camps, and the difficult journey home. The girls all agreed to tell their stories with their faces uncovered, literally and figuratively.

Escape in a trunk

Malika Tazhenova, aged twenty-seven. Lived in Syria for five years and returned after escaping from ISIS.

I was born and grew up in Atyrau Oblast, in the city of Kulsary. I'm twenty-seven now, and I'm bringing up three young children. I grew up in a good family – my father was a police officer, a major, and my mother was a housewife. She was always at home and looked after us – my older sister, younger brother, and me. As a child, I loved going to school and joined several educational clubs. I had a lot of friends in my yard. When I think about those days now, I understand it was really a wonderful dream.

I finished only nine grades of schooling, and then, with my parents' permission, I decided to leave for the city of Atyrau, to join the Faculty of Finance and Credit at the Caspian Modern College. I was always numerate. Around this time, some important events started happening in my life. I lived in rented apartments, which I shared with girls who had come to the city to study, like me. These girls were different. They were religious, adhered to an Islamic lifestyle, and prayed five times a day. I accepted their lifestyle and behaviour as a good thing – they didn't hang out or drink. Without noticing it, I became interested in religion, too. I began to perform *namaz*, and covered myself. My social circle began to change. And now I realise that my new social network had a radical outlook.

One of my then-closest friends urged me to marry a fellow believer, which meant doing *nikah* [marriage contract] without the need to get any other marriage permits or documents. I listened to her and, in 2010, I married a man from Atyrau who was born in 1987. At the time, I was already in my second year at college, but I never finished my studies. My husband insisted I stop attending classes, and so I listened to him, stopped paying for my education and 'gave it the finger'. To me, my marriage seemed normal – we lived like everybody else. We would host people and see them off, kept up family relations, and nothing particular was happening, except that I began wearing religious dress that covered the whole body, and it was all one colour: black.

In 2012, my husband decided to go to Egypt to continue his education. He had broken it off earlier for reasons that I'm unaware of. I don't remember exactly when it was, but we went to Egypt. We already had a child, an eighteen-month-old girl, whom we took with us. After staying there for seven months, I decided to come back to Kazakhstan with the child because the strikes that had begun in the country were turning into riots. My husband stayed and intended to return home as soon as he finished studying.

But everything turned out differently. He found an illegal channel and people who were ready to help him go to Syria to do so-called jihad. After quite a while, he contacted me on a Skype video call and, when I began asking, he said he was already in Syria. He asked me to join him, saying it was a good life out there, and that fellow believers help each other. He also said the family should be reunited. I don't know why or what for, but I listened to him and went to Syria to join him, although already then I understood it was a big risk for me and the child. Now, with hindsight, I can explain it by my religious illiteracy at the time. I think that my misinterpretation of the faith, deception, and my young age all played a part, and all this played into the hands of false sheikhs.

And so, in autumn 2013, I and my little daughter found ourselves in Syria. The first thing I saw was ruins, lots of weapons, hunger, heat… And a constant feeling of cold inside me. I gave birth to our second child in Syria.

While I was waiting for the better life my husband had told me was about to materialise, and which he was waiting for too, he was killed in a bomb raid. After his death, I tried to escape several times, but every attempt failed. I will explain so it's easier for you to understand: there is war going on around, people are ready to die for their convictions, that is why they all came here. In truth, nobody really had any intention of living there. Those who wanted to return home were killed, the women were raped and the children sold into slavery. Nobody believed anyone there, everyone was only looking out for their own interests.

In 2018, I found people willing to help me and my children leave Syrian territory. Like me, these people realised there was a war of interests going on there, but they were reluctant to take me with the children because they were afraid they would be executed. They were afraid I might be a covert agent trying to find out their plans for leaving Syria and that I would report them as traitors. Sobbing, begging, I managed to win their trust. They told me their plan and we began preparing for our departure.

It was unbearable. I wouldn't wish this on anyone. In the space of a couple of days, we passed 170 checkpoints guarded by the local Syrian army, or sometimes by Kurdish militia. All this time, we were hiding inside a trunk 1 x 2 metres, and the children had been given sleeping pills so we wouldn't be discovered. It took me five months to leave Syrian territory.

I couldn't help crying for joy when we crossed the Syrian-Turkish border. The only thing I said to myself then was: 'we did it'. In Turkey, representatives from the Republic of Kazakhstan's embassy began their work straight away, and soon managed to obtain all the necessary documents, and so we were deported to Kazakhstan. In August 2018, I flew into Atyrau. I was so happy, words can't express it. We were home. No danger, clear skies over our heads, and the constant inner cold disappeared.

On the journey I had been thinking about my relatives, thinking shame and disgrace were waiting for me and my children. But I was wrong. We were received very warmly, helped with rehabilitation, employment, restoring the children's documents, and help in getting them a place in kindergarten.

I would like to take this opportunity to thank everyone who helped us and to say thank you to the Department of Religious Affairs of the Atyrau Oblast, and to Mr Kairolla Kushkaliyev personally for the help and support he provided.

But above all I want to say the biggest 'thank-you' to you, Kazakhstan! Thank you for not forgetting us, because you are our Motherland, and I regret that I betrayed you. Yet you were able to forgive and take us back.

The long road to myself

Balzhan Abdrakhmanova, aged twenty-six. Lived in Syria for seven years and returned during the Jusan-2 Operation.

I was born in western Kazakhstan. My parents got divorced when I was very young, and I stayed with my mum, who soon remarried. My stepfather did not welcome me into his family, he would humiliate me in every possible way, and beat me. I was only five but he did not care that I was just a kid. I still don't understand why he behaved that way with me... My mum had no choice, she had to send me off to her parents. But they didn't want me either, so every day I was beaten and insulted.

In 2006, my mum died, and that was when I met my father. He lived in Aktobe Oblast at the time. My mother's parents tried to cause all sorts of obstacles in our relationship, plus I was officially registered with my grandma and grandpa, so my father didn't have any legal right to take me. In 2009, I met a girl called Aigerim, and now I understand that she was following a destructive religious movement. But at that time, in that friendship, I found the support and comfort that I had so missed in my childhood and adolescence at home. I began slowly getting entangled in this web.

I covered myself, began performing *namaz*. At home, everyone was against my hijab. And my girlfriends advised me to marry a man who would share my beliefs. So, at the age of sixteen, I married a man from Atyrau Oblast. He also followed destructive movements, and attended clandestine classes in safe houses, where they persuaded him to go and study in Egypt. They argued we would get more reliable knowledge about Islam there and learn to speak Arabic fluently. They also promised us full financial support.

After several days, we were ready to go. The journey took us from Atyrau by taxi to Uralsk, then from Uralsk by train to Moscow. In Moscow we bought plane tickets to the Sharm El-Sheikh resort. We were met when we landed. They put us on an intercity coach and, six hours later, we arrived in the capital of Egypt, Cairo. We were met by Kazakhs there, and they immediately arranged for us to join a local *markaz* [language centre] to study Arabic. In Egypt there was open propaganda for jihad all over the world, and especially in Syria.

Believing the promises of a better life, in April 2012 we agreed to go. We were bought tickets to Istanbul, and from there we flew to Gaziantep. We left the airport, took a taxi, and drove to the village of

Reyhanli [in the south of Turkey] which is right on the border with Syria. In Reyhanli, we were met by guides, and there were already other people who, like us, were waiting to be taken to Syria.

They gathered us all together and we set off on foot. We walked 300 metres, stepped over some barbed wire, and were told: you are now on Syrian territory.

New arrivals were met by militants; my husband and I were taken to the Chechen commander Omar al-Shishani [his real name was Tarkhan Batirashvili; a leader of the Jaish al-Muhajireen wal-Ansar (JMA), he then joined ISIS. One of the leaders of the Islamic State, he was a native of Pankisi Gorge; his mother was Chechen-Kist, and his father Georgian. Batirashvili converted to Islam in prison and fought in Syria. His death was confirmed in 2016 – *author's note*].

So, my peaceful life ended and life in war began. Seven long, pointless years, during which I experienced every aspect of war, hunger, cold, loss, humiliation, prison, and captivity. It was a time when I realised how precious my Motherland is. I was in Raqqa during the siege and in al-Sousa, where I saw atrocities committed by ISIS militants who were killing women and children.

In 2018, after walking fifteen kilometres through quicksand in the desert, I voluntarily surrendered to Kurdish self-defence brigades. In May 2019, I was evacuated from Syria with my children in the Jusan-2 operation. When I arrived, I wrote a letter to the President as a sign of my gratitude for our salvation. I also wrote a book about life during the war in Syria to protect young people from making the kind of mistakes I made. I want to open the eyes of people who want to go there. Now, I have begun a new life, a life more filled with joy and happiness. I am studying, working, bringing up my children, making progress, and setting myself new goals. I want to thank the author of this book. Dear Erlan Tynymbaiuly, thank you for your work, and especially for your part in the Jusan special operation, which gave us another chance.

Under the black flag

Tolganai Mukysh, aged twenty-eight. Lived in Syria for five years, returned during the Jusan-3 Operation.

Meeting my future husband

I am from the Pavlodar Oblast, the Bayanaul region. I was born there and went to school there. Then I left for Karaganda and started a technology-engineering course at the Polytech [Karaganda State Technical University]. That's where I met my future husband. He was in the same class as me. I didn't know much about religion then. I followed some Kazakh traditions that we practised at home, like any normal Kazakh woman. I would say that I was a Muslim, but that was it. I wasn't deeply religious. My future husband had already started reciting *namaz* but I hadn't. He would tell me about religion – we talked a lot about it and went to the mosque together. One day, he said he wanted me to perform *namaz*, too. So, we were friends like that for about a year, and officially married in January 2011.

When I began dating him in 2010, I began covering myself. Now I'm trying to analyse this. I think I was naive at first. I fell in love with him, deeply. Listened to what he was telling me. I wanted him to like me. In the mosque they also used to say I should read namaz and wear the hijab. He was saying he wanted to me to cover up so that nobody but him could see me. And so I was happy to put on the hijab and proudly said I was Muslim. My parents were against it. I tried to explain that this is the right way, that it is pure – nobody can see you, you only show yourself to your husband. They were strongly against it at first, but I didn't take my scarf off. And then I said I was getting married. They didn't take it all in at first, but, when our parents met, they somehow got on well together straight away, and my parents later agreed to the marriage. They made us promise we would graduate from university, that we wouldn't drop out but would get our degrees.

My husband and I studied full-time. In my second year, I gave birth to a son, and to a daughter the following year. I was a good student; after all, I got in on a grant, so I was able to fit everything in. We lived with his parents, they helped us. In his fourth year, my husband met some guys, and now I understand that they were probably Salafists. They were Kazakhs, older than us. I don't know where they were from, I didn't pay much attention at the time. My husband would say that we were apparently practising Islam incorrectly, it should be like this, not like that. To be honest, I didn't pay much attention to what he was saying, I didn't have time: small children, study. And we were writing our dissertations, too, that was important for me. One day, some 'brothers' came to visit. When they left, my husband said: 'They said they are going on *umrah* [small *Hajj*].' So, it turns out that he didn't know them for very long and they brainwashed him in just a few days.

My husband was the eldest of two brothers. His parents were happy that their son didn't drink or smoke and recited *namaz*, that we didn't quarrel or fight, that we spent time with each other, listened to our parents, spent a lot of time at home, that we were friends and that I listened to my husband. When they saw our Islam, they liked it. Then, when we were about to get our degrees, in the fourth year, he suddenly left. We were visited by the authorities, who told us that he is there [in Syria]. We were shocked at first. He knew the family would be against it, so he didn't tell anyone beforehand. He left in 2013.

Then he called me and said that apparently you have to do it if you are a Muslim. I was against it at first. I threw tantrums, cried. Then I started feeling bad without him. But he kept calling and said that the wives of all the other 'brothers' were already there with their husbands. 'You come, too, to me,' he would say. He was talking me into going there for eighteen months. He would call on the phone and through Skype. He would say that everything is fine there, everyone lives with their families. I missed him, I wanted to be with him. I loved him very much…

Running away to Syria

Things were relatively quiet in Syria when we left. My husband would call and say they had everything there. He would send photos showing he could walk everywhere, and life seemed to be pretty much peaceul. He said everything was working – shops, and parks where everyone takes walks with their families as if there is no war at all. I decided to go and join him eighteen months later, in 2014. Everything happened spontaneously. I didn't even have a passport, so I went to the PCS [Public Service Centre], got a passport and, several days later, I left for Almaty. I didn't say anything to anyone, just took the children and ran away. Just left. I even left my phone at home so they wouldn't look for me.

Back then I had been at home with the children and had a little bit of money. One day, when everyone went to work, I left home in the morning, too. I bought a ticket and flew to Almaty, and the same night I flew to Istanbul, where I was met. Three days after I left Kazakhstan, I was already with my husband. But first, from Istanbul we were taken to Gaziantep and, from there, to the border. There were other women, too, but no Kazakhs. They were from Dagestan and other nationalities, and we all piled into the bus. I didn't speak to anybody, I didn't know anybody, I just went with everyone else where I was sent. I was in touch with my husband by phone. We crossed the border. It was calm. We didn't run, we didn't even hide. And so, we found ourselves in Raqqa [unofficial capital of the Islamic State] and, as my husband had told me, it really was more or less civilised there then.

Each family was given a flat. We were welcomed so warmly! I had the feeling that I had landed in a place where there was real Sharia, where everyone lives according to the rules. At first everything was fine – we were given a home, furniture, everything you need in life. Every family was given an allowance, a larger one at first, around

200 US dollars a month. I was looking after our children at home, he was going out on some business. It was only later that he said he went on military operations, to patrol the border.

When I first arrived and saw him, I was shocked – he was armed with a submachine gun and wearing military fatigues. I asked him: 'What, are you really fighting?' and he said: 'Yes, we have to. That's why we came here.' He hadn't said anything like that when I was in Kazakhstan, he had just said we'd be together. I hadn't even thought about all that, I had just wanted to be with my husband. But when I arrived – there he is, in military fatigues, and I realised this is war.

When we arrived, all the women had to dress in black, that was the rule there: covered face, clothes covering all your body. They said that, according to Sharia, no strange man should even know the colour of a strange woman's skin. We lived in the Kazakh Jamaat. It was big. I don't know exactly how many families were there, but I would guess several hundred. The Kazakhs all lived close to each other, and we all moved together, too. Many Kazakhstanis came to Syria that year.

After a while, we moved to the city of al-Shaddadah. It was almost a Kazakh village. We were given this place for the whole Jamaat. Everyone was given a flat there. At first it was quiet there, too. The first bomb raid happened in 2016. That was the first time I saw what it was like. I had already seen videos about what was happening in other cities. Then the air raids began happening far away, not very close to us, but then one day it happened in our village. I got frightened and ran to the next house where there was another Kazakh 'sister'. We didn't know what to do, we were sitting there frightened, waiting for it to be over.

When it was over, they said that a 'sister' whom we knew had died. An artillery shell hit their house. We felt really bad. After that event, we were transferred to another city, Rawa, in Iraq. At first, it was quiet there. My husband would go out to patrol the border and come back. Then that began repeating all the time – quiet at first, then a bomb raid, so we would leave that place in search of a new, safe one. And conditions were getting worse and worse… In Raqqa there were good flats. We lived in big houses in Iraq, too. They gave one villa for two families. In 2017, things were already bad. There weren't enough houses for everyone, and those that were available were in a terrible condition.

In 2015, my husband took a second wife. It was common practice there – everyone was taking second or even third and fourth wives. My husband married a Kazakh woman whose husband had been killed. She was older than him, she was thirty-two. She had three daughters. Out there, they were always saying that it is good to take a wife, 'You'll enter Paradise and feed orphans.' It is a godly deed for a Muslim.

And so, he decided to marry. He didn't ask me. Just came and said he'd got married. I was in shock, crying. I kept asking him why? What for? He would say: 'You have to keep *sabr* [patient], help others.' He said that the woman was alone, she had three daughters and that I have to accept it, too. He consoled me, saying: 'I'm taking an adult woman, not one that is younger than you.'

Then there was a third wife, also older than him but younger than the second. I knew her, she was from Pavlodar, like me. I was ready for this. I knew he would take a third, and a fourth one. Yes, it was difficult, but I thought it was all temporary. Especially when there are bomb raids, you think: soon we'll all leave. Why should I fight with my husband needlessly? One of us might die, and then we'll be sorry that we didn't make up. I tried not to throw tantrums. Initially, all the wives lived in separate houses, but in the end everyone lived together.

Losses

In December 2017, my husband went to visit our neighbour's house where the men used to gather. I could see the house from my room. I had tucked the children into bed and gone to sleep when I heard the sound of shells exploding. The house was hit by a missile and everybody was killed. I looked out of the window and saw the house was gone. I knew in a flash. I became hysterical. In the morning, they told me my husband had been killed. I didn't believe it. I was crying, thinking maybe he had managed to get out of the house in time. Then I was shown a photo of his body, a frightening photo. I was shocked.

It took a long time for me to come round. I already had four children then – I gave birth to two more in Syria. They wanted to put us in a widows' house. I said I wouldn't live with my husband's other wives any more and decided to live in the house of some 'sisters', acquaintances whose husbands had also died. It was probably due to jealousy; two of his other wives were crying, reminiscing, telling stories. I didn't want to listen to it all.

In 2018, my oldest son was six and a half. He was hit by a motorbike. I was going from hospital to hospital. They put a plaster cast on his leg, it wasn't easy. One day, in summer, in July, I needed to take my son to the hospital in the morning. We took a taxi, but I had to take him back again after lunch for physio. Some 'brothers' came – it was normal for them to come to where widows lived and ask if we needed anything. I said I was tired but that I had to take my child to the hospital again after lunch. They said: 'If you're tired, we can take him ourselves, you stay at home.' I agreed. They had a small motorbike with a sidecar. As soon as they drove away from the house, they were hit by a rocket… That is how I lost my son. Maybe it was a targeted strike, I don't know. They hadn't even managed to get far. I heard the sound of a missile exploding, got dressed and ran out, asking where it had struck, but they didn't let me go any further, saying: 'Your son was killed…'

I didn't remarry. I couldn't bring myself to. At first, I observed mourning for my husband, then for my son. Usually, it lasts four months and ten days, but of course it depends on how you take it. Our Kazakhs already had three-to-four wives each. They suggested I marry them, too, but I didn't want to. Many Kazakh women married Arabs because they were well-off. I thought that, if there was a chance, Kazakhs would stick together and head in one direction, and what would I do if I was with an Arab? I decided it was better to stick with our own. We weren't forced to remarry but they said it would be good if we did.

Then we began contacting our parents, saying we want to go home. ISIS was being driven out, there were bomb raids every day. Every day somebody was killed – you know a 'sister', speak to her today, and tomorrow she is no more. It was hard. I was in touch with my parents and heard from them that there was a way back… I told them my son had been killed, and they said it was my fault… They scolded me, of course. And then I decided I wanted to go home.

Returning

After the Islamic State was pushed back to al-Baghuz, we were left living in tents on the street. We wanted to leave but they were saying that the roads were mined – if you wanted to leave, you had to know the exact route. Some tried to escape by themselves but got blown up. You had to find a guide, but they were expensive, and we didn't have any money. There was no food. We ate grass. There were a lot of us crowded together, really a lot of women and children. If anyone found something, we would eat it. We begged on the street. The children were sick and emaciated, and nobody even had the strength to walk.

It was winter. It was raining. And we slept on the street. The men didn't know what to do to help us. Bomb raids, hunger, cold, fear. You're walking along, bullets whizzing around, someone is hit, someone else isn't. We lived in al-Baghuz for three or four months. On the street. We stayed there until the end, we witnessed those terrifying bomb raids. I was ready to die, praying all the time. I was asking Allah not to leave my children without me or me without them. Many were killed. So many. I was really afraid, I always kept my children beside me. Some women found guides and left to surrender themselves, but they often returned because someone got blown up and there weren't any good roads.

And then ISIS decided to negotiate with the Kurds so that the women could surrender, since it wasn't possible for us to stay there any longer. So, they agreed to temporarily suspend the bomb raids so we could leave. They sent large trucks for us, the kind used to move livestock. We were taken to the al-Hawl camp. We lived on the street there, without blankets. They knew we were very hungry and taunted us by throwing us water and bread. They would throw sweets to the children, the kids would run and pick them up, and they would film us and laugh. It was the same tent camp, only surrounded by guards, essentially a prison. The camp had bars all round it, and we were inside. The Americans handed out humanitarian aid, I think they were from the UN. They gave out rice, grains, and butter. We left al-Baghuz in March and lived in that camp for another three months.

When we got in touch with our parents in Kazakhstan, they told us about Operation: Jusan, but we thought it wasn't true. How could they come for us here? One day we heard that Kazakhstanis were being called for deportation. They said: 'You go, Kazakhs. They've come for you.' I thought it was unlikely they could come for us here, but all us Kazakhs gathered our children and went. We looked, and saw such handsome, fair men in sunglasses. Then we thought: they are probably Americans.

I went up, and he asked me in Kazakh: 'So, Tolganai, do you want to go home to Kazakhstan?' My heart almost jumped out for joy, I was shocked. 'Are you a Kazakh?' I asked. 'Yes,' he said. It was such a joy. And we were always asking: 'When will you take us away? When?'

That was mid-April. First, they made a list, and then they left. Then they came a second time, but I didn't make it that time. That was Jusan-2, as I understood – they were taking the wounded, pregnant and very ill. I was on the third list, at the end of May.

I remember that day. They told us that ours had come. We ran and saw it was true, it was ours. They warned us we shouldn't take much with us, just a change of clothes. They told us not to take big bags, that we would be given everything. They told us to take food, too, because we might have to spend a couple of days in another camp. They left, and the Kurds bussed us to another camp, Ayn Issa.

We spent the night there. They began checking exactly who had come, taking photos. As if they were our blood brothers, Kazakhs came to us, asking: 'Did you eat? Is everything OK? Do you need anything?' We had enough food for the first day but not for the second, so we kept asking when we would leave. They said we had to wait one more day, and brought us food. There were over thirty women and many children, and they brought food for everyone. We were happy that they treated us like that. At first everyone thought they would call us terrorists, but they didn't.

They took us by bus, and we boarded a plane. And we arrived in Aktau. My younger son was very ill, so they put him in hospital along with other children. Ten days later, we were taken to a rehab zone. We spent a month there, working with psychologists and theologians.

The staff of the Chance Foundation helped us a lot. Those who had nowhere to go were given accommodation. They bought clothes for the children, and grocery baskets and things for us. Their lawyers helped us a lot with the paperwork, which was complicated, but they worked very hard. We had to prove that the fathers of our children had been killed, but we couldn't get any death certificates from anywhere. I was helped by a very good lawyer, Irina Dyerdyevna. I had to go through a divorce court. I had to divorce in order to get support as a single mother, and she helped me with this.

At first, I went to Pavlodar, to my parents. I lived there and they were happy. I thought my father would scold me, but no, it was OK. I took an accountancy course – we were told we could do a course. I graduated and got a job in my village of Bayanaul as an assistant accountant.

I sent my children to kindergarten and school, and it turned out my middle son had a problem with his kidney. He had stones and needed an operation. They refused to do it in Pavlodar – complicated case. We wrote to Astana [the capital, now called Nur-Sultan]. But because the children's birth certificates weren't ready yet, they didn't admit him into the hospital. Then we found a good urologist professor in Karaganda, and he agreed. And so, I found myself in Karaganda. My husband's parents are there.

The boy had his operation and spent two months in hospital. He had to be under observation for another six months because he had internal bleeding. And so, we decided to stay here with my mother-in-law. They were missing their grandchildren... My husband was their favourite son. By the will of Allah, we returned. When my son got better, I went to work at the hospital. I am trying to keep what we went through to myself. At work they don't know my story at all.

When I went back home to Pavlodar, my mother was horrified and insisted I take off the hijab, and so I did, to calm her down. After I left for Karaganda, I was quietly preparing my parents for the fact that I would put it on again. I told them I felt bad without it. My mum said: 'You understand everything yourself now. You suffered so much.' My parents gave their permission, they only asked that I didn't wear black.

Now when I think about everything that happened, I think I would do it all differently... If I could go back in time, I probably wouldn't follow my husband, no matter how much I loved him. But on the other hand, it is a test. I want to forget it all, I don't tell anyone about my life, I want to live differently.

Disappointment

When we got there, they told us we must live according to Sharia and keep the rules, but in fact it wasn't like that at all. I saw a lot of injustice and deceit there. When I said goodbye to my husband when he left for military operations, each time I risked not seeing him again. If they won, they would often bring trophies back and the Arab emirs took them all for themselves, saying to our husbands: if you take the trophies, your *sawab* [reward for doing a godly deed in Islam] will be smaller. They took cars, electronics, carpets, valuables. They had everything, they lived in luxury villas and ate their fill. People like my husband, ordinary people, were tricked. Like many of the other Kazakhs, my husband was just fighting in someone else's war.

They took all boys over the age of twelve to the *muaskar* for military training. They didn't ask the parents, everyone had to train there. One year, in one of those *muaskar*, in Raqqa, cases of paedophilia were discovered. It was covered up at first, but then the boys' mothers began to panic, because this is a dreadful sin according to Sharia law. It looks as though the boys came home over the weekend and told their mothers. I was extremely worried too, as my sons were growing up. We kept telling our husbands to look into it. But, when they did, it turned out it was the older boys who started it, and the teacher didn't know at first, but then he was covering it all up. As a result, the *muaskar* was closed down, but everything was hushed up. Our women didn't really want to talk much about their sons being abused.

ISIS had its own rules for bringing up children. It was forbidden to buy children dolls, soft toys, any toys with eyes that represented living beings. Mothers taught their children the alphabet, reading and maths at home, and they went to school from the age of eight, but education was in Arabic. While my husband was alive, I didn't need that language much but, when he was killed, I had to go to the shop, to the market, and so I began practising speaking. Like it or not, you'll learn it there.

Cartoons, films, music, books – everything was forbidden. You couldn't show the children cartoons on the phone. You could only watch videos they produced, they had their own cartoons in Arabic. Mobile phones were allowed but, because the connection was weak, you had to go to an Internet café to connect to the Web. We were in touch with our parents, but in order to get permission to contact them you had to say that your parents were believers. I said that mine were. TV was forbidden. They distributed their own magazines and newspapers.

I began to realise that things weren't fair there. If everything were according to Sharia, everyone would have lived in fairness. But there was no justice in the Caliphate. I was always asking my husband, why is it like this, and not like that? This isn't according to Sharia law, it's not right. He would say: 'I don't know, I don't know, I don't get it myself.' Then, in 2017, my husband confirmed it himself: 'It turns out that there is no Sharia here. It's better to leave.' He wanted to send me back home. 'I shouldn't have called you here.' He was regretting it already.

Some people were profiting at the expense of others there, killing their own Muslim brothers. Those who dared to doubt whether there was real Sharia law in ISIS were imprisoned and then executed. If we said that there was no Sharia there, no Dawlah [*ad-Dawlah* – the Arab name for an Islamic state], we would have been imprisoned. After some time in prison, they would ask the person if they repented, and if they didn't they would execute them. Many Kazakhs were executed there for saying it wasn't true Sharia there, and not taking their words back. That is why, in his last days, my husband tried to get me out of there.

It was much more difficult for men to leave, they would be killed at once. The women would be punished, yet they had more chance. That's why he tried at first to find a way for me to leave with the children, but he didn't manage it. After he was killed, I only had one goal: to find a way out and leave.

Executions were done in public. They would say: 'Look what happens to those who talk like that.' They would drag them to a market. I remember one terrible story. One Kazakh woman whom I knew well was saving up money to escape. She saved 10,000 dollars. She had four children. Other women killed her for this money, so her children were orphaned. ISIS militants found the ones who killed her, three Kazakhstani women. During the interrogation, they admitted that they wanted to leave, and that's why they killed her, to take her money. They were condemned and publicly executed.

I didn't go to that execution, I didn't want to see anything like that. But once I witnessed such horror anyway. I was walking in the market and saw a big crowd. It turned out that father and son were being executed. The guy was about eighteen to twenty years old – I think they were Turks. I ran away home, shocked, and forgot what I had gone to the market for. When they killed someone, they left the body for a day or half a day, for everyone to see.

They had their own police, *amnayat,* and their court. I tried not to say anything in public, people informed on each other. If women ran away, they were caught and put in prison for several months, where they were beaten. Then they had to say they repented and ask for forgiveness. But, if they were caught again, they could be killed. Once or twice a week, lecturers would come to the widows' house where we lived, and explain what we could and couldn't do, so we didn't transgress, otherwise we could have been punished too. There was a constant atmosphere of fear. I think we were deliberately intimidated so we couldn't go elsewhere.

… Now I am here in Kazakhstan, and my social circle is more secular. I am a believer, but I am by myself. I have dreams – first I want my own flat so I can live there with my children. I am educated as a technical engineer, so according to my profession, I have to work in a mine. I submitted my CV. My goal is to find a good job. I want to be helped and to help others, and I don't want to remember the past any more.

In the Syrian cauldron
Gulpari Farzieva, aged thirty-two. Lived in Syria for seven years, returned during the fourth stage of Operation: Jusan.

First love

I was born and raised in the village of Moyinkum, Shu district in the Zhambyl Oblast. When I was eighteen, I married my classmate, Kassym. He had another brother, and their father had died. When Kassym was a kid, his mother remarried, and his relationship with his stepfather didn't work out, so his paternal grandmother took him and raised him. He was an Azerbaijani, like me. I can't say that I married him for great love, but he was a good man, he didn't smoke or drink, was quite handsome and clever. He was religious from childhood.

At school, we hung out together as classmates. I think he noticed me when I started getting interested in religion. I was brought up strictly and in modesty, right from childhood. There were four of us – my brother, then me, and two other sisters. A normal family. Our father died in 2008. We grew up according to certain rules – you can't do this, you can't do that. We always saw how Granny did *namaz*. My mother's younger brother was religious. He lived in Kyrgyzstan; when I went to visit him, I saw everything.

His house was not far from the Islamic University in Bishkek. To be honest, I liked the covered girls. They looked beautiful and modest to me. When I visited there during my school holidays, I put on hijab and began performing *namaz* when I was nineteen. It caused a stir at home, let alone in the whole village. Everyone was talking about it. Even if my dad was against it, he didn't show it, he stuck up for me.

I finished school, passed Unified National Testing, and wanted to go and study, but my father didn't let me go. So, then I went to my uncle in Kyrgyzstan, worked there as a nanny in a private kindergarten and came back home for new year. Kassym proposed. I liked him so I married him. But true love developed during our marriage. He was a good husband and friend. I never regretted saying yes.

We lived with his grandmother and his older brother, who wasn't yet married. We were busy with household chores and the family. Then we left for Kyrgyzstan where he joined some theological faculty at the Islamic University, and I worked as a seamstress. We lived at my uncle's in Bishkek. We didn't have any children. At first it didn't work out, and then, when we got tested, it turned out that Kassym couldn't have children. But that didn't stop us living together for nine years.

To be honest, village life was not for me. And he preferred to study, too. At home he was studying Arabic using online courses. We decided to go to Bishkek because there were no other options. Several months before his first year at university, Kassym met a Russian guy who was religious, too. He had his own shop selling men's clothes. He suggested growing this business further with my husband in Turkey. My husband passed his first-year exams, and they left for Istanbul. He would send photos, saying: 'It's so beautiful here, I'll fetch you soon.' Those were our plans.

Once, he wrote that he was going somewhere and there would be a poor connection. Later he called and said: 'Remember I told you I was travelling? I was going from Istanbul to Gaziantep.' He said he had crossed the border to Syria and was going to war.

That was in 2012. We were shocked. I cried a lot. I couldn't believe it. But to be honest, I was such an obedient wife... He calmed me down. Probably any man can calm his wife down.

As far as I can tell, he really went to Istanbul for work and was waiting for me there. Later, when I asked why he left Turkey, he said that they watched lots of videos from Syria there and decided to go. That guy paid all his expenses – moving, the flight, and dressed him in clothes from his shop and gave him spending money. Maybe he was a recruiter, as I understand it now. They entered Syria together, and he bought all the uniforms and equipment for my husband. Two weeks later he left, and after that we didn't see or hear anything from him. I only know that he lived in Turkey, and his wife was there.

Syria

Kassym rarely called from Syria and, when he did, it was just to say he was alive. I would ask, and he would reply briefly: 'It's war here.' Later, when we talked, he told me he really regretted going there. Those videos and that guy influenced him. The videos showed local people calling: 'Muslims, where are you? We are being killed!' They showed children dying, that was all. He went out of pity. He decided he should help. He went to protect Muslims and that was it.

After a few months, he called for me. He said I would live in Turkey and he would come and visit me. Back then, it was no problem to cross the border. Many men who were in Syria visited their wives in Turkey once a week or so. My mum would tell me: 'Don't even think of going anywhere! Stay in Turkey and I will come and join you later.' So, I took a flight and went to him.

I lived in Istanbul for three days. He called me and told me to put on niqab [dress that covers the face] and gloves. I bought it all there. Three days later he wrote to me saying he'd bought a ticket to Gaziantep and that I should fly out there straight after morning *namaz*. Then I figured it all out, argued and cried. He replied that it was no big deal, that there are safe places in Syria, that I would live in one of them and that he would go out just as if he were going to work, and then come home to me.

When I flew to Gaziantep, he met me at the airport. I hadn't seen him for almost six months and I really missed him. Later I was told that I was obsessed with him…

We drove to the Syrian border, but it was only a border in name because all the fences were cut and nobody was guarding it. We crossed a field, and a local taxi driver was already waiting for us there. I was already dressed head-to-toe in black, which was very inconvenient, you are always stumbling, it's hot and you can't see anything. The taxi driver took us to a Syrian Turkmen village. We were met very warmly. The locals were eager to welcome Muslims from all over the world. Kassym's friends, militants, arrived. They had long hair and submachine guns. We drove to the city of al-Bab.

At that time, there was one general jamaat – Kataib al-Muhajirin [a group that fought against Bashir al-Assad's forces and consisted mainly of foreign fighters from the CIS]. There was no ISIS yet in Syria and everyone who came joined the jamaat. For the first time I saw weapons and the whole situation. We were taken to settle. I thought that, because there was war, we would live in some hovel, but we drove to a new multistorey building. My husband was given a large, three-room flat, brand new. Nobody had moved in yet. Only Arabs lived in those houses, and our flat was right at the top, on the fourth floor.

When I arrived, I was given $300 as a gift. And, every month, they gave him $100 and me $50. Everything was cheap then, and it was quite enough for us.

Kassym stayed with me for three days, bought groceries, and then left for another town – he worked in Anadan, almost two hours' drive from al-Bab. I didn't know the language or the neighbours, nothing. I was only the third 'muhajir' woman who had arrived in Syria then. I had nobody to socialise with. Believe me, I didn't leave the block of flats for six months. I was cooking, sewing, reading, doing something… My husband would visit me a couple of times a week.

It was relatively calm, but the city of Aleppo was nearby. It was heavily bombed, and I already felt that the war was very close.

Everyone loved and respected Kassym, and the local people treated us very well. My husband told an adult Arab, a neighbour from the first floor, that his wife had arrived, and that he should look after me if anything happened. There were six flats on our stairwell, and everyone began coming one after another to visit me, saying something in their language. We communicated with gestures, and slowly I got to know everyone on the stairwell and we lived as one big family. Little by little, I began studying the language, and by the end of six months I could speak it tolerably well.

There was Internet connection and telephone. I told my mum that I had gone to Syria. She was very upset and cried a lot. If I didn't get in touch, she would think I had died. She was asking me to return, but it was already too late… Although, no, probably then it would still have been possible to return, but my husband somehow convinced me to stay, I trusted him. To be honest, I was never scared there, even when planes were flying and a rocket landed right under the window. I don't know why, maybe it is faith… My husband wasn't a fighter. He knew languages and mainly worked as a translator. He was even complaining that they wouldn't let him go on military operations. They kept him as somebody useful, mainly at the headquarters.

Second wife

About a month after I arrived, I noticed my husband started dropping hints that he wanted a second wife. It turned out he had been looking for one even before I came. Maybe if I had known about that, I wouldn't have gone to Syria. And although I was madly in love with him and was jealous, I told him: 'Marry if you want to, I can't forbid you to if even Allah allows you to.' He said he was joking. Then I found out that he was just testing my reaction, and after a month or so he came clean and said he had married a local girl, his friends' sister. He had local Syrian friends, five brothers. That girl was four years younger than me and had been betrothed to a local, but something happened and he broke it off, and the brothers suggested Kassym marry her.

When I found out, I was hurting a lot – why hide it now? – but I put on a brave face. Even told him I wanted to see whom he had married. He was happy and brought her to me the next day. But he himself went away somewhere. I already knew the language a bit, and I had a dictionary, so I could explain to her what I needed. The reason he got married was because he wanted children. He didn't want to believe it was his fault that we couldn't have children – probably like every man. And he told her: 'I love my wife very much, but I want children, and that is why I am marrying you.'

Honestly, it was very difficult for me. Until recently, I couldn't accept it. And although I kept myself in check, never quarrelled or fought with him, it wasn't easy. The fact that there was a war played into his hands, because each time he went away, I knew that he might not return.

After several months, he took us to Anadan and rented a house there. One week I was with him, the other week, she was. It was as if we lived in one house, but in turns. We cleaned and cooked together. In the evening he came and, if it was my night, he would take her home. If it was her night, he would take me to a flat. They didn't manage to have children, either. She knew that he loved me more. According to Sharia law, he had to be with her for the first three nights. She said he was crying all night, felt he was betraying me, felt bad... Well, that's how it was fated to be...

Sometime later, my husband was offered the post of mayor in a small town on the border with Turkey. He was clever and responsible and so he inspired trust. When he was taken there, he rented a flat and would fetch us there. One day, he took the second wife and I remained in Anadan. The wife stayed in the flat and he went to work. He was sent to the desert somewhere, where they were surrounded by the military.

A that time, ISIS was already getting stronger, and Kataib al-Muhajirin, which Kassym was a member of, split into those who supported ISIS and those who didn't. The locals knew that my husband was one of the Muhajirins, and thought he was probably pro-ISIS.

While I was in the flat, those who accused him of collaborating with ISIS tried to capture me. The Syrians protected me. The military arrived and wanted to enter our stairwell, shouting that I was a traitor's wife and they wanted to take me away. The locals came out and protected me, saying that they know Kassym and he is not like that.

In the morning, the neighbours whisked me away. A relative came to the border of the town – you already couldn't enter it, even then. The neighbours gathered, took their children and several women to make it look as though the locals were going to visit relatives in another town. I was dressed as a local – the women there wore tighter clothes, so they took me out as one of theirs. They are a very friendly people. They saved me, I'm sure of it. The relative met me and took me to the flat where the second wife was.

My husband broke out of the military ring and came to us. We lived there. It was an OK time. There, we swapped every three days. He wasn't there for days at a stretch, and she and I would be busy doing something at home.

Caliphate

About another nine months passed, and the Caliphate was proclaimed in Syria. That was Ramadan of 2014. According to Sharia, a caliphate is a place where all Muslims are obliged to go. I remember there were a lot of killings around that time. Some supported ISIS, others didn't. Local groups simply shot those who supported it. Even if you showed just a little sympathy towards ISIS and they found out about it, they would kill you. ISIS was capturing city after city.

It was a new page. There were new rules for women, too. If on this side, women could go out without socks, without gloves or even in trousers and a tunic – the main thing being that they wore a headscarf – in the Caliphate that wasn't possible. You had to be completely covered. Even if you were in niqab with a fine net over your eyes, they would reprimand you. I would say I had bad eyesight, and they would reply: 'You should wear glasses, then.' They had special people, mainly men, who checked for compliance. You're out walking on the street or in the market and just want to look at the goods from under the niqab and remove the net, and they immediately shout at you: 'Woman, hide your eyes!'

My husband didn't support ISIS. Neither did I. He simply went to the Caliphate, and didn't say anything to me. One day, he was with the second wife. I was with my female relative, and she runs in with big eyes and says she is going to Turkey with her husband. Her husband worked on the border with Turkey, meeting new arrivals. I said: 'How is that possible?' I rang my husband and he said we were leaving the next day, too. I told him: 'What do you mean, leaving?' He said we are going to al-Bab. And then I couldn't contain myself. 'What do you mean, al-Bab? That is already Caliphate land, al-Baghdadi's territory!' I cried a lot. It was terrible. I was telling him: 'Give me a divorce. I won't go! You have a wife, so you go together!' and he replied: 'How can I be without you?'

Why was I against it? I read the Arab scholars who explained that this is not at all the true Caliphate. They knew that it was a game or a trick, that something was wrong.

But the situation turned out to be more complicated. Kassym's friend was killed, shot by a gun with a silencer right by his house. One day there was a shoot-out in the men's *makar* [dormitory]. Someone said it was in support of ISIS. They called for reinforcements, and a whole column arrived, and they shot people. My husband was always very anxious about something, suspicious, he would check the car every day. Saying it wasn't safe here, that we were preparing to go to Turkey.

And that night, when he told me we were leaving for the Caliphate, they called him and said he was being hunted and should be killed – because there was a rumour that he wanted to leave, and they thought he was going to the Caliphate, not Turkey. We quickly gathered the essentials – we had a car, a Toyota Hilux. We loaded our stuff and drove off.

There was another man with us. We drove through the desert. The road was long and very dangerous. Someone was always calling him and telling him where to go. He told us: 'Pray! If they see that we have bags, then they'll kill us for sure.' And so we drove for several hours like that.

Then there was some checkpoint. The man got out. At the checkpoint, there were some people with long beards and uncut hair, with submachine guns. And I'm thinking: If they kill him, then we'll be captured, and that is the end. More and more cars kept coming and coming. A motorbike arrived, and everyone was coming towards us. Yet another guy arrived, got out, and I saw he was hugging my husband, they greeted each other. It turns out this was the border of the Caliphate, and he was an acquaintance of my husband who had settled on the other side and came to meet us. It was a terrible sight – fighters, black flags of ISIS… so that's how we ended up in the Caliphate.

When men arrive in Syria, they are taken to a *muaskar*. The Caliphate had its own rules. Men were taken to *muaskar* for two months. Our husband was taken for one month because he had already done training. Fifteen days' training, fifteen days' religious lessons. Brainwashing, as I see it now. During that time, we whitewashed and painted the house, tidied up.

He left us wives a bit of money and, while he had still been with us, some 'brother' came and gave us more. There was no problem with that there. You could say to any 'brother', 'I will be away and need someone to look after my family,' and they would.

My husband came back. We lived there for a couple more months, until one day a rocket hit a house nearby. Our house became uninhabitable. There were bomb raids, winter was coming, and we moved to Tabqa. A pretty little town, very quiet. Or it was. My husband worked in the town of Hama, he didn't come home much. And so, another year passed.

He visited me and the second wife in turns. According to Sharia law, one should not ignore any of the wives, although many men didn't observe this. But Kassym stuck to the rules. If for example he bought a phone for me, he would buy exactly the same phone for her, including the same cover, too. I remember once he bought a battery for my phone, but I didn't need it. Then I found out that the second wife's phone battery had broken, so he bought one for her, and he bought one for me, too, to be fair. If he gave us pocket money, it was the same. If he bought groceries, he bought them for both of us. He was fair…

In 2016, we moved to Raqqa and one day – it was in May – he told me: 'I want to be with you properly. Not for a day, but longer. Let me stay with the second wife for nine days and then I'll send her to her parents, and after that we can have a nice time together.' And so he did. On the ninth day, I woke him up in the morning and said: 'Time's up.' He had sort of taught me, and I loved him and supported him, too, and what's more, when you know it is a sin to deprive the second wife of attention, then you don't want your loved one to be punished, so you observe these things. He was thoughtful those days. We always had a good relationship, but those days he was particularly attentive, as though he had some foreboding. He was always looking at me, was kind of strange, and kept sending me tender messages.

He left that morning and never came back. He was killed that day with his friend – we all lived in the same house. And the friend's wife was telling me too: 'Parina, mine has either already married or is planning to marry, he's being too good.' But it turns out that's how they were before they died…

That day our husbands left for work. We got up in the morning, tidied up and cooked. We sat and waited, but they didn't come. Normally, they came home about seven, but it was already midnight. We began asking around, calling their friends. And finally, we were told that they had both been killed. My husband and his friend were responsible for checking arms reassembled from old parts outside the city. They would go out and check whether they worked or not. And there was an explosion while they were there, either because of a drone strike, or for some other reason. The first 'brother' died on the spot, but mine was wounded and was still crawling. A nearby shepherd said he heard the screams but was afraid to come close. So Kassym died in this way, on 30 May 2016…

I stayed in that house, mourning. It was terrible. I cried every day. For some reason, the very day he died he left his phone at home, which he never normally did, and took all the money from his pockets. My heart sank. I took the phone, and, after the funeral, I asked to be taken to an Internet café, from where I sent a photo and a message to my mum telling her I was now a widow. And I saw his second wife on the phone, the one he should have picked up that day, sending messages to him: where are you? How are you? And so I told her, too. Kassym was $500 in debt, so we sold some of his stuff and paid off the debts. We divided what was left evenly between us. At that time, they were giving $1,000 per widow, but we were given $500, and so I divided that between us, too.

Abdulla

I mourned for four months and ten days. Then an acquaintance, a Dagestani woman, came to visit and said jokingly, 'Soon we'll marry you off. *Iddah* [mourning] is almost over'. I didn't want to get married. I wrote to my mother, telling her I wanted to come home and asking for help. It cost $3,000 to get back, you had to pay the guides. Mum had been hiding the fact that I was in Syria from all our relatives, and she didn't have that money herself.

Saida, the woman from Dagestan, had lived with her husband for five years but they didn't have any children: 'My husband wants to marry,' she told me. 'I know you, you are good.' I was making up excuses. There were many suitors of all ethnicities and ages, from all over the world. Saida's family moved from Dagestan in full force – husband Abdulla, his two sisters with their families, their mother, his father, who later died in Syria. When Saida left my place, her sister-in-law came and began trying to talk me round. In short, everyone was putting pressure on me, and talked me into meeting him.

He worked with weapons, too, and was visually impaired – he was blind in one eye. Everyone is wearing niqabs there, so if there is any intention to marry, you had to go with a chaperone. You can go on a 'date' like that three times, and then you have to decide. I agreed to a meeting. He came with a witness. Normally, it is man, and he was sitting turned away so as not to look at a strange woman. Abdulla saw me and was just sitting and looking in silence.

He was the same age as my husband, neither handsome nor ugly, the recommendations were good, I had been told everything about him. Moreover, it's important to have a husband in wartime, it's your business card. It often happened during emergency evacuations that everyone ran away – women were taken but widows were left. If you had a husband, you would be helped, driven away, and taken in. I had little choice. One could only escape from the Caliphate, you couldn't leave just like that. I didn't have the money to escape, and it's dangerous to escape blindly. That is why I agreed to that meeting.

He asked for a second meeting after the first one. It was later that I found out that Abdulla told his sister that he liked me very much, but it was dark in the room and he had problems with his eyesight. So, then they organised a second, and a third meeting. You can only have three before *nikah*. He would just sit silently and look. I didn't have much to ask, either. On the first date, he briefly told me about himself and asked if I had any conditions. I said that I know what polygamy is and the only thing I asked was that I wanted to live separately from the first wife. He agreed.

Before *nikah*, you have to do a test for hepatitis and AIDS; there had been cases. We did the tests, and they were fine. And so, we married. It took a long time for me to get used to him. It was very hard for me. I kept having visions of my first husband, whom I was madly in love with. The second turned out to be very fair and attentive, too. He stuck to the rules, didn't treat me badly. In my second marriage I wasn't jealous like I had been in the first. We lived in Raqqa. It was really interesting – he and Saida had been together for five years without children, I had been married for nine childless years, and the very month I got married to him, Saida got pregnant. But she had a miscarriage in her sixth month.

One evening my new husband came and said: 'The Americans are planning to blow up the dam in Tabqa and, if they do, everything will be flooded, including Raqqa. We have to move to another city.' He left for work in the morning and we were evacuated urgently. They have special people there who look after each family or the women if their husbands are not at home. We were taken towards Iraq, to the village of Mayadin. It was dusty and dirty. We were all crammed into one house, seven other women as well as us. The dam wasn't blown up, may Allah be praised, but we stayed there for another three months or so. But they began bombing that place, too.

And so, we moved to the next settlement. It was very hot there in the summer. We slept on the roof. There are roofs like that all over Syria – they are arranged like rooms but without a ceiling. That night, an assault helicopter came in. There was bombing, shrapnel was flying everywhere. Our husband was on watch duty, guarding the warehouses. There was no light anywhere. We barely survived that night. He came and fetched us. We all lived together. And then, I remember, we decided to sleep on the roof all together, far apart, so that neither I nor Saida would feel spurned.

The situation was getting worse. The city where we lived before had already been taken, so we had to leave there, too. My husband was sent to guard warehouses in another village. There were bomb raids all over, everyone left, but we were the last family in the village. At night, a car came for us – we all gathered – two sisters-in-law, mother-in-law, lots of children, two wives. We all climbed in and drove away. It was a terrifying night. You are driving along and see someone's severed head lying there, terrible scenes.

We were evacuated by a special group that normally carried out emergency evaluations of militants' families. We were taken to some house, but there was nothing there at all, no beds, no furniture, it was cold, and fifty or sixty women were inside. Then they brought us some stuff, and food. And for a time our husband lost us. He was told his family had been evacuated but he didn't know where they had gone.

Two nights later, we had to run again. OK, I took a backpack and set off. But other people had children. Such a rush and confusion, a crammed bus, no idea where they are taking us. I remember one woman who was sitting next to me with two children asked: 'Sister, do you have children?' I said I didn't, and then she said: 'If we have to run, will you take one of mine?' I burst into tears, I looked at these women and these children and thought, what are we all doing here…?

Again, we found ourselves in some empty house… so we continued wandering like that and finally found ourselves in the village of Kishma. The village was divided by a river. There was nowhere else to run, the only way was to cross the river. And then, suddenly, they began evacuating everybody at night. Children, widows, everyone who wanted. We wanted to stay with our husband [the family had by then been reunited]. He worked in that village, guarding a warehouse. Saida and I decided: if we have to die, we'll die. How long can you run for?

Gradually, they evacuated everybody. But then they started bombing Kishma. We didn't have a car back then, we had a big motorbike. My husband said: 'We have to go.' We started packing and heard an explosion. He came in and said: 'Is there a shovel in the house?' 'Why do you need a shovel?' we asked. It turned out that some young, handsome guy had been killed by a shell, and we had to bury him, there was no one else. Oh Allah… He was so heavy… We barely managed to drag him. We buried him in some hole. It looked as though somebody had been digging a trench for themselves. It was terrible…

The rest of the family had already been transported across the river and housed in mosques. We found a new house in the same village and lived there, looking after a woman in her sixties, a Dagestani. She had a grandson, a boy of ten, and she refused to leave, too.

When the mop-up operation began, they attacked from the air, and with tanks. They bombed every centimetre. That's why there was no chance of surviving, and everyone ran to a safe place. One day, when the bombing started, we found our husband and decided to flee along the river. He took us to the riverbank on his motorbike and we joined the queue for the boat. Abdulla went back for the woman and her grandson. Everything around was burning, like in the movies – tanks, rocket launchers, aircraft, closer and closer. And he was driving with this woman and child, and behind them – fire.

The women, including Saida and me, were taken to the far bank, and the men were waiting for a boat on the other bank. The boy, the grandson of the Dagestani woman, had a pair of binoculars. I took them and began looking for my husband, and saw that a helicopter was coming. Do you know what that means? A helicopter is more terrifying than an aircraft. Normally, they threw awful home-made bombs from the helicopters. They made them from metal barrels or fridges. They mined them and dropped them. And so, I saw that a huge barrel like that was dropped right there where people were waiting to cross the river. I saw smoke everywhere, everyone wounded and screaming, and so I said: 'Saida, I think he died.' She was crying, I was looking through the binoculars but didn't see him. Some of the wounded were being dragged towards the boat. The helicopter was flying towards us and I was sitting under a tree. They started shouting: 'Run! Run!' And as soon as I ran out, a rocket hit the spot where I had been sitting. My husband was no more, I was running to the riverbank, and they were yelling to me: 'Don't go there, nobody's left alive!'

We were all loaded into a car and taken who knows where. We didn't know which mosque the family was in, we had no husband. Such a mess. Wounded. Groaning. Screaming. Everyone was dirty, and so were we. Through acquaintances, we found the family – our mother- and daughters-in-law. We arrived at the mosque in tears. The mother-in-law came out and asked: 'What happened?' and we replied: 'Your son was killed.' She was in shock, poor thing, he was her only son.

We took off our jewellery and prepared for mourning. *Iddah* had already started. Everybody was feeding us, looking after us. We had no possessions, no food, nothing, and the whole Dagestani jamaat was in that mosque, and everyone was commiserating…

By the evening, a boy came running in and asked: 'Are your names Saida and Parina?' 'Who is calling?' 'Abdulla is calling.' 'What Abdulla?' 'Your husband!' We were running out, in shock. He's standing there, dusty and dirty and looking at us… It is said that if the time has not come, the person won't die. His motorbike exploded and I thought he had been blown to smithereens, but he survived, he wasn't even wounded. I told him: 'You are the real Terminator!'

We found new houses in another village and began living there… This was our last lull. In December 2017, after all the eleven years I had been married, I got pregnant. My husband was very happy and proud that he was the father. Several days later, Saida felt ill. We thought it was gastritis and she was taken to hospital. But she was pregnant, too. So, in one month, we both found ourselves in the same position. Everyone was shocked, friends and acquaintances.

The pregnancy was difficult. There was less and less food. They brought only one or two truckloads, and even that had to be bought for an extortionate price. We took vitamins that were handed out free in the hospital. Ultrasound showed that Saida and I were carrying children of different sex. We didn't find out who had what. We were told that there was one month's difference, and that I should give birth in September and she in the beginning of October. But Saida gave birth before me – and, exactly one week later, it was my turn. That was something. My daughter was called Attika (my husband named her), and Saida's son was called Abdurahman, after his father.

Three months later, in December, they began storming this village, too, and so we had to move on.

Battle for al-Baghuz

We were always having to move. One day here, two days there. No water. The stream, if there was one, was under fire. We sewed nappies for the children ourselves. At some point Abdulla's family was evacuated – his mother and sisters with their families. My mother-in-law and elder daughter-in-law were wandering for four months and finally ended up in Turkey. The younger sister and her family were caught, and they were locked up in prison in Damascus. Their older, seven-year-old girl was taken from them and deported, but the other children were left there in prison, too…

Abdulla, Saida and I stayed in Syria; there wasn't enough money for me and Saida to escape. We kept moving from place to place, running away from the bombs. We were pushed and pushed, and finally found ourselves in the last ISIS stronghold, al-Baghuz.

The area was surrounded. Kurds to right and left, and behind us – the river [Euphrates]. And across the river, the Bashar al-Assad army. And on the remaining fourth side, mountains. There was a field, so we dug our own trenches, and lived there, like in burrows. A trench a bit less than one metre deep for a room, covered with plywood and a tent. If you lie down, there is a chance that the shrapnel will fly past, but if you're sitting up it can hit you.

A three-day truce was announced. During that time it was possible to surrender, but our husband wouldn't let us go, and it was dangerous for men to surrender; we didn't know what they would do to them. There was no food. People were starving. One kilo of flour cost $100, simple canned food was $50, there was only bran, with straw and rubbish. Several weeks passed. We lived in trenches, getting by on whatever we could find. There were almost no trees, nowhere to get firewood, and so the fire was made out of whatever possessions were left. Al-Baghuz was bombed. We decided to surrender to the Kurds.

With our last money, we bought a packet of dates, divided it in three and put one portion in each backpack. We baked bran cakes for the road. While we were getting ready, we were told that the truce would end at 6 p.m. that evening, which meant they would start bombing again. We had been unaware of that earlier. There was no longer any way any more. Our husband told us: 'Prepare to die today. They will kill anyone who has not surrendered.' For two days and nights, there were dreadful bomb raids. Our husband told us to lie down and not get up, but we had to go to the river, at least to get water to drink and change the children. Beyond the river were snipers who would kill anyone, as if they were shooting at figures in a computer game.

On the third day, it went silent. No explosions to be heard. If you sit in a trench, it comes up to below your shoulder, so we were sitting, the children were lying on a mattress. They were four months old. Then suddenly there was such a loud explosion in the middle of this quiet day! And I saw that something was flying into my chest. I didn't feel any pain, only a blow. And my eyes went dark. A rocket-propelled grenade had hit the ammunition dump not far from us. Explosions started, and a shard ricocheted and hit me. Blood gushed out, I fell down and thought: 'This is the end.' I started asking for forgiveness from everyone around and prepared to die.

Our husband wasn't around, he had gone to look for food. Not far from our trench, an Arab family we knew had settled. And that 'sister' stood up and began shouting: 'Help!' Her husband and some other man and my husband's friend put me on a blanket and dragged me into hospital, risking their lives. Wounded and corpses were lying by the hospital, so many people… I couldn't breathe any more. I was in pain. I was left on the porch. My husband's friend stayed with me.

The hospital didn't have enough medicine or drips, and everyone was given just a little bit. I was dragged into an office. There was an Arab doctor. They were saying: 'Forgive us, sister, forgive.' And I was thinking: 'O Allah, I'm dying. What do they want from me, again and again?' It turned out that they had to cut my clothes and were asking forgiveness for that. They found a shard under my armpit. I had internal bleeding, so they inserted a tube to let the blood out. Meanwhile, my husband came. They injected me with a little bit of painkiller and handed me over to him. And then they brought in the next woman, screaming and all covered in blood…

My husband was dragging me to a shelter. Everyone was screaming, everything was exploding all around. I was put on the floor in some little house. Since I was 'in critical condition' they left me there and found a drip from somewhere. One of the 'sisters' was dissolving sugar, and pouring it into me, teaspoon after teaspoon. I will never forget that. It turns out that they had said, if I survived that night, then there was hope. Apparently, I was meant to live. Then they dropped a phosphorus bomb. I came round because Saida was covering me with a blanket, saying we might get poisoned. It was hell on Earth. So many people died there. Al-Baghuz is a wound. Effectively, we were left there to die...

Captivity and return

There was another lull. They said there was a road, and so we surrendered. Went towards the mountain, where Kurds were sending big trucks. They loaded us into them and took us somewhere. Half an hour later, they announced they were going to separate men and women. We got frightened, thinking the men would be shot. My husband said nothing. He helped me get out and said: 'Go and don't look back...' They were taken to one side, we were taken to the other, in columns. And searched. That was the last time I saw Abdulla...

They kept us in that field until nightfall. Cars arrived in the evening. Surprisingly, the Kurds were not aggressive. Now I think that if the situation were reversed and they had been captured by ISIS, they would have been slaughtered immediately. But when they met us, they gave us water and food and didn't treat us roughly. Maybe they were a bit harsh with the men, but not with us. The trucks were high, and I said to someone: 'How will I climb up there?' and he said to me: 'I don't know, sister, we'll think of something.' 'Sister!' After all, I am counted as his enemy, or at least the wife of his enemy.

They tossed me up, and the shard inside me must have moved. I thought I would surely die in that packed truck. I felt so bad. I will never forget that journey; we boarded at night and only arrived after lunch the next day. There was no food. They gave us water, but not much. Saida was breastfeeding our children in turn... And I felt every bump. There was no space, nothing to breathe. Each time I felt my soul was departing…

Somehow, we arrived at the camp. I was placed in a large ward for the wounded. Actually, it was a mattress on the floor. Saida and the children were beside me. I was examined, given an injection and told they would take me to hospital. But, in the end, I lay there on the floor for two weeks. It turns out the men were taken to prison. There was a Red Cross journalist, a lot of people. It was impossible to sleep at night. The wounded were moaning, and it stank.

Finally, I asked to be given some medicine. I was so weak, I couldn't even get up. One of the paramedics looked at me and said: 'She is dying. What are you waiting for?' I was on a drip for two days, and that made me feel better straightaway. Eventually, I was taken to a hospital and spent four days there. You had to pay for food in the hospital, and I didn't have any money. So, I didn't eat. A cleaner took pity on me, bought me a banana, an orange and one shawarma. I divided them into pieces and so I managed to last out. All my life I weighed 65–70 kg, but during those four days I went down to 50 kg. Eventually, the wound was sewn up, but they left the shard inside; it didn't bother me so much any more.

I returned to the camp. We were issued IDs with our personal data and number of children, so we could get food and a tent with this card. After that, I lived there with Saida and the children for three months in more or less normal conditions.

The military usually announced when some country came to take their citizens. But I didn't hear the announcement about Kazakhstan because we lived right at the end of the camp and, since I was wounded, I didn't go out. It turns out I missed the day when they were compiling the list of Kazakhstanis.

My mum wrote to me, saying I should go to the gate and make an application. Somehow, I managed to get to the gate, but I was told ours were not there, and I should go the next day. I went the next day and asked if the Kazakhs were there or not, and they said, no. Beyond the gates there was a camp for Arabs, it was freer. They had a market, and phones were allowed. Many from our wing of the camp lied, said they were going to be deported and ran to the market. That is why the guards were suspicious.

They saw that I wasn't Kazakh, and didn't want to let me. I said: 'What is the difference? Not only Kazakhs live in Kazakhstan. Let me go, I know that they are signing up for deportation there.' The guard didn't even look at me, and there were lots of women there. Everyone wanted to get out.

I began asking another guard. He asked me: 'Where are you from?' I said I was from Kazakhstan. To be honest, when you say you are from Kazakhstan, they treat you better. If you say you are from Russia or Turkey, they got very aggressive. So, he was looking at me, trying to see my eyes through the net, because I was in niqab, and I was saying: 'I'm not a Kazakh. Please let me go.' So they let me pass. I crossed to that side and saw our people. O Allah! I was overjoyed. They were from Arystan, sitting in a row. They were not aggressive, and behaved with restraint. Everyone was serious. And you know, on their table I saw 'Kazakhstan' sweets and chocolate. In Syria. It was so nice…

They wrote down all my details. Then said to wait and to come to the gates when the evacuation started. We went to the camp and got ready to leave. After that, they took Jusan-3. But I was left behind. Allah… I was very nervous during that month of waiting because there were rumours that they would not fly in any more. Can you imagine? There were so many women in the camp, so how much speculation there was!

Finally, they began announcing: '*Kazakhstan!*' The whole camp knew that I was waiting, so everybody was shouting: 'Parina! Your Kazakhs have come for you!' We all gathered together and began getting ready. From there, we were taken by bus to the Ayn Issa camp where we spent several nights, and then we were taken to a base.

A huge plane came for us. They gave us food and drink. I remember there was one doctor who asked: 'Are you wounded?' 'Yes,' I replied. And then he said to me: 'No problem, we will cure you at home.' And it was such a special feeling… 'at home'. Right up until the last moment, I couldn't believe it.

And finally, we flew in, home. Honestly, while we were flying, we thought we would be imprisoned, but it seemed better to sit in prison at home than… *there*. There, they played with us, used us, betrayed us, and sold us. Now I am at home with my mother and the child.

A letter from my husband arrived in al-Hawl [the refugee camp where Gulpari had been held]. They took a photo of it and sent it to me. He wrote that he was alive and well, being fed, and was in prison. He said that, if I had the chance to leave prison, I should take it and not wait for him. He doesn't even know where I am. When I returned to Kazakhstan, I thought I would wait for five or six years, just in case, although I understood it's unlikely we could see each other again. Even if they release him, don't execute him or put him in prison for twenty years or so, we wouldn't be able to meet, anyway.

I went to the local muftiate and they divorced us there. They gave me three months, after which I was free. I'm already thirty-two, I need to have children and build my life. You have to make decisions like that in life… Now I have to go on living. I kept my hijab, nobody asked me to take it off, but I dress in light colours. Psychologists from the Chance Foundation worked with us. There was a Russian man, a psychologist, and for some reason he understood me, a Muslim woman, very well. He helped me a lot. We were well received. All our documents were reissued. We were given medical help and they created a programme for us… A lot of work was done.

You know, every night I dream about my captivity, that fear, those explosions… Every night. I close my eyes and see it all. What they did in ISIS, that is not Sharia. They did such *zulym* [evil] to people. They killed Muslims, separated them into Arabs and everyone else. But, in Islam, it is not allowed to divide Muslims into nationalities. The Arabs in al-Baghuz didn't starve, but our husbands were holding their trousers up with ropes, they lost so much weight. There was a lot of injustice. Our husbands were simply lured in, used, and abandoned.

Even in al-Hawl, women were divided into those who defended al-Baghdadi and those who were disillusioned with him. They would come at each other with knives. 'Sisters, you don't understand,' we would say, 'We were betrayed, you were betrayed.' They defended him, saying that he didn't know anything. And, after that, a video with Baghdadi came out, where he says: 'I followed your every step in al-Baghuz.' He apparently left his commanders there.

Those who are for ISIS still wear black and gloves there, but our girls put on the hijab, just lighter-coloured ones. There were those who didn't want to return. But most understood long ago, in Syria already, that they had made a mistake. They wanted to leave but it was too late, there was no way out.

VII

REHABILITATION: WHAT COMES NEXT?

Today, the problem of radicalisation has taken on a global nature. And although the number of terrorist attacks is decreasing, the geographical range is increasing. For example, in 2017, there were 23 per cent fewer terror attacks in the world than in 2016. However, the number of countries in which terrorist attacks took place increased: from sixty-five in 2015, to seventy-seven in 2016, and 100 in 2017.[1] The number of people convicted for terrorism and religious extremism grows year on year. Once a country has encountered terrorism, it develops its own methods for fighting this problem, and the question of rehabilitating those involved in radical activities deserves special mention in that gamut of measures.

However, international experts admit that 'the fight against radicalisation is a "science in development." Faced with the challenge of modern terrorism, nobody can claim anything for sure.'[2] Some

---

1. 'State Department: Kazakhstan limits freedom of religion in its fight against "extremism"': https://rus.azattyq.org/a/29499770.html.
2. 'Terrorist act in Strasbourg: why France's preventive measures aren't working': https://inosmi.ru/politic/20181213/244230938.html.

observations, however, can be made, based on experience gained in the course of such work. Staff at centres specialising in working with those who support destructive ideas argue that a radical can be persuaded to change their mind. This can usually be done after the sixth or seventh talk, provided that it is an average case, not a severe one. In the course of the initial ten to fifteen minutes of the first conversation, the specialists determine which radical religious movement the person follows. There are special methods for working with each movement. Nevertheless, around 7–9 per cent of 'victims' who went through programmes in special centres still adhere to their radical views. They are mostly leaders or activists in their cells. According to psychologists and theologians, they tend to stand their ground not so much because of their ideological convictions but because, owing to their status, they cannot depart from what they are saying.[3]

In addition, international experience shows that around 10 per cent of those who have gone through rehabilitation nevertheless return to antisocial groups. According to the latest research, 5–7 per cent of those convicted for terrorism were later found to be involved in terrorist-related crimes again. For example, data analysis of 199 jihadi terrorists convicted in Spain between 2004 and 2018 showed that fourteen of them were recharged with terrorism. In Malaysia, from 2001 to 2011, thirteen out of 240 inmates relapsed. In Indonesia, twenty-five radicals out of 300 convicted terrorists became involved in crime again.[4] In Tajikistan, thirty-four out of seventy-two militants given amnesty returned to the ranks of ISIS.[5]

---

3.   'Theologian at Akniet rehab centre tells how radicals are being dissuaded': https://informburo.kz/novosti/kak-pereubezhdayut-radikalov-rasskazal-teolog-reabilitacionnogo-centra-akniet.html.

4.   Thomas Renard. 'Overblown: Exploring the gap between the fear of terrorist recidivism and the evidence': https://www/ctc/usma.edu/overblown-exploring-the-gap-between-the-fear-of-terrorist-recidivism-and-the-evidence.

5.   'Jihadists from ex-Soviet Central Asia: where are they? Why did they radicalize? What next?': https://www.russiamatters.org/analysis/jihadists-ex-soviet-central-asia-where-are-they-why-did-they-radicalize-what-next.

One of those involved in the terrorist act in Aktobe in June 2016 had previously been convicted for taking part in terrorist activity and was serving his sentence in a correctional colony. After his release, he underwent rehabilitation in a specialised centre. According to theologians who worked with him during the rehabilitation programme, he showed a change in his radical views. But, despite this, he later took part in a terrorist attack. Many professional psychologists insist that rehabilitation requires an individual approach; they deem it more effective.

To date, rehabilitation programmes, in particular ones dealing with people convicted of extremism and terrorism, have been established in one form or another in more than forty countries around the world. There are no common templates, of course, as each country has its own approach.

The government of Saudi Arabia, for example, provides social support for former inmates. This help is very extensive – they buy them an apartment, a car, furniture for the new house, give them money for a wedding, etc. The first specialised rehab complexes for radicals were opened there between 2004 and 2006, and psychologists and prominent religious figures worked with them. The centres themselves were well-appointed and expensive, with swimming pools, sports halls, computer classes and comfortable rooms. According to open sources, about 4,000 people passed through one of these centres alone; 86 per cent renounced their extremist views.[6]

One well-known programme is the Aarhus Model (named after the Danish city where it was instigated). The model was developed as early as 2007, but was implemented only in January 2015, with fighters returning from Syria and Iraq. The key principle of this model is maximising the ex-fighters' environment in the rehabilitation process. Police, social services, teachers and parents control the process, while at the same time performing the role of mentors. However, this

---

6. 'Lavish rehab centre for terrorists in Saudi Arabia': https://trinixy. ru/153754-roskoshnyy-reabilitacionnyy-centr-dlya-terroristov-v-saudovskoy-aravii-6-foto.html.

model has been criticised for its soft-touch approach towards former terrorists.

The deradicalisation of women and children is a separate item in such programmes. Resocialising children is a complex and multi-stage process, and not every country has a general understanding of what needs to be done. There is really no easy solution to this problem. Work is already underway in this direction, and there are some general approaches. For example, nobody denies that the children need the systematic help of psychologists and theologians. In January 2018, the UN Office on Drugs and Crime published 'Guidelines on working with children recruited and exploited by terrorist and extremist groups: the role of justice systems'. This was the first UN publication on this topic. Austria, Canada, Denmark and Switzerland provided financial support for the dissemination of these guidelines. In March 2019, three textbooks on treating children recruited and used by terrorist and extremist groups with violence were presented at the UN.[7] That is, there is a clear understanding at the global level that such an acute issue calls for a serious and balanced approach.

Often, the specifics of the local situation simply force some countries to pay close attention to this problem. In particular, the New Dawn Rehabilitation Centre in Pakistan has treated hundreds of children. This project reintegrates minors into a peaceful life. Government forces found many of these children in special training camps for suicide bombers. Specialists maintain that children brought to the rehabilitation centre are frightened and don't know what to expect. Staff say it usually takes several months to gain their trust.[8]

---

7. 'UN ODC and Japan gather representatives for the protection for children, victims of terrorism and violent extremism from countries of Central Asia, the Middle East and North Africa': https://www.unodc.org/unodc/ru/frontpage/2019/March/unodc--japan-gather-countries-from-asia--the-middle-east-and-north-africa-to-protect-children-affected-by-terrorism-and-violent-extremism.html.

8. 'Deradicalizing boys in Pakistan': https://www.csmonitor.com/World/Asia-South-Central/2012/0525/Deradicalizing-boys-in-Pakistan.

Minors who experienced continuous military action do not emerge unscathed. For example, relatives of children evacuated from Iraq back to Russia say that, at first, they were afraid to go out onto the street, terrified of the sound of cars and planes. 'Hadija sometimes talks about these horrors – how they were being killed and poisoned there, how dead children were lying all around,' her grandfather says. 'She tells all her friends, but I ask her not to, I ask her to forget it all.'[9]

In countries where active military conflicts are raging, children who gained a sad experience of war are left to their own devices. In particular, in Iraq, many children who took part in the military actions against ISIS before they turned eighteen are now returning home. They are physically and mentally damaged. Some admit that,

> [T]he Iraqi government restricts the ages of those who can be considered part of the militias, now a semi-formal part of the Iraqi security forces. Anybody younger than eighteen is not supposed be part of the militias and therefore cannot receive wages as a member, or any compensation for injuries.[10]

In the Iraqi province of Anbar alone, there were around 550 fighters under eighteen at the time of the battle, but they were excluded from any compensation programmes or any other payments financed by the government.[11] Local authorities acknowledge the existence of such problems and are trying to resolve them so that these young people will not succumb to radical sentiments and become a new generation in the extremist underground. At the same time, the official authorities in Syria, where active fighting is still ongoing, plan to open specialised centres throughout the country, such as schools for rehabilitating children who joined radical groups. One such centre is already up and

9. 'Children in Trouble': https://russian.rt.com/world/article/489315-irak-siriya-deti-vozvraschenie.

10. 'The teenage soldiers who fought extremists, now deserted by their country': http://www.niqash.org/en/articles/security/5975/The-Teenage-Soldiers-Who-Fought-Extremists-Now-Deserted-By-Their-Country.htm.

11. Ibid.

running in the city of Aleppo, and 2,700 children are studying there, including 400 from single-parent families.[12]

There is, then, no universal recipe for the rehabilitation of former radicals. Each country looks for the best approach to resolve this very pressing issue by itself, and Kazakhstan's experience in this regard is very special. According to the Pravo Public Foundation, the first child was returned to Kazakhstan in 2015, and is currently studying in the seventh year, and all issues relating to his rehabilitation have already been resolved.[13] As for the rest of the evacuated children, it is too early to give a general assessment or draw preliminary conclusions.

However, Operation: Jusan acted as a catalyst for the development and implementation of a systematic programme for the rehabilitation of women and children who arrived from armed conflict zones. And, as was noted above, the decision to go ahead with the operation was taken only after this programme had been tested (coordinated by the Ministry of Education and Science of Kazakhstan). Under the auspices of the Ministry, an inter-departmental group was created that developed and implemented step-by-step action plan for organising work with repatriated women and children. It included the following steps:

First: On arriving from Syria, 140 women and 406 children were housed in specifically-created adaptation centre on the territory of the Flamingo Children's Health Camp in the Mangystau Oblast on the Caspian Sea. They were housed in fully-equipped, comfortable cottages. Five meals a day were provided, and the menu was drawn up taking religious requirements into account, while special dishes were prepared for those with diabetes. There were separate offices for medical examinations and educational work within the adaptation, including work with scholars of religion and theologians.

For children of school and pre-school age, a temporary school and kindergarten were set up with experienced teachers, educators and

---

12. 'In Syria, children who grew up among terrorists are beginning a new life': https://www.tvc.ru/news/show/id/151063.

13. '39 families return from Syria to Kazakhstan': https://bnews.kz/news/39_semei_vozvrashcheno_iz_sirii_v_kazahstan.

child psychologists. There were also playrooms and playgrounds at the centre. All those who arrived remained in the centre for three-four weeks and, once the quarantine period was over, they were all taken to where they had previously lived.

Second: A comprehensive medical examination was organised with the help of local authorities for all repatriated women and children. They were tested for dangerous infections and diseases. Furthermore, anti-epidemiological, disinfection, and disinsection measures were also taken. During this quarantine period, medical staff undertook scheduled daily visits. If an infectious disease or cold was detected in any of the women or children, an appropriate course of treatment was prescribed.

It came to light that one wounded woman had a piece of shrapnel lodged near her heart. She was operated on in Nur-Sultan. Several children were also operated on. In particular, many wounded arrived in the Jusan-2 operation in May 2019. They had ended up in Kurdish camps after the fall of al-Baghuz, the last town held by ISIS. The militants put up a desperate fight for the city, and consequently there were many wounded among the women and children who walked out of the encirclement.

Third: All women and children were given clothes and basic necessities, including outer garments, footwear, children's clothes, toys and personal hygiene products. During the Jusan-1 operation, everyone was handed winter clothes on board the aircraft. That stage of the operation was completed in January. Everything was prepared in advance.

Fourth: With the assistance of the Ministry of Internal Affairs and the Ministry of Justice, all women were issued ID documents, and birth certificates were reissued for their children. For children born outside Kazakhstan, birth certificates were issued based on DNA tests.

Fifth: Comprehensive psychological rehabilitation work was carried out. Experienced psychologists conducted individual talks, training, and psychological tests with children and adults. Individual social and religious portraits were created based on the results of a questionnaire and interview. Child psychologists, teachers, and educators, including those experienced in working with so-called difficult children and teenagers, were involved in the work of rehabilitating children. The centre organised performances by the Aktau Puppet Theatre, and the Nurmukhan Zhantorin Regional Music and Drama Theatre. Specialised theologians from the Akniet Information-Religious Centre also worked with the returnees.

Sixth: Work with the returnees was continued by social services of local executive bodies once the quarantine period was over and the returnees had gone back to where they had previously lived. Most of the work to rehabilitate women and children was caried out by NGOs: the Akniet Foundation (theological work) and the Pravo Foundation (social and psychological work). It was decided that the state would not be the sole provider of this rehabilitation outreach. For example, in some regions, the Pravo Public Foundation established centres for the 'socio-psychological and legal support for women and minors'.

These centres encompass two structures: a children's hotel where repatriated families could receive medical and social assistance, and a legal office. Here, help was provided for the reissuing documents and obtaining benefits for the loss of a breadwinner; children who had been taken out of the country were eligible for this because of the death of their fathers. Rehabilitation centres also deal with finding employment for the women and offer them the chance to attend vocational training.[14]

In addition to psychological and theological work, these centres provide substantial legal and judicial assistance for the returnees, in particular, by liaising with government agencies to resolve issues regarding the payment of benefits.

Olga Ryl, Director of the Pravo Public Foundation says:

When a woman is repatriated, she has no residence permit, no housing, in other words, no circumstances whereby she can get used to [life in Kazakhstan]. Especially if they have been there for a long time. How long they stay in the centre depends on rehab – it can be a year, or six months. It's important to understand

---

14. '39 families return from Syria to Kazakhstan': https://bnews.kz/news/39_semei_vozvrashcheno_iz_sirii_v_kazahstan.

that it takes quite a while to reissue the documents – just the trial takes three months, and that has to be done before changes in the certificates of civil status can be made so that the child can receive a birth certificate. There are women with kids, but the children have no documents at all. These cases require DNA tests, and that takes a month, and only then will the registry office issue the child's birth certificate.[15]

The Akniet NGO in Nur-Sultan helps women find work, providing them with references and employing them in a tailoring workshop at the centre itself.[16] In the Pavlodar Oblast, a women's club, Inabat (meaning honour, consciousness, respect in Kazakh), at the Centre for the Analysis and Development of Interfaith Relations, has been up and running since October 2017. The club hosts various events for women, aimed at reintegrating them into society. For example, girls can join cooking classes. Meetings with theologians and psychologists are also held here, and this is an important part of the work.

Women repatriated during Operation: Jusan take part in charity events of their own accord. In summer 2020, when the state of emergency and quarantine were introduced in the country to combat the spread of coronavirus, some of the women made and distributed medical masks for free. In particular, with the support of the Shapagat Centre for Assistance for Victims of Destructive Religious Movements in the city of Atyrau, fifteen women sewed up to 300 medical masks a day, and these were then distributed to orphanages, nursing homes and low-income families.[17]

---

15. Ibid.
16. 'Kazakhstani specialists pay more attention to the problem of radicalisation of women': http://carmo-pvl.kz/ru/article/kazahstanskie-specialisty-udelyayut-bolshe-vnimaniya-probleme-radikalizacii-zhenshchin.
17. 'In Atyrau, women repatriated thanks to Jusan Operation give out free medical masks': //www.zakon.kz/5014738-v-atyrau-zhenshiny-vernuvshiesya.html.

Women in the Inabat centre, November 2018[18]

The Kazakhstani authorities took a systemic approach to the problem of rehabilitation. As well as organising the work of state bodies and collaborating with NGOs, they carried out external evaluations on an ongoing basis. Stevan Weine, an American psychologist, was one of the first to arrive in Kazakhstan and meet with women and children who had returned from the active combat zone. The involvement of international consultants is a welcome addition to the national programme, as it helps gain an independent third-party evaluation of the ongoing efforts.

Dr Weine has twenty-five years' experience working with refugees and other groups of people who have suffered as a result of migration, disasters or political violence; his research interests focus on PTSD and problems of violent extremism. He is a professor at the Department of Psychology, University of Illinois at Chicago. He visited Kazakhstan twice in 2019, immediately after the Jusan-1 operation, to meet officials from the Ministry of Foreign Affairs and the Ministry of Education and Science of the Republic of Kazakhstan, as well as psychologists, lawyers, theologians, teachers, directors of all seventeen regional rehabilitation centres, and mothers and children. These meetings aimed to evaluate the needs of the national rehabilitation programme. He then conducted staff training at regional centres,

18. 'Kazakhstani specialists pay more attention to the problem of radicalisation of women': http://carmo-pvl.kz/ru/article/kazahstanskie-specialisty-udelyayut-bolshe-vnimaniya-probleme-radikalizacii-zhenshchin.

based on the results of this preliminary analysis. After meeting the returnee Kazakhstanis, Dr Weine shared his impressions:

> No other country has done what Kazakhstan has done. I was impressed. I also noticed that the centres are facing serious challenges. Staff told me that local residents had expressed reservations about children aged ten–thirteen. They think that the teenagers could have been taught to handle weapons, that they might know about suicide weapons and could have been involved in combat, torture, or murder. They also could have been brainwashed, sworn oaths of allegiance to ISIS and may now be hiding their convictions. However, I should point out that Kazakhstan is fully aware of these risks, and sees the children and mothers as deserving the chance to return home and rebuild their lives.

> They need to be helped to renounce violence. Even if they still hold some extremist convictions, their psychological traumas should be healed and their ability to make decisions should be nurtured. They did not have normal schooling in Syria. Many of them do not speak Russian or Kazakh. Here, children are attending summer school and evening classes to catch up and not be bullied by the local kids.

> Like the toddlers, the older children need trauma rehab, too. Because they probably remember their pre-ISIS childhood, some will have positive memories that could become the building blocks for new relationships, new identities, and new lives. Children usually imitate their peers, and this can help them forget what they learned abroad.

> I heard that returnee teenagers are already wondering about ISIS, about how the Caliphate did not live up to their dreams. They can think about the decision of their parents, which forced them to leave a normal life for the war zone. Undoubtedly, with the help of counsellors and theologians, children could help their mothers or other family members work through such issues. Ultimately, returnee children have a chance to heal and change before they

grow into teenagers and adults. While many countries are still harbouring doubts, Kazakhstan is already helping women and children rebuild their lives. This is an example for all of us who will, sooner or later, face similar problems.[19]

Working with pre-school age children is considerably easier. Psychologists and theologians can be quite effective if they begin their rehabilitation work earlier. Children's psyches and consciousness are malleable when they are young, meaning that young children can respond very well to resocialising. Of course, one should not overlook deradicalising those children's mothers. Most of the children returned during Operation: Jusan were under school age yet had suffered multiple psychological traumas due to witnessing violence, losing loved ones, and experiencing the bitterness of separation. In addition, many were forced to be constantly on the move and adapt to new environments, which adds further stress to a child's psyche.

About 90 per cent of the children displayed some signs of impaired psychological development. Many children had been compelled to take on the role of 'parents' as they were obliged to take responsibility for younger siblings as though they were their guardians. Psychologists believe that this is also a trauma that impacts of the child's further development as they grow up. Out of 420 children, thirty-two were orphans. Thus, the national rehabilitation programme focused above all on helping these children to adapt to their new lives.

The state sees these children as victims of adults' misdemeanours. Yerzhan Yersainov, former deputy chairman of the Committee for Children's Rights Protection of the Ministry of Education and Science of the Republic of Kazakhstan, commented as follows:

These children are victims. They were taken out illegally. Now we have to do everything we can so that maximum resocialisation happens and they reintegrate into society. They grew up in a

---

19. "'Nobody is helping their children" – American psychologist talks about the Jusan': https://mix.tn.kz/mixnews/nikto-ne-pomogaet-svoim-detyam-amerikanskiy-psiholog-386858/.

different environment and society. They do not pose a threat to the children of Kazakhstan.[20]

The Ministry of Education and Science adopted a special deradicalisation programme to achieve the maximum socialisation of these children. Alim Shaumetov, an expert from the Akniet organisation, shares his experience of working with such children:

> These children spent a long time in flashpoints on the Syrian-Iraqi border, and emulated their fathers, brothers and uncles, and performed *namaz*. They still pray now. At the same time, they show no traits that could be considered dangerous. They are normal children who play games, go to school and are happy that they live in a peaceful environment and live a peaceful life. They are glad they left. Talks with children aged eight to nine are held on a one-to-one basis, while three-year-olds visit specialists accompanied by their mothers. These are small children, there is no question of them having been radicalised.[21]

Most of the children did not go to school in Syria or Iraq. To help them adapt quickly to their new social reality, summer and then evening schools were set up. The Ministry of Education initially also provided payment for tutoring services. However, owing to the low literacy rate, 80 per cent of children were enrolled in classes one year lower than their peers. NGO specialists working with children maintain that the children will need the help of tutors going forward. Only 67 out of 205 pre-school age children in the care of the Pravo Foundation were placed in kindergarten; eighty are still under three,

---

20. 'ME RK asks for 200 million tengi to rehabilitate children returned from Syria': https://informburo.kz/novosti/200-mln-tenge-poprosil-mon-rk-na-reabilitaciyu-detey-vernuvshihsya-iz-sirii.html.
21. 'An expert talks about the deradicalisation programme for children returned from Syria': https://informburo.kz/novosti/eksperty-rasskazali-kak-prohodit-deradikalizaciya-detey-vernuvshihsya-iz-sirii.html.

while fifty-eight were not enrolled for various other reasons.[22] As Vice Minister of Education and Science of the Republic of Kazakhstan, Bibigul Assylova, says:

> Today, organisations within our educational system are carrying out complex and comprehensive educational work with all the children who have returned from zones of terrorist activity. One hundred and ninety-eight school-age children are effectively attached to the educational organisations and are on distance learning. They are assigned to responsible people – school psychologists, teachers. As for the range of measures conducted *in situ*, we have regional quality assurance departments. At present, the work is being continuously monitored, in all regions and with all children. In other words, this process is constantly being evaluated by the Ministry of Education.[23]

In March 2020, the government submitted a draft law to Parliament, 'On introducing amendments and additions to some legislative acts of the Republic of Kazakhstan on the issues of motherhood and childhood protection'. This bill calls for giving the Ministry of Education and Science of the Republic of Kazakhstan powers to establish the parameters for rehabilitating children who are victims of terrorist activity.

However, a lot depends on the children's mothers and relatives. According to the director of the Regional Centre for Social and Legal Support, Karina Polyakovich, children are highly dependent on their mothers:

> If a mother has a positive attitude and responds to outreach, the children will be responsive, too. Children study in normal schools but, at the same time, they struggle to understand the Russian

---

22. Information from the Pravo public foundation.
23. 'Kazakhstan working out rubric to help children returned from zones of terrorist activity': Kazinform: https://www.inform.kz/ru/v-kazahstane-razrabotayut-pravila-okazaniya-pomoschi-detyam-vernuvshimsya-iz-zon-terroristicheskoy-aktivnosti_a3644592.

language, and even the Kazakh language, because they speak Arabic, English and Turkish.[24]

Like their mothers, the children have a very superficial knowledge of religion, and many even resist working with theologians, whom they do not see as righteous Muslims.[25]

A study by the International Penal Reform on the dissemination of radical views and ideas in the penal colonies of Kazakhstan (presented in 2017) shows that there are currently no religious scholars, theologians and psychologists in the country who have experience in working with radicalised children.[26] Seven minors were convicted in Kazakhstan for crimes of an extremist nature in 2017.[27] And so, in 2019, the Ministry of Information and Social Development, in collaboration with the National Security Committee, launched a training programme for theologians who will be dealing with Kazakhstani children returned from conflict zones.

The state and all departments concerned have gone to great lengths to ensure that those repatriated can return to a peaceful life. However, in order to see results in this difficult task, the state must not slacken its attention to this issue and to the returnees themselves, and must ensure the rehabilitation programme continues. As soon as government agencies working with these women and children switch from priority mode to an inert, autocratic approach, all the painstaking hard work that has been done before will have been for nothing. This calls for a continuous, critical analysis of the measures and efforts, and then, step by step, we will be able to return our fellow citizens to a peaceful life, and win the fight for their minds and their future.

---

24. 'Over 90 Kazakhstani children returned from "hotspots"': https://1tv.kz/bolee-90-kazahstanskih-detey-vernulis-iz-goryachih-tochek/.

25. From the brief report the 'Programme for the rehabilitation and reintegration of repatriated children and mothers in Kazakhstan' by Stevan Weine.

26. 'Why is the fight against terrorism coming apart at the seams in Kazakhstan?': https://bnews.kz/ru/news/pochemu_borba_s_terrorizmom_v_kazahstane_treshchit_po_shvam.

27. Ibid.

VIII

WERE WE RIGHT TO REPATRIATE OUR CITIZENS FROM SYRIA?

The public response to Operation: Jusan was generally positive. But, at the same time, fears have been voiced that women and children returned from the conflict zone may bring their radical ideology with them to Kazakhstan. Some citizens are rightly asking questions. Is there a guarantee that these people will not take up arms tomorrow and turn against their own country, their own compatriots? Why did we need to save those who voluntarily renounced their homeland? Was the state aware of all the risks and threats when they repatriated all these people?

Although some time has elapsed since Operation: Jusan's completion, questions of this kind are still being raised in discussions at various levels and on various platforms. Just the fact that, as a result of the operation, several hundred children were returned should have outweighed any doubts. Given the difficult situation in camps in Syria – overcrowding, lack of sanitary conditions or proper medical care, and, most importantly, high crime rates – we could not postpone returning the children any longer. According to data from various international bodies, in 2019, 371 children died in the al-Hawl camp alone.[1] Other sources maintain that 'lack of resources and security dynamics meant that, from January to September 2019, 409 children died in al-Hawl, thirty-five as a result of malnutrition and disease'.[2] This does not include children who died of malnutrition or hyperthermia on the way to the camps.

Can there be any other more important mission than saving children? in this chapter, then, I would like to explain the main goals of Operation: Jusan once again. Why, after weighing all the pros and cons (and there are always both), did the state vote in favour of repatriating Kazakhstanis? First of all, I want to underline that, despite the mission's humanitarian nature, the country's leadership took the decision based on matters of national security. And this decision was neither spontaneous nor ad hoc. Long before the situation in Syria changed, intelligence agencies analysed the conditions of women and children in ISIS structures and were working on scenarios to repatriate them. This work was carried out primarily to prevent potential threats that could have been aggravated, had our compatriots stayed over there.

First, it was necessary to return children who, as I have already mentioned, could tomorrow join the ranks of radical groups. Most terrorist organisations view militants' family members, particularly children, as potential and already ideologically prepared recruits. The armed conflict in Syria is likely to be protracted, and that means that opposite sides, including ISIS and other groups, will need to constantly replenish their ranks; they will need a new influx of fighters. Moreover, the fact that ISIS lost its positions on the territory of Syria and Iraq does not equate to its complete defeat and the disintegration of the group. ISIS quickly regrouped as an underground terrorist network and, a year after losing the town of al-Baghuz in Syria that was

---

1. 'The Children of ISIS Detainees: Europe's dilemma': cgpolicy.org/wp-content/uploads/2020/06/CGP-Children-of-ISIS-June-2020.pdf.
2. Aaron Zelin: 'Wilayat al-Hawl: "remaining" and incubating the next Islamic State generation': www.washingtoninstitute.org/uploads/Documents/pubs/PolicyNote70-Zelin.pdf.

considered its last stronghold, the group is active again. According to some evaluations, it has restored its activities to 2014 levels.

Aaron Y. Zelin @azelin · 6 дн. ∨
IS made a huge leap in claimed attacks in April compared to prior months in Iraq and Syria:

Jan: 88
Feb: 93
Mar: 101
Apr: 151

Map is for April.

*Map of ISIS activity in Syria and Iraq from January–April 2020
(Twitter account of Jihadology.net Aaron Zelin)*

This means that ISIS needs to replenish its ranks, just as before, and will not accept that its ex-members are being held in prisons and camps in Syria. That is why, in jihadi chats, ISIS propagandists often bring up the subject of their former followers returning to their homeland and frighten them with the threat of possible persecution by the authorities, thus trying to thwart the exodus of ISIS members. Moreover, in September 2019, shortly before his assassination, ISIS leader Abu Bakr al-Baghdhadi released an audio address in which he called on his followers to make every effort to liberate arrested ISIS militants and refugees, calling this task a 'most important and serious issue'.[3] In May

---

3. 25th report of the Analytical, Support and Sanctions Monitoring Team submitted pursuant to Resolution 2368 (2017) on ISIS (Daesh), Al-Qaeda and persons and organisations related to them (20 January, 2020).

2020, official ISIS spokesman Abu Hamza declared in his audio address that captured ISIS fighters and their relatives will be liberated sooner or later. Foreign experts warn that ISIS may indeed attempt to free their fighters and members of their families:

> Prior to its capture of Mosul in 2014, ISIS initiated a campaign to release sympathetic prisoners from poorly guarded facilities across Iraq. The campaign swelled its ranks with hardened supporters. Camps like al-Hol and Roj are at serious risk of serving as a ready-made recruitment buffet for the group. It is evident that ISIS is acutely aware of the situation regarding the camps, given that they were featured in an audio address last year by the late caliph Abu Bakr al-Baghdadi. European women and children are vulnerable to being churned back into the group's ranks if they remain in the camps across Syria.[4]

Such interest on the part of ISIS leadership in the fates of the families of their former militants is not accidental. Fighters' families are an important source of human resources for this war. Therefore, all the more reason not to forget that the number of ISIS children was increasing constantly. Women remarried when their husbands died, meaning that, on average, three to five children lived with each woman. These children grew up in harsh conditions, and were familiar with weapons from an early age. By the age of eleven or twelve they could take part in combat on a par with adult militants.

Children who emigrated with their parents to the Middle East in 2012–13 underwent military training three to four years later, when they became teenagers. Some took part in executions. Similarly, pre-school children in refugee camps in Syria could replace their older brothers in five to six years' time and, a few years later, could become fully combat-ready units in the ISIS army. Intelligence agencies understood that such numbers of children could not have gone unnoticed by radical forces, left without care and attention. According

---

4. 'The Children of ISIS Detainees: Europe's dilemma': cgpolicy.org/wp-content/uploads/2020/06/CGP-Children-of-ISIS-June-2020.pdf

to Bakhytbek Rakhymberdiev, head of NSC RK, these facts could not be ignored:

> [W]e need to think about who these children will grow up to be, abroad, if we leave them without help. They will most likely replenish the ranks of the same terrorists. By bringing them home, we are solving this issue, so it will not bother us in the future.[5]

The intelligence agencies were right to be worried. Not only ISIS but also other groups were considering liberating radicals' families from Kurdish camps. For example, the Hay'at Tahrir al-Sham group (HTS), fighting ISIS, accused Kurdish groups of forcefully repatriating detained ISIS fighters to Kazakhstan and Uzbekistan. In summer 2019, former emir of al-Qaeda-affiliated Katibat Tawhid wal-Jihad (KTJ), Abu Saleh al-Uzbeki, announced on the group's site that those repatriated would face persecution and torture in prison when they returned to their homeland.

Former emir of Katibat Tawhid wal-Jihad, Abu Saleh al-Uzbeki

---

5. 'Kazakhstani intelligence agencies disclose details of Jusan-2 covert operation': www.caravan.kz/gazeta/kazakhstanskie-specsluzhby-raskryli-podrobnosti-sekretnojj-operacii-zhusan2-540830/.

In his statement, al-Uzbeki also acknowledged that leaders of Central Asian and Caucasian jamaats in the Syrian province of Idlib took steps to free the wives and children of ISIS fighters from Kurdish captivity. According to him, the leader of Hay'at Tahrir al-Sham, Abu Mohammad al-Julani, initiated negotiations with the Kurdish group SDF, offering them money, and tried to make a deal to move the families of ISIS fighters to Idlib – an HTS-controlled zone. However, according to al-Uzbeki, the Kurds rejected this offer. Earlier, in 2017, HTS allegedly managed to ransom over 700 ISIS fighters' wives and children from pro-Assad forces in Hama Province.[6]

The concern of HTS leaders with returning ISIS fighters' wives and children is, in reality, motivated not by sympathy to their plight. This is one manifestation of ideological wrangling between various radical groups (ISIS and al-Qaeda) for the hearts and minds of jihadi communities with a view to replenishing their own ranks. The fact that HTS leaders attempted to free ISIS fighters and their family members from captivity testifies to the serious intentions of groups affiliated with al-Qaeda. Mostly likely, they plan to take advantage of the weakening of ISIS to strengthen their own positions by replenishing their ranks with immigrants from Central Asia. Consequently, potential new recruits play an extremely important role in this struggle. This is also confirmed by a corresponding information campaign, and certain attempts that have been made. It is quite possible that the active efforts of the intelligence agencies of Kazakhstan and other countries to some extend hindered the plans of jihadi groups.

However, recent data show that followers of al-Qaeda are nevertheless managing to ransom some women from the camps. In 2019, members of this group in the Syrian province of Idlib began an online fundraising campaign to liberate prisoners. The fundraising was carried out using the encrypted app Telegram. According to American experts, one incident came to light when around thirty women with children were freed during this campaign. According to

---

6.   Uran Botobekov: 'Why does al Qaeda oppose the repatriation of ISIS prisoners to Central Asia?': https://moderndiplomacy.eu/2019/07/27/why-does-al-qaeda-oppose-the-repatriation-of-isis-prisoners-to-central-asia/.

the same analysts, there is nothing strange in al-Qaeda raising money to free family members of fighters belonging to its sworn enemy – ISIS. In this way, 'al-Qaeda is trying to win the women over to their side once they are smuggled out'.[7]

One way or another there was a chance that several hundred Kazakhstani children who had not the faintest idea of their homeland, who found themselves in unfavourable conditions and were growing up in a very different reality, would become a potential instrument for destructive forces, and their ethnicity would be used against Central Asian countries. It is quite possible that these children could have been organised into some sort of brigade or fighting unit. After training in military camps in Syria, the children of Kazakhstani radicals could have spread all over the world. Adult militants, who had once left Kazakhstan for Syria and Iraq, were, in one way or another, constantly kept in the operatives' sights. Whether they were moving within the territory or switching from one group to another, the radicals' activities were always monitored. However, monitoring the movements of children, most of whom had no documents and would consequently be difficult to identify, is problematic. As such, it was risky to leave such large numbers of children in Syria and Iraq. Threats associated with their potential radicalisation would have multiplied over time. The children simply had to be returned in order to forestall the risks they posed to national security.

Second, another argument in favour of the covert operation was the growing role immigrants from Central Asian republics played in international terrorist groups. According to various sources, natives of CIS and Central Asian countries made up one third of foreign fighters in ISIS. Before the war in Syria, such numbers of Central Asian citizens were not registered in any other conflict zone (Caucasus, Afghanistan). Recent reports by UN experts also note Central Asian groups' growing activity in Syria and Iraq. In particular, several large groups are active in Syria: Turkestan Islamic Party; Katibat Tawhid

---

7.   Aaron Zelin: 'Wilayat al-Hawl: "remaining" and incubating the next Islamic State generation: www.washingtoninstitute.org/uploads/Documents/pubs/PolicyNote70-Zelin.pdf.

wal-Jihad (KTJ); Katibat Imam al-Bukhari (KIB); Islamic Jihad Union (IJU). According to a UN expert, the ranks of KTD alone swelled to up to 500 members and the group now comprises three factions headed by migrants from Uzbekistan, Kyrgyzstan, and Tajikistan.

Central Asian groups such as the Islamic Movement of Uzbekistan (now part of the Taliban forces), Katibat Imam al-Bukhari, the Islamic Jihad Union, the Islamic Movement of East Turkestan, and the group Jamaat Ansarullah, have also become more active in Afghanistan.[8] At the same time, a certain Hikmatov, former deputy of the IJU, became the new leader of KTD in Syria, and this indicates a fairly high level of interaction and coordination between Syrian and Afghani cells of Central Asian radical groups.[9]

It is especially worth noting that, in recent years, citizens of Central Asia have increasingly taken part in terrorist attacks around the world. From 2016–17 alone, Central Asian radicals carried out several major terror attacks on the territory of other states.

In April 2020, German authorities reported the arrest of four people suspected of links with ISIS. The alleged members of the group, identified as Azizjon B., Muhammadali G., Farhodshoh K. and Sunatullokh K., were charged with planning attacks on US military installations in Germany. All four men were from Tajikistan. According to experts, the suspects initially planned to carry out the attack in Tajikistan, but later decided to attack the military installations. The members of the group were in contact with high-profile figures in ISIS in Syria and Afghanistan.[10]

---

8. 24th report of the Analytical, Support and Sanctions Monitoring Team submitted pursuant to Resolution 2368 (2017) on ISIS (Daesh), Al-Qaeda and persons and organisations related to them (15 July, 2019).

9. 25th report of the Analytical, Support and Sanctions Monitoring Team submitted pursuant to Resolution 2368 (2017) on ISIS (Daesh), Al-Qaeda and persons and organisations related to them (20 January, 2020).

10. 'ISIS has recruited a base of followers from Central Asia': https://www/fdd/org/analysis/2020/04/22/germany-disputes-isis-plot-for-us-military.

Terrorist Acts Involving Citizens of Central Asia

2016–17				
Date	**Country**	**Terrorist act**	**Participants**	**Victims**
29 June 2016	Turkey, Istanbul	Three explosive devices were detonated by suicide bombers at the Atatürk Airport.	According to Turkish authorities, they were citizens of Russia, Uzbekistan and Kyrgyzstan.	As a result, 45 people were killed and over 200 wounded.
1 January 2017	Turkey, Istanbul	Abdulkadir Masharipov broke into the Reina Club in Istanbul on New Year's Eve and opened fire.	Masharipov left Uzbekistan six years ago and is wanted for connections with a terrorist organisation in Afghanistan.	39 people died (including 16 foreigners) and 65 were wounded.
3 April 2017	Russia, St Petersburg	An explosion went off between Sennaya Ploshchad and Technologicheski Institute metro stations right in the centre of St Petersburg.	The State Committee for National Security of Kyrgyzstan reported that the terrorist attack was committed by a native of their country, Akbarjon Jalilov, born in 1995, who had received Russian citizenship.	16 people died.
7 April 2017	Sweden, Stockholm	A truck was driven into people on a central street in Stockholm. It drove 550m and crashed into the Åhléns shopping centre.	The authorities reported this was a terrorist attack. A 30-year-old citizen of Uzbekistan, Rahmat Akilov, confessed to committing this crime. Swedish police detained five men	Four people were killed, 15 were injured, some more seriously than others.

2016–17				
Date	**Country**	**Terrorist act**	**Participants**	**Victims**
			from Uzbekistan and Kyrgyzstan between April and October 2018. At least one of them was in contact with Akilov.[11]	
31 October 2017	USA, New York	A truck driver drove into pedestrians in the south-eastern part of Manhattan.	According to US media, the truck driver who rammed the crowd in New York was 29-year-old Saifullo Saipov, who had arrived in the US from Uzbekistan in 2010. He had an expired green card. In recent years, he had been living in New Jersey, near New York. He left a note in the car stating that he was carrying out this attack on behalf of the ISIS terrorist group.	Eight people were killed and more than 10 wounded.

11. 'Immigrants from Uzbekistan and Kyrgyzstan accused of terrorism in Sweden': https://knews.kg/2018/12/28/v-shve tsii-vyhodtsev-iz-uzbekistana-i-kyrgyzstana-obvinili-v-terrorizme/.

In January 2020, UN experts announced that Central Asian nationals were already trying to join ISIS cells in Africa. In particular, movement of Central Asian militants from Syria to African countries – Guinea-Bissau, the Central African Republic, Egypt and Sudan – was noted.[12] According to information from a number of states, some citizens from Central Asia may be transiting through these countries with a view to joining ISIS affiliates in West Africa and the Sahel. If this information is correct, it means that the goals of Central Asian jihadis are becoming more global. Having begun in the North Caucasus and Afghanistan, the Central Asian radicals then headed for the Middle East, made themselves felt in Europe, and are now trying to join jihads in Africa.

According to Western experts, Central Asian militants are 'becoming prominent players in the arena of international terrorism, some of them having climbed to authoritative military positions in ISIS'.[13] In the summer of 2019, an Analytical Report for the President of the UN Security Council stated that a thirty-one-year-old Tajik citizen, Sayvaly Shafiev, had become the leader of a 200-strong ISIS-affiliated unit, all of whom were natives of Uzbekistan, Tajikistan and other Central Asian countries.[14] Tajik intelligence agencies confirmed this information. According to the report, Shafiev is also a member of the top leadership – the ISIS Khorasan Council (ISIS declares all the territory of Afghanistan to be part of its Khorasan province). Earlier, in 2015, another Tajik citizen, Gulmurod Khalimov, is known to have become one of ISIS's military commanders in Syria.

---

12. 25th report of the Analytical, Support and Sanctions Monitoring Team submitted pursuant to Resolution 2368 (2017) on ISIS (Daesh), Al-Qaeda and persons and organisations related to them (20 January, 2020).
13. 'Jihadists from ex-Soviet Central Asia: Where ARE THEY? Why did they radicalize? What next?': https://www.russiamatters.org/analysis/jihadists-ex-soviet-central-asia-where-are-they-why-did-they-radicalize-what-next.
14. 'Tajik man emerges in Afghanistan as leader of IS unit of central Asian fighters': www.rferl.org/amp/Tajikistan-islamic-state-central-asia-leader-sayvaly-shafiev/3015372.html?_twitter_impression=true.

Central Asian militants never lost sight of their own region; today they are dying in the territories of other states, but tomorrow they may come to fight in their own countries, even using their own women and children. As the presence of Central Asians in the ranks of ISIS and al-Qaeda grew, so did the volume of propaganda content directed at our region. Propaganda videos and addresses were also published more frequently. The further advancement of Central Asian nationals in international radical groups could facilitate their relatives and people from their close social circles joining their ranks. Leaning on the support of 'veterans' from Central Asia, young child recruits detained in temporary camps in Syria might have formed a new generation of leaders of the world jihadi movement. It was important not only to deprive the radical groups of this new draft from family members of Central Asian militants, and from Kazakhstan in particular, but also to prevent the formation of a new generation of trained radicals capable of taking leading roles in the future.

Third, repatriating ISIS fighters' families was in keeping with an in important goal: to choke any attempts to institutionalise Kazakhstani radicals. Kazakhstan first encountered international terrorism in the early 2000s, and radicals have since attempted to emigrate first to the Caucasus and then to Afghanistan. During all these years intelligence agencies nevertheless managed to achieve what was most important: they thwarted attempts to create stable groups or organisations involving Kazakhstanis, although such attempts were made.

In a short time, emissaries from the al-Qaeda-affiliated Union of Islamic Jihad managed to form several militant groups which would conduct terrorist acts in Uzbekistan, i.e., in Tashkent in spring 2004. However, the whole network was exposed and eliminated. Some group members managed to escape and, several years later, they gathered new followers. Consequently, it was their associates who organised the 2011 and 2012 terrorist attacks in Kazakhstan. These actions were not, however, coordinated by a single centre but represented isolated attempts by separate cells. Intelligence agencies once again successfully prevented them unifying. That is why any new attempts to coordinate were done abroad.

Efforts were made to create an independent brigade of Kazakhstani radicals in Afghanistan – the Kazakh Islamic Jihad (KIJ). Kazakh fighters were dissatisfied with their position in the Islamic Jihad Union (IJU) which was dominated by ethnic Uzbeks, and this prompted them to join forces. Constant conflicts and disagreements resulted in the Kazakhstanis leaving the IJU. Owing to lack of funds, however, they were later forced to return under its banner.

Unwilling to accept this situation, some members of the KIJ colluded with al-Qaeda operatives and, with their help, in 2011 created a new group, Jund al-Khalifa (Soldiers of the Caliphate) in the Afghan-Pakistani border region. Moez Garsallaoui, a Belgian citizen, became its leader. French, Turkish, Saudi, and Tajikistani nationals also joined the group. But it was Kazakhstani nationals who were the most active. The terrorist attack in Atyrau in October 2011 was planned and executed with their participation. It was Kazakhstanis who initiated the release of video addresses on behalf of the Soldiers of the Caliphate with threats directed at the government of Kazakhstan. Thus, Kazakhstani radicals tried by any means to assert themselves and attract new followers. However, these attempts failed, too. After the death of Moez Garsallaoui in 2012, the group disbanded.

The war in Syria became the next step in the Kazakh radicals' attempts to institutionalise. Right from the outset, Kazakhstanis in Syria sought to present themselves as an independent community, hence the corresponding titles of videos about Kazakh militants in ISIS – '150 Kazakhstanis in Syria', 'Kazakh Jamaat in ISIS' and so on. A community of Kazakh militants did indeed exist in ISIS. But divisions within the Caliphate into independent – and, even more so – ethnic groups was not particularly encouraged. Kazakhstani fighters who joined the Hay'at Tahrir al-Sham hostile to ISIS, formerly Jabhat al-Nusra, did not succeed in creating a separate cell, either, and had to take part in active combat within the ranks of other, larger brigades – the Turkestan Islamic Party, Tawhid wal-Jihad, etc.

Kazakh radicals' attempts to assert themselves by creating independent groups or ethnic organisations ended in failure each time, thanks in part to the intervention of intelligence agencies, who thwarted such plans at the very early stages. Nevertheless, we cannot rule out the possibility that the idea to create such an organisation may have been inspired not just by the radicals themselves, but also by third parties keen to influence the situation in the Central Asian region.

Hundreds of Kazakh ISIS fighters' families held in refugee camps could have been used to artificially institutionalise the jihadi movement. Such large numbers of women and children would not have been left 'unsupervised'. Many women who returned during Operation: Jusan said in their interviews that representatives of the a certain foundation visited them and talked to them in the refugee camps. They gave them the chance to emigrate to Turkey.

The foundation presents itself as the Cultural Research Centre for Immigrant Affairs. It turns out that in fact it focuses on providing social help to families of ex-fighters: providing them with temporary work and education in a specialised school. Many women, widows of Kazakhstani fighters, had previously spent time in Turkey in the care of this foundation, which played an active role in several public campaigns championing the protection of militants arrested by Turkish law enforcement agencies while trying to enter Syria via Turkey. For example, it provided legal assistance to Kazakhstani radicals – Eldos Kunshugarov, deputy emir of the Kazakh Islamic Jihad, and Usen Chilmanov, a member of the IJU.[15,16]

There are many similar centres and foundations that present themselves as human-rights or charitable organisations. For example, one of the Kazakhs involved in creating Jund al-Kalifah, Rinat Habidolla, was detained in Turkey in 2012. The campaign for his legal defence was conducted by a different foundation.[17] As a result, Habidolla was not extradited to Kazakhstan but escaped and hid in Syria, where he joined the ranks of Jabhat al-Nusra (now Hay'at Tahrir al-Sham).

---

15. 'Kazak kardeslerimiz olume yollanmasin': https://www.imkander.org.tr/m/y.

16. 'Kazak multeciler iade ediliyor': www.pressmedya.com/m/turkiye.

17. https://dogruhaber.com.tr/mobil/haber/30072-twitter-kazak-usseeni-ipten-aldi/. https://istanbul.mazlumder.org/tr/main/faaliyetler/basin-acikla malari/1/av-abdulhalim-yilmaz-multecilerin-yasadigi-ha/11526.

Thus, by repatriating Kazakhstani radicals from Syria, intelligence agencies prevented them being used in new attempts to unify under the banner of some group. Otherwise, Kazakhstan would have faced a far more organised terrorist threat than it is facing now.

Fourth, the unstable military and political situation is ongoing in Syria and, at any moment, fighters and their families captured by Kurds could escape the prisons or leave refugee camps and spread around the world. In this scenario, our intelligence agencies may lose the ability to track them, resulting in new threats in the future.

The events that followed Operation: Jusan showed that Kazakhstan not only acted correctly in repatriating its citizens from the zone of active combat, but also that it acted at the right time. A few weeks after the final phase of Operation: Jusan, the area our citizens had been evacuated from was engulfed by major hostilities involving almost all main players in the Syrian conflict.

On 9 October 2019, Turkey announced the beginning of its 'Peace Spring' military operation. The goal was to create a buffer zone that would form a protective belt against Kurdish brigades on the Turkish border.[18] Ankara explained that this operation was necessary to neutralise the terrorist threat posed by Kurdish armed groups. The operation began with Turkish air force strikes, after which detachments of the Turkish army, supported by units of the so-called Free Syrian Army (FSA), were able to advance 30–35 km into Syrian territory. The Kurdish People's Self Defence Forces (HXP) and Syrian Democratic Forces (SDF) were forced to surrender a number of settlements under their control and retreat from the Turkish-Syrian border.

Ankara's actions led to a sharp escalation of the situation in Syria. Announcing that it had no intention of getting dragged into this new conflict, the US withdrew its military from the area. On 13 October, the American military left its bases in Kobanî and Manbij. The US also announced it was prepared to introduce tough economic sanctions against Turkey. Washington threatened to end trade negotiations with

---

18. 'Turkey launches offensive against U.S.-backed Syrian militia': https://nytimes.com/2019/10/09/world/middleeast/turkey-attacks-syria.html.

Turkey, increase duties on Turkish steel from 25 to 50 per cent and impose personal sanctions on some Turkish politicians – ministers of defence, energy and domestic affairs. A number of European countries – Germany, France and Italy – froze the supply of arms in response to Ankara's military actions.

To contain the onslaught of the Turkish army, on 13 October Kurdish brigades were forced to forge an agreement with their other enemy: Damascus governmental forces. As a result of negotiations held at the Khmeimim Russian military base, Syrian army units entered Kurdish-controlled areas and, on 14 October, took several large settlements: Manbij and Kobanî. And on 16 October, the Syrian army entered the city of Raqqa. Russian military police began patrolling Manbij.

On 17 October, US then-Vice President Mike Pence and Turkish President Recep Tayyip Erdoğan agreed Ankara would suspend military operations for three days so that the US-backed Syrian Democratic Forces could retreat from the border, thereby enabling the Turkish military to later create a security zone there.

On 22 October 2019, the presidents of Turkey and Russia held talks in the Russian city of Sochi. They reached an agreement to give Kurdish brigades 150 hours to retreat from the Turkish border and be replaced by Syrian border guards. It was also agreed that Russia and Turkey would jointly patrol territories vacated by the Kurds. As a result, 395 settlements fell under Turkish control, and a 2,200 km² security zone was established.[19]

In this way, the Turkish military operation upset the applecart, radically changing the balance of military power in the north of Syria. As a result of all these manoeuvres, Kurdish positions were weakened, Russian and Turkish influence increased, and US presence in the region also decreased. The fight against ISIS naturally took a back seat. Moreover, military escalation led to a weakening of the security regimes in prisons holding ISIS militants. As we have already noted, several camps and prisons were located in northeastern Syria on Kurdish-controlled territory. After the Turkish military operation

---

19. Turkish military operation 'Peace Spring': https://ria.ru/20191016/1559864.

of October 2019, the security situation in these prisons and camps deteriorated, as Kurdish militias sent the bulk of their fighters to the front line, resulting in a decrease in the number of prison guards. According to some sources,

> [W]ith the Turkish advance, the YPG redeployed over one third of the guard unit for al-Houl camp to the front near Tel Abyad. This reassignment left only 150 YPG security police (Asayish) officers and 200 YPG fighters in charge of perimeter security. Around 200 ISIS-linked women, along with dozens of children, escaped from al-Houl in the weeks following the Turkish incursion, hoping to reach the Iraqi border.[20]

On 13 October 2019, the Telegram channel Directorate 4 reported that 785 people had escaped from a prison near the settlement of Ayn Issa where ISIS fighters were being detained with their wives and children. This happened after Kurdish militia followed the American military and left the town following artillery shelling from pro-Turkish groups. Reuters reported that, a day earlier, 12 October, five ISIS fighters had managed to escape from a prison in Qamishli, northeastern Syria. In November 2019, Turkey accused the Kurdish People's Self-Defence Forces of releasing 800 ISIS militants in Tel Abyad (near Raqqa).[21]

Escaping terrorists present new threats. They can rejoin their underground ISIS cells or leave for other regions – Libya, Afghanistan – or even clandestinely return to their own countries. In autumn 2019, a number of Turkish media outlets reported that around 959 foreign ISIS fighters had been detained by intelligence agencies and were being held in special centres. They included 147 minors who lost their parents in Syria. Among the detainees were eighty-two people from Uzbekistan, twenty-three from Kyrgyzstan, twenty-one from

---

20. Elizabeth Tsurkov, Dareen Khalifa: 'An unnerving fate for the families of Syria's northeast': https://carnegieendowment.org/sada/80950.
21. 'Turkey accuses YPG and PKK of freeing over 800 ISIS militants in Syria': https://mk-turkey.ru/bezopasnost.

Tajikistan, six from Turkmenistan, and ten from Kazakhstan.[22] All of them tried to take advantage of the unstable situation in Syria and disappear into third countries. Corruption was also a problem among the ranks of various groups. As international experts noted, the rapid increase in SDF numbers triggered a rise in corruption. Cases of bribery in exchange for facilitating the release of prisoners are quite common.[23] According to Vera Mironova, a research fellow at Harvard University, 'a lot of people escape, and when they escape, we don't see any trace of them. As long as governments don't take their citizens back, or actually track them, these women can disappear into thin air.'[24]

That is why the deterioration of the military and political situation in Syria in one way or another makes it more difficult to repatriate ISIS fighters' families from refugee camps and camps for displaced people. Now, it would be difficult for countries who decide to repatriate their nationals from Syria to do so successfully. Due to ongoing armed clashes in this region, missions such as Kazakhstan's Operation: Jusan are all but impossible.

Fifth, repatriating fighters' families helped reduce the aggression radical communities felt towards the state. Of course, we are not and should not be under any illusion about supporters of radical ideas being so impressed by Operation: Jusan that they instantly abandon their views or become more loyal to the authorities. Nevertheless, the humanity the state has shown towards those who supported radical ideas in the past deprives those promoting jihad of many arguments. For example, their rhetoric that the state is pursuing an extremely harsh

22. 'Deport listesinde 959 DEASli': www.hurriyet.comtr/amp/gundem/deport-listesinde-959-deasli-41372790?twitter_impression=true.

23. Jean-Pierre Keller: 'ISIS after the US repositioning in the northeast of Syria: camps, women and children, and leadership revival': https://dam.gcsp.ch/files/images/Syria-Transition-Challenges-Project-Discussion-Paper-6.

24. Louisa Loveluck: 'In Syrian camp for women and children who left ISIS caliphate, a struggle even to register names: www.washingtonpost.com/world/middle_east/Syria-al-hol-annex-isis-caliphate-women-children/2020/06/28/80ddabb4-b71b-11ea-9a1d-d3db1cbe07ce_story.html#click=https//t.co/tXtCh4cRYj.

repressive policy towards adherents of some religious movements is no longer justified. Most women returnees were not prosecuted for having left Kazakhstan and joining the Islamic State. Moreover, the state helped all the repatriated women obtain the necessary documents and receive social benefits, training and further employment.

One of the women who returned during the Jusan-2 operation later wrote a letter. The author's style has been retained:

It probably isn't just necessary but also my duty to write about the people who helped me draw a line under the 'black page' of my life, turn it over and start a new chapter. As a still-silly eighteen-year-old girl, I followed my husband and left for Syria. My ideas of good and bad turned upside down. I was skilfully manipulated by agitators who pursued their own sordid ends. There is no need to describe all this, but it is my duty to thank all those who extended their helping hands. I am very grateful to the people who took part in Operation: Jusan – pilots, intelligence agencies, theologians, psychologists, educators all contributed greatly. I am especially grateful to our First President, Elbasy Nursultan Ábishuly Nazarbayev, and the incumbent President, Kassym-Jomart Kemeluly Tokayev, as well as to my family who, despite all odds, waited and believed I would return and did not turn away from me, but surrounded me with their love and support. I want to especially emphasise the role of my father who motivated me to go on, and served as a source of energy and strength for me. Papa, I could not have done it without you. Thank you, how wonderful that I have you. I am very proud of my country, which did not abandon us but managed to understand and forgive. I was very proud when they announced in the camps that Kazakhstan was collecting its citizens, and I saw the eyes of other captive women full of tears, longing and sadness, and heard their words: 'Kazakhstanis are lucky people.' I promise you, I will do my utmost to justify all the hopes you invested in us.[25]

---

25. From Balzhan Abdrakhmanova's Instagram account: www.instagram.com/p/B_u6RI-FsiW/?igshid=r8zavvkvlm2I.

According to NSC RK, on 20 June 2020 the preliminary results of the work with 160 repatriated women show that thirty-eight completely abandoned their radical convictions. They returned to a secular way of life and practised traditional Islam. Ninety have made significant progress in abandoning their radical worldview, and only fifteen women still adhere to their previous views. Seventeen have been convicted or are still under investigation for committing terrorist crimes while in Syria or Iraq, but have already given up their previous views. Some women voluntarily got involved in explaining the state's measures to reintegrate and rehabilitate people returned from the conflict zones. Examples of the state's concern even for citizens who once renounced their country are better than any propaganda and agitation. At the very least, when taken together, all these actions are checking the rise of those supporting radical ideologies. In today's environment, winning time in the fight against extremism is already half the battle.

In this way, while humanitarian in nature, the large-scale Jusan special operation simultaneously served the specific goals and objectives of protecting the interests of national security. Yes, there are risks. Nobody denies that. But, I repeat, had the state not repatriated the militants and their families, these risks would have increased exponentially. Our intelligence agencies risked losing track of those who, just yesterday, were living under the black flag of the Islamic State. Most likely, these people would have made their presence felt after some time, and we would have found ourselves facing a much more *large-scale* and *organised* threat.

At present, the *ultimate* success of Operation: Jusan rests largely on how effective the rehabilitation programmes are, the ongoing socialisation of repatriated Kazakhstani families, and public opinion. Radical ideologues can easily replenish their ranks when there is a dividing line between friend and foe. The state showed compassion to its citizens who once stumbled, and gave them another chance. Now it is up to everyone else – psychologists, experts, relatives, neighbours, colleagues, strangers on the street – in other words, each and every one of us. These individuals need our joint support.

ABOUT THE AUTHOR

Erlan Karin (b. 1976) is a Kazakhstani politician, and has been an assistant to the President of the Republic of Kazakhstan since 2020.

He has held posts in several Kazakh agencies over the past two decades, including as Deputy Director of the Institute of the Russia and China; Director of the Central Asian Agency of Political Research; Director of the Centre for Counterterrorism; Head of the Department of Internal Policy of the Administration of the President of the Republic of Kazakhstan; and Director of the Kazakhstan Institute for Strategic Studies. He has also been Chairman of the Board of Qazaqstan, the country's national broadcasting corporation.

He holds a doctoral degree in Political Science from Al-Farabi Kazakh National University in Almaty. Since July 2020, he has been a Visiting Professor at The American University in Washington, DC. Previously, he was an Honorary Professor at the International Institute of International Studies in Shanghai.

His previous book *The Soldiers of the Caliphate: Anatomy of a Terrorist Group*, was published in Kazakhstan in 2016.